MW00658392

# ELECTORAL GUERRILLA THEATRE

In liberal democracies across the globe, where the right to vote is framed as both civil right and civic duty, disillusioned creative activists run for public office on satiric, ironic and iconoclastic platforms. With little intention of "winning" in the conventional sense, they use drag, camp and stand-up comedy to undermine the legitimacy of their opponents and sometimes the electoral system itself.

This revised and updated edition of *Electoral Guerrilla Theatre* explores the phenomenon of the satirical election campaign, and questions the purpose of such public political performances. Drawing on extensive archival and ethnographic research, this is an entertaining and illuminating read that will be invaluable to students and scholars working across a variety of disciplines, including performance studies, the social sciences, cultural studies and politics. New case studies for this edition include:

- Reverend Billy's run for Mayor of New York City in 2009;
- Stephen Colbert's run for President in 2012;
- Candidates including Superbarrio, the Best Party, Antanas Mockus, and Einstein the Dog.

**L.M. Bogad** is professor of political performance at the University of California at Davis. He is the author of *Tactical Performance: The theory and practice of serious play*, and the plays *Haymarket*, *Tahrir*, *COINTELSHOW: A patriot act*, and *Economusic: Keeping score*. He is the founding director of the Center for Tactical Performance.

# ELECTORAL GUERRILLA THEATRE

## RADICAL RIDICULE AND SOCIAL MOVEMENTS

Second edition

L.M. BOGAD

Routledge
Taylor & Francis Group
NEW YORK AND LONDON

First published 2016
by Routledge
2 Park Square, Milton Park, Abingdon, Oxon OX14 4RN

and by Routledge
711 Third Avenue, New York, NY 10017

*Routledge is an imprint of the Taylor & Francis Group, an informa business*



First edition published by Routledge 2005

*British Library Cataloguing-in-Publication Data*
A catalogue record for this book is available from the British Library

*Library of Congress Cataloguing-in-Publication Data*
Bogad, L.M.
Electoral guerrilla theatre: radical ridicule and social movements/
L.M. Bogad.
pages cm
Includes bibliographical references and index.
1. Performing arts–Political aspects. 2. Political satire–History–20th century.
3. Theater and society. 4. Political campaigns–History–20th century.
5. Radicalism–History–20th century. 6. Social movements–History–20th century. I. Title.
PN1590.P64B84 2016
306.4'84–dc23
2015035176

ISBN: 978-1-138-18418-3 (hbk)
ISBN: 978-1-138-18417-6 (pbk)
ISBN: 978-1-315-64536-0 (ebk)

Typeset in Janson
by Florence Production Ltd, Stoodleigh, Devon, UK

MIX
Paper from responsible sources
FSC
www.fsc.org
FSC® C013056

Printed and bound in Great Britain by
TJ International Ltd, Padstow, Cornwall

Wise fools:
To the front; in all directions!
We are everywhere!

# Contents

# Illustrations

# Acknowledgments

This project would not have been possible without the advice of Tracy Davis and Sara Monoson, who provided consultation and encouragement as I formulated the theory and parameters of "electoral guerrilla theatre." Dwight Conquergood was a brilliant guide and teacher throughout my graduate studies and beyond. His integrity and dedication were inspiring; his untimely passing was an enormous loss to the field and to the communities for which he advocated.

Special thanks also to Talia Rodgers for her enthusiasm for this project, and her support for an updated second edition. In the ten years since the first edition, many more radical pranksters have taken to the campaign trail with a parodic premise; I have pointed at a few favorites in this update, but it does not pretend to be an exhaustive list. Please add your own favorite examples to the conversation.

The Woodrow Wilson Foundation's Charlotte W. Newcombe Dissertation Year Fellowship enabled me to focus on finishing this work in a timely manner. A Teaching Fellowship at Northwestern University's Center for the Humanities provided me with much needed funding and a wonderful community of scholars with which to discuss my research. Travel grants from Northwestern's Center for International Comparative Studies, and from the Graduate School, enabled me to make major research trips to Sydney and Amsterdam, respectively. As an "Arts and Controversy" Postdoctoral Teaching Fellow at Carnegie Mellon University's Center for the Arts in Society, I was able to further revise and develop this work. An earlier version of Chapter Three appeared in the Summer 2001 issue of *TDR: The Drama Review*.

Without the translation skills of Saar Frieling and Anneliese Nassuth (1921–2015), my research on the Kabouters would have been impossible. Anneliese was a generous and compassionate friend and anti-fascist literary activist; I wish we could have met one more time over butter cookies and Provo/anarchist theory.

I am enormously indebted to my consultants in Amsterdam, Toledo, Chicago, and Sydney, including Coen Tasman, Guy Kilian, Simen de Jong, Luud Schimmelpennink, Gabriel Gomez, Simon Hunt, Garry Convery, and many others.

Elspeth kydd (1966–2013) left us far too soon; she will be remembered and honored for her brilliance, kindness, commitment, and her beautiful films. Her generosity with her personal archive and insights made Chapter Two of this book possible.

Many thanks to these dear friends: Andrew Buchman, Dean Campbell, Scott Edelstein, Jenn Fitter, Kerry Glennon, Rachel Hamilton, Philip Howard, Brad Krumholz, Tavia La Follette, Rupa Marya, Jason Montero, Kelly Moore, Ben Shepard, and James Wengler.

I am most grateful to my parents, Walter and Suzanne, to Marjorie Bogad (1907–2001), to Gail Evra; and for the inspiration of my comrades in such high-powered, efficient, and solemn organizations as Reclaim the Streets, Absurd Response, Billionaires for Bush, and the Clandestine Insurgent Rebel Clown Army.

# Introduction: Electoral guerrilla theatre in recent democracies

## Speaking mirth to power

> Don't vote – it only encourages them.
>
> (Anon.)

> If voting could change anything, it'd be illegal.
>
> (Anon.)

> [Incumbent Sheriff] Sherman Block has been working for the past thirty years to bring order to Los Angeles [. . .] I've been working during that time to bring disorder. I'll leave it to the voters to decide who's done a better job.
>
> (Elisha Shapiro, Nihilist Party Candidate for LA County Sheriff, 1994)

On 14 April 2000, guerrilla filmmaker Michael Moore and about forty supporters showed up at the New Jersey State Division of Elections in Trenton to register their chosen candidate for US Congress in the 11th District. They had 211 signatures, 11 more than the minimum needed. However, the Division of Elections refused to put their chosen candidate on the ballot because it was a potted ficus plant. Furthermore, the Division ruled that the Ficus 2000 campaign slogan, "Because a Potted Plant Can Do No Harm," was too long for the ballot.

The activists, wearing hats and buttons saying "Ficus for Congress," made their counter-arguments; Ficus was a resident of New Jersey, after all. Mr. Moore argued that the incumbent Congressman, Republican Rodney P. Freylingheysen, was running unopposed and at the very least should be required to face an opponent whose main platform was to provide oxygen for all creatures – whether campaign contributors or not.[1] However, they had to admit when challenged that they had no proof of Ficus's residency, and that Ficus was not a registered voter in the state. When told that they could still vote for Ficus as a write-in candidate, the activists immediately began calling for all voters in the 11th District to write in Ficus, the photosynthesis candidate (Jackson 2000).

Using the (now defunct) Ficus 2000 website as a virtual base of operations, Moore and his movement launched Ficus candidacies across the United States during the 2000 election cycle, primarily against conservative members of Congress who were running unopposed. None of the plants won, but the campaigns generated some press coverage for Moore's lampooning of what he saw as a largely closed, duopolistic US electoral system.

This study examines a relatively recent innovation in the tactical repertoire of modern social movements: the satirical electoral campaign, or electoral guerrilla theatre. Across the globe, in countries where liberal democracy has taken root, where the right to vote is seen as both civil right and solemn civic duty, certain marginalized political combatants have chosen to run for public office on sarcastic, ironic, and iconoclastic tickets and platforms. With little intention of winning in the conventional sense, drag performers, anarchists, and others on the political margins execute their electoral campaigns using the aesthetics of camp, agit-prop theatre, and the stand-up routine to undermine the legitimacy of their opponents and sometimes the very electoral system in which they are operating.

What is the purpose of such public political performances? What theatrical devices and aesthetic sensibilities do they draw on to enhance their satirical effectiveness? How do these guerrilla electioneers create their public personae and platforms, and which audiences and subcultures are they playing to and/or against? How do parodies and the "respectable" political performances that they mock interact?

Furthermore, what does this phenomenon reveal about voter frustration and dissatisfaction across a range of political systems and nationalities? Do these satirists pollute and abuse the electoral discourse and system, wasting public resources and media time with their outrageous performances, or is this "offensiveness" necessary for galvanizing marginalized communities? While many people in developing nations still struggle for the right to vote, is this primarily "developed nation" phenomenon just another appalling symptom of political disillusionment and cynicism in post-industrial democracies, or is it an unexpectedly constructive response, an innovative method of political engagement?

These performances defy generalization. They are situational responses to specific grievances and desires. However, there are some connections and patterns, and many practitioners of this art have been inspired by each other's examples. Electoral guerrilla theatre is often an expression of the frustration felt by individual citizens and social movements who feel excluded from the real decision-making process in current democracies. Many feel that without an enormous amount of money they cannot hope to influence public policy. Some also feel that there is something fundamentally crooked and unrepresentative about the way elections are organized and executed, particularly in the United States following the fraudulent debacle of the 2000 Presidential election (Lantigua 2001).

Perhaps even more disturbing is the sense that corporate globalization (represented by agreements such as NAFTA and GATT) has greatly weakened national governments' power to regulate the activity of multinational conglomerates, rendering the results of elections less and less relevant anyway. This perception has heightened the old debate within progressive politics between direct and indirect democracy, and between working "within the system" versus working outside of it. Electoral guerrilla theatre is an ambivalent, hybrid measure that merges the traditions and techniques of "third-party" electoral intervention with grassroots direct action and performative disruption.

The term "electoral guerrilla" contains that contradiction. It is the volatile combination of two seemingly incompatible elements. *Electoral* activists work within the state's most accepted and conventional avenues in an attempt to reform the system peacefully. *Guerrillas*, in the military sense, exist on the extreme margins of the social system, constantly on the move, violently attacking the state, running and hiding (hence the coining of the term *guerrilla theatre* in the 1960s). This contradiction is what makes electoral guerrilla theatre a wild card in the repertoire of resistance, both for the target and the activist performer. It is a fraught, unstable, and problematic combination which can take all players involved by surprise.

Winning office is rarely the primary goal. Rather, these campaigns usually aim to simultaneously corrode and rejuvenate different elements of the civic body, much like the degrading and regenerative aspects of Rabelasian carnival (Bakhtin 1968). They satirize the dominant political center and expose its unacknowledged exclusionary devices and ritualistic nature (Brecht 1964). This can create a moment of theatricality in the public sphere, disrupting assumptions of dignity, fairness, and legitimacy (Davis 2002). At the same time, these campaigns echo, entertain, and energize the performer's base community(ies), and communicate grievances from that marginal position to the center through parody and irony. Sometimes an electoral guerrilla's motivation is more immediately tactical; to serve as a spoiler, using humor to agitate specifically against one of the "mainstream" or "serious" candidates in the hopes that a "lesser evil" will win. Simon Hunt, whose "Pauline Pantsdown" campaign helped to defeat far-right parliamentarian Pauline Hanson in Australia, is a key example of this (see Chapter 3).

The positive, community-building aspect of these performances seems integrally connected to their often withering attack-humor. This is serious play. Electoral guerrillas mock the "straight" system of capitalist liberal democracy and the laws and economic structures that impede the effective, strategic, serious participation of marginalized communities. They direct their parodic platforms and personae at subcultures who have experienced that frustration and who will hopefully *get the joke*. Irony is subculture-specific, but it can also "cross over" and appeal to a wider audience. Guerrilla electioneers ask specific publics, as the active consumers of the humor, to *catch* the irony and, perhaps, deliver an extra punchline by voting for them. Thus, dissatisfied voters have the option of joining in the act as active spectators, or, as Augusto Boal puts it, "spect-actors" (1985), by exercising their franchise (socially constructed as a serious civic privilege and duty which must be solemnly enacted), in support of patently irreverent candidates/parties with names like Jello Biafra, Pauline Pantsdown, Sister Boom-Boom, or the Rhinoceros and Monster Raving Loony Parties. While electoral success and actual immediate access to mainstream parliamentary power are unlikely, a marginal community is activated or even defined through active participation in such a campaign. This is an indirect, ironic, nonviolent approach to social-movement organizing that, through parody and symbolic inversion, poaches on the electoral system and the media coverage it can generate. Oppositional, collective identity and resistance are encouraged and enacted as the guerrilla electioneers' absurdist participation exposes the theatricality and symbolic ritualism of an electoral system which defines itself as natural, optimal, and democratically inclusive of all of its citizenry.

Why target elections? It is the ritual nature of the electoral process that makes it an economical, efficient target of counter-symbolic manipulation by the satirist. Elections are a familiar cultural phenomenon, intensely covered by the mainstream media. When the satirist engages this ritual by drawing on popular genres such as stand-up comedy and parody, a satirical performance results that can be understood and appreciated by far more spectators than a street protester might otherwise be able to reach. Part of the guerrilla electioneer's performance is to set up the conventional candidates as the unwilling or unwitting *straights* in his/her routine. Traditional candidates are forced to repeat the same lines over and over again as a necessary element of the "sound bite" or "getting the message out." This can leave the more powerful candidate vulnerable to viciously effective satire when the guerrillas provide the punch lines.

But at what price to already eroded social contracts? Many conventional politicians have charged that "frivolous" campaigns are a waste of public resources and time, mocking the system while benefiting from its protection. The more effective these satirists are at ridiculing earnest politicians, the argument goes, the less likely it is that citizens will choose to run for office, for fear of public humiliation. The campaigns of Jello Biafra (see below) and Pauline Pantsdown resulted in legal responses that attempted to limit or fully outlaw such campaigns. Such restrictive measures may satisfy those who wish to enforce a respectful, solemn tone within electoral politics, but at an obvious cost to the democratic ideal of free speech.

Beyond the immediate electoral context, there is a larger ethical question at play: how can different subcultures communicate and coexist in a representative democracy in which some groups perceive themselves to be marginalized? Do satirical electioneers further polarize an electorate, corroding trust in parties, platforms, and representative democracy itself? Do they deepen and reaffirm the fragmentation of the public sphere into many rival, irreconcilable, and clashing counterpublics? Or is this phenomenon just a performative reflection of that social balkanization? These performances bring these ethical questions to a head as they intrude upon the electoral system's reified rituals, introducing disrespectful rhetoric that may reflect a deep despair about current, collapsing social contracts.

This book documents an understudied topic. Electoral guerilla theatre is a newly modified, modular technique for activists, an innovation in the "repertoire of contention" – the bag of tricks and tactics that a movement inherits, innovates, and implements for collective anti-establishment action (Tilly 1995; Tarrow 1998). It is an example of people using established parodic devices in a new context in many countries around the world. Through such parodic public performance, marginalized, resource-poor groups may incisively desacralyze and satirize the electoral ritual: a ritual which they feel effectively and unadmittedly denies them the option of earnest participation. We may see more electoral guerrilla theatre in the future, from all marginalized sectors of society: left, right, or "other." While in the past such performers have been dismissed as irrelevant cranks, this study investigates the possible efficacy and agency that their nonviolent, absurdist methods obtain. Of course, like all movement tactics, electoral guerrilla theatre may become stale through unimaginative over-use or co-optation by opponents.

In this book, I document and analyze performers' motivations and political and aesthetic tactics, how they use performance to create a spectacle that compels and/or repels audiences. I study the props, costumes, speech styles, and other aspects of representation that guerrilla electioneers employ to create parodic public personae. This study examines the municipal and federal campaigns of the Dutch Kabouters in 1970 and 1971; Joan JettBlakk's campaigns for Mayor of Chicago and US President in 1991 and 1992; and Pauline Pantsdown's bid for the Australian Federal Senate in 1998. These case studies vary in terms of campaign objectives, performative tactics, the size and nature of the electoral guerrilla's backing organization, and greater national, cultural, political, and legal contexts. These variations offer informative contrasts and some provocative commonalities. In order to examine how these performers' tactics are affected by variations in the electoral systems under which they operate, I have chosen case studies located in the US's two-party, winner-take-all system and in the more proportional or majoritarian systems of the Netherlands and Australia. I include descriptions of each national electoral system so the reader can better understand the rules and strategic terrain within which these mock-candidates operated.

Electoral guerrilla theatre appears to occur for the most part in recent liberal democracies. In authoritarian contexts, such satirical work is very dangerous, and might seem frivolous in the face of more earnest military and political resistance to oppression. In many authoritarian countries, there is no electoral system that can be engaged satirically. Though it has roots in the more earnest-toned protest campaigns of suffragettes and other people struggling for the franchise, this tactic may seem out of place where disenfranchised people are locked in a deadly struggle for the right to vote. It is more likely to be taken up by people who have the right to vote, are disillusioned with the efficacy of that vote to advance their interests within their given system, and are now struggling for the right to a vote that is *meaningful* to them.

## Brecht, Bakhtin, Boal, and candidate drag

> Another thing that makes for freedom in the actor's relationship with his audience is that he does not treat it as an undifferentiated mass. He doesn't boil it down to a shapeless dumpling in the stockpot of the emotions. He does not address himself to everybody alike; he allows the existing divisions within the audience to continue, *in fact he widens them.*
>
> (Brecht 1964: 143, my emphasis)

Electoral guerrillas are political actors and performance artists, guided by aesthetic concerns and theories as well as sociopolitical agendas and grievances. To be politically effective, their work must entertain and engage their chosen audiences. Brechtian distantiation, Boalian spect-actorship, and the Bakhtinian carnivalesque intermingle in this complex exercise.

Bertolt Brecht was heavily influenced by the Marxism of the German Old Left. From this perspective, he developed his theory of artistic distantiation (the *Verfremdungseffekt* or *V-effekt*), a device intended to serve the class struggle. Brecht wrote that the conventional theatre of his time had

> degenerated into branches of the bourgeois narcotics business . . . the sort of theatre which we face . . . has been fully able to transmute our optimistic friends . . . into a cowed, credulous, hypnotized mass . . . it shows the structure of society (represented on the stage) as incapable of being influenced by society (in the auditorium).
>
> (Brecht 1964: 179–89)

Naturalist acting in the bourgeois theatre generalized and dehistoricized human experience and conflict, overwriting the dialectical, class-based specificities, tensions, and struggles of history. Lead characters were written as universal, and performed with such emotional investment that the audience was led to identify with these protagonists (regardless of their class position), to root for them, and, in the end, to abandon their critical engagement with both history and contemporeneity in the ongoing spectacle.

For Brecht, this universalization of humanity was anathema, layering the comedic/tragedic masks over the class divisions and clashes of interests in society. Brecht's epic theatre was to be a dialectical, historicized theatre that exposed reified class conflict and oppression in everyday and political life. *Verfremdungseffekt* would "make the familiar strange" in this way through a new method of acting that alienated the "social gest" (Brestoff 1995: 149).

To achieve the *Verfremdungseffekt* in performance, actors were to demonstrate and comment upon their carefully constructed and entertainingly portrayed characters, but not to identify with those roles. This would encourage the audience to withhold empathy, and thus to maintain a critical attitude toward all characters and the decisions they made as the plot progressed from contingency to contingency. Brecht wanted to take "common, recurrent, universally practiced operation[s] and [try] to draw attention to [them] by illuminating [their] peculiarity" (1964: 145). This is what he meant by alienating the social gest: "The social gest is the gest relevant to society, the gest that allows conclusions to be drawn about the social circumstances" (1964: 104–5). Through an alienated gesture or staging, audience members were to be surprised into thinking about an unmarked power relationship or everyday ritual in a new, critical way. To ensure that the audience would never get so swept up in the theatre magic that they might forget that they were watching an act of cultural production, Brechtian work exposed the operation and mechanics of lighting/set/sound effects and other trappings of the theatre. Thus, the socially constructed nature and *strangeness* of the familiar was to be illuminated.

Electoral guerrillas use *Verfremdungseffekt* to disrupt the unmarked ritual of the liberal-democratic capitalist election process through ironic and/or parodic participation. They ape the "straight" candidates, repeating their performances with a critical distance (Hutcheon 1985). They direct attention to the electoral mechanisms by using them in an off-kilter way. Even if they are not *revealing* this aspect of the electoral process for the first time to a supposedly "hypnotized" group (their audience may be savvy enough to have figured these things out for themselves at some point), they nevertheless provide a sharp and entertaining *reminder*; people can often lay aside or partially forget the critical assessments they have made of their own society's rituals. David Kertzer explains that

> [t]his is understandable, since our own rites, our own symbols, are the most difficult to see. They seem like such natural ways of behaving, such obvious ways of representing the universe, that their symbolic nature is hidden. Here indeed, is one of the sources of power of rites and symbols, for insofar as they become dominant they create a convincing world; they deflect attention from their contingent nature and give us confidence that we are seeing the world as it really is.
>
> (1988: 184)

Thus an unexpected dose of *V-effekt* injected into a social ritual can serve as an amusing and/or disturbing wake-up call for an audience that has internalized the symbols in question.

Electoral guerrilla theatre can be further analyzed in terms of Tracy Davis's concept of "theatricality" as a disruption of sympathy with an individual or social convention. For Davis, "theatricality is not about a relationship of theatre to lived reality, but rather the comparability of spectating to civil society" (Davis 2002). Theatricality is the moment when the citizen/spectator chooses to withdraw sympathy, or identification, with a societal phenomenon: "I am, therefore, arguing for the enabling effects of active dissociation, or alienation, or self-reflexivity in standing aside from the suffering of the righteous to name and thus bring into being the self-possession of a critical stance" (2002). This emphasis on distantiation to enable critical reflection is aligned with Brecht's *Vefremdungseffekt*. Davis helps to complicate this model and recognizes the agency that lies in the hands of the citizenry/audience as interpreters of social rituals and disruptions.

The electoral guerrilla's mission is to provoke, cajole, invite, or incite the citizen/spectator to create a moment of theatricality in the electoral ritual, to recognize its constructed nature and withdraw their sympathy from it (Davis 2002). The electoral guerrilla does not, as a vanguard force, reveal this objective truth upon the supposedly sleeping, hegemonized masses. The agency is in the hands of the ironizing audience, who may think: "'the system fails, producing this result, and the system is mine' . . . in public life, the onus for instigating this theatrical moment is on the spectator, who by failing to sympathize and instead commencing to think, becomes the actor" (Davis 2002). So, electoral guerrillas work as catalysts or facilitators rather than enlighteners. Agency is on both sides of the performer–audience dialogue.

Brecht's concept of *Verfremdungseffekt* informs my analysis, when tempered with Davis's "theatricality" and its emphasis on the agency of the audience/citizenry. Linda Hutcheon's idea of irony must also be incorporated into Brecht's model, since it emphasizes the risk of unintended interpretation. Brecht is more interested in asking questions and provoking thought in his audience than providing pre-digested answers. Nevertheless, he seems to propose that a proper *V-effekt* will enlighten the audience, while allowing for a desirable polarization based on class and other social divisions. Hutcheon recognizes that an audience composed of many individuals, who are members of diverse and overlapping discursive communities, will ironize a speech-act as they choose, or will refuse to ironize at all. Thus the radical electoral guerrilla's performance may fall flat, be ignored, or be interpreted in unintended ways.

Identifying the relegation of the audience to the passive role of spectators to be "the first oppression," and influenced by Paolo Freire's *Pedagogy of the Oppressed*, Augusto Boal's Theatre of the Oppressed (TO) breaks down the performer–audience division, encouraging the audience to take an active role in the performance as "spect-actors." The spect-actors learn to act as protagonists in image-based exercises ("Image Theatre") and improvisational scenario-workshops ("Forum Theatre") with the goal of applying these self-taught lessons to their real lives (Freire 1989; Boal 1985). A description of Boal's work directly applied to the electoral sphere may illuminate the contrast between his work and that of the electoral guerrilla. In 1992, Boal ran for local office in Rio de Janiero on the Workers' Party ticket (Boal 1998: 6–18). The campaign was meant as a carnivalesque, joyous street performance, a promotional effort for the Workers' Party as a whole, rather than as an earnest campaign. The slogan was "Have the Courage to be Happy." However, Boal was elected, against his original intention, to a position he hadn't wanted. He and his co-workers in the Center for Theater of the Oppressed started to adapt TO exercises to a new form: the direct, dialogical solicitation of legislative programs from the spect-actors of his new constituency. After getting a number of laws passed that were crafted during these theatre workshops, Boal lost the next election. However, his "legislative theatre" activists continue to operate, drawing up laws based on their workshops and lobbying for them with the local politicians (Boal 1998). Boal's "legislative theatre" is an impressive phenomenon, but it differs from the ironic, poach-and-run of electoral guerrilla theatre. Indeed, Boal's work serves as a valuable counterpoint. His example of earnest, constructive engagement with the electoral system from the margins may serve as a position from which to critique or question the value of the efforts of electoral guerrillas.

In celebrating the "carnivalesque," Mikhail Bakhtin might prefer Boal's anti-spectacular, participatory model to Brecht's Marxist demonstrations of the *Verfremdungseffekt*:

> Carnival does not know footlights, in the sense that it does not acknowledge any distinction between actors and spectators. Footlights would destroy a carnival, as the absence of footlights would destroy a theatrical performance. Carnival is not a spectacle seen by the people; they live in it, and everyone participates because its very idea embraces all the people. While carnival lasts, there is no life outside it. During carnival time life is subject only to its laws, that is, the laws of its own freedom.
>
> (Bakhtin 1968: 7)

The "carnivalesque," as a liberating phenomenon for the "lower orders" of society, includes abuse and laughter, which degrade at the same time that they renew. Grotesque realism exaggerates the material body and the "lower bodily stratum," inverting the hierarchies of elite taste and decorum and the symbols of hierarchy. This is not an exercise in rational, Brechtian satire, but a frenetic, celebratory, and ideologically ambivalent performance mode which breaks down the bodily boundaries of the idealized bourgeois individual, "polluting" and collectivizing the human condition in a joyous, outrageously humorous demonstration that has some potential for rebellion (Bakhtin 1968).

Bakhtin has been qualified and critiqued by theorists such as Kertzer, Peter Stallybrass, and Allon White. While finding Bakhtin's work useful, they have noted his tendency to romanticize the carnivalesque. Stallybrass and White argue that while there are some clearly transgressive aspects of carnival, and that at times it has been the catalyst for open rebellion against hierarchy, it also can serve as a sort of "steam valve" for the frustration of the oppressed, ultimately stabilizing and legitimizing the hierarchy that it temporarily inverts. They conclude with the "banal but often ignored truth that the politics of carnival cannot be resolved outside of a close historical examination of particular conjunctures: there is no a priori revolutionary vector to carnival and transgression" (Stallybrass and White 1986: 16–19). While more strongly emphasizing its revolutionary potential, Kertzer agrees that carnival can go either way:

> The rites through which people cope with crises and conflict are not just products of a political elite . . . such rites . . . provide a means for the powerless to take power . . . undoubtedly [they] did often vent pent-up political hostilities in a way that dissipated them without threatening the political status quo. But the very fact that the rituals encouraged mockery of the politically powerful made them a prime occasion for launching more direct threats to the political order.
>
> (Kertzer 1988: 144–50)

Carnival, thus, is situational. Symbolic inversion can trigger actual rebellion, but Kertzer also acknowledges the argument that carnival can be used as a demonstration of just how unfit the lower orders are to rule. Electoral guerrillas risk the same interpretation of their work. Their outrageous performances may appear to some spectators merely as proof of the admirable tolerance and openness of the system; others may conclude that the dissidents are incapable of making positive contributions to public discourse.

Bakhtin's carnivalesque is often evoked in contemporary writings about subversive performance. The current global justice movement (which opposes corporate globalization in favor of a more egalitarian globalization from below) often convenes in massive, festive, creative street protests, and has consciously theorized itself using terms such as "Carnival Against Capital" (Notes From Nowhere 2003: 185). However, there are important differences between modern oppositional performance that evokes the carnivalesque and the phenomenon that Bakhtin was exploring. Feudal carnival was a calendrically circumscribed event (the word derives from *carne*; this was the meat-eating festival), tied to the harvest and religious schedules of agrarian-Christian societies still influenced by their pagan pasts. The beginning and end of the carnival were predetermined by the established rhythms of the society, and the event itself was part of a commonly shared cultural and religious vocabulary. The oppositional "carnivalesque" protests of today take place when and where the protestors choose: sometimes in reaction to "establishment" events, sometimes not. They may be ideologically complicated and ambivalent events, but they still tend to be more focused and specific in their social critique than most feudal era carnivals. In this sense, there is more tactical agency in contemporary "carnivalesque" protest, but it also tends to draw on a narrower, more specialized appeal and participation than the all-community carnival of feudal times. While those who dance, sing, and party in current street protests may share an experience of the joyous and outrageous carnivalesque, the entire "village" does not take part. Thus there is an inherent performer–audience divide in current carnival protest, and indeed the event as a political protest is partially framed in terms of how spectators receive it, either on the street or even more so through the mass media. For this reason, I would distinguish between Bakhtinian carnival and what I call the *tactical carnival* of today.[2]

However, there is a calendrically demarcated, routine event that is central to the rhythm of modern capitalist liberal democracies. Like feudal carnival, it, too, has been exalted as an event where the floodgates open up, when the masses can freely express and liberate themselves. It has also been denounced as a mere steam-valve for dissent which further legitimizes a hierarchical system while being utterly unable to change that system's basic structure for the better. I am talking, of course, about the election.

In modern democracies, elections have a similar ambivalent, complex, and situational status as feudal carnivals did in their societies. The laughter is canned, and the mass experience is largely mediated and bereft of play, but the structural function in society is similar. While electoral victories can produce important reforms, they very rarely achieve lasting or major changes to fundamental power relationships in society. Through their mechanisms, there is a great exchange of rhetorical energy, but ultimately power is transferred between elites, conferred and confirmed by those in the middle, and endlessly deferred by the low. However, also like feudal carnivals, elections can sometimes serve as an opening for more serious tactical resistance, as moments of breakthrough or advance for a subjugated or marginalized group, where visions of more fundamental change can be playfully put forward. Electoral guerrillas attempt to make the election into just such an occasion.

Operating more in the mode of tactical carnival than Bakhtinian feudal carnival, electoral guerrillas' work is not always fully participatory. There is often an actor–audience divide in their staged, bounded events. While these subversive performances tend to have more specific ideological focus than the ambivalent carnivalesque, they do share the same double-edged quality, with their multivalent irony. Like carnival, they degrade their "straight" candidate opponents, and the electoral system itself, with bawdy earthiness and grotesque realism.

Electoral guerrillas' radical, subversive, and ironic performance acts share, in varying proportions, aspects of Brecht's *V-effekt*, Boal's spect-actorship, and Bakhtin's carnivalesque. Though none of these elements occur in a "pure" form as conceived by their original theorists, their influence is present in this art form.

## Counterpublics

> The isolation of the voting booth provides thoughts as well as separations.
>
> (de Certeau 1984: 112)

> For bourgeois democracy emerged with a class which, whilst indeed progressive in its best political aspirations, had encoded in its manners, morals and imaginative writings, in its body, bearing and taste, a subliminal elitism which was constitutive of its historical being.
>
> (Stallybrass and White 1986: 202)

An overview of some theoretical conceptions of the public sphere will help us to better understand the larger context in which electoral guerrilla theatre takes place. Nancy Fraser's concept of the "subaltern counterpublic" is a progressive response to Habermas's "bourgeois public sphere." Fraser complicates and questions Habermas's exclusionary privileging of the public activity and culture of the white, male bourgeoisie over that of other, less powerful groups. Fraser argues that the latter groups have had the agency and intelligence to develop their own public spheres – discursive home bases for community-building and protest – for at least as long as the bourgeoisie.[3]

While Fraser sees the idea of the public sphere as a valuable construct, she questions Habermas on several grounds. She takes strong exception to Habermas's idea that power relations between speakers can be "forgotten" by the *as if we were equals* postulated by a coffeehouse's cordial atmosphere. If anything, this *as if*, by bracketing power differentials in a context without actually eliminating them, serves the purposes of the oppressor, whose best-case scenario is to retain elite power while being able to pretend that such power does not exist, that all are equal, and that the system is thus legitimate and just (Fraser 1997: 77–8). Fraser aptly argues that Habermas's liberal model wrongly assumes that

> a public sphere is or can be a space of zero-degree culture [. . .] with perfect neutrality. But [. . .] in stratified societies, unequally empowered social groups tend to develop unequally valued cultural styles. The result is the development of powerful informal pressures that marginalize the contributions of members of subordinated groups both in everyday life contexts and in official public spheres.
>
> (79)

In this sense, Fraser's critique of Habermas's bourgeois public sphere parallels Brecht's criticism of the universalizing bourgeois theatre. Fraser also describes the political-economic context in which corporate control of the mass media affects participation in the public sphere (a point corroborated by Chomsky (1989) and Bagdikian (1990)):

> Moreover . . . in (the bourgeois) public sphere, the media that constitute the material support for the circulation of views are privately owned and operated for profit. Consequently, subordinated social groups usually lack equal access to the material means of equal participation. Thus political economy enforces structurally what culture accomplishes informally . . . *Liberal political theory assumes that it is possible to organize a democratic form of life on the basis of socioeconomic and sociosexual structures that generate systemic inequalities.*
>
> (Fraser 1997: 79, my emphasis)

This *as if we were equals* is impossible, and not even desirable, in the context of dominance and subordination. Habermas's *as if* has the same potentially obscurantist ramifications as Stanislavsky's "magic if." These *ifs* both have the undesirable potential to obscure the concrete, live context of the speech-act or performance and its attendant power-relationships in the actual moment of the utterance.

Fraser notes that, while Habermas acknowledges in part the exclusivity (racism/(hetero)sexism/classism, etc.) of the bourgeois public sphere, he ignores the existence of competing, non-bourgeois public spheres, which formed side by side with the bourgeois sphere. This led him to idealize the bourgeois public sphere:

> virtually contemporaneous with the bourgeois public there arose a host of competing counterpublics, including nationalist publics, popular peasant publics, elite women's publics, black publics and working-class publics. Thus, there were competing publics from the start . . . *Habermas's account stresses the singularity of the liberal model of the bourgeois public sphere, its claim to be the public arena in the singular.*
>
> (Fraser 1997: 74–80, my emphasis)

Fraser thus introduces the idea of a *subaltern counterpublic*, or competing public sphere, which serves as a sort of home base or tenuous, safer space for marginalized and/or oppressed groups to "formulate oppositional interpretations of their identities, interests and needs" (81). Since an *as if* of equality is problematic without first addressing social and political-economic inequality, the oppressed need a space from which they can organize their own networks and articulate their own grievances and discourses. Fraser's illustrative example is the late-twentieth century US feminist subaltern counterpublic, with its huge array of alternative media and meeting places, alternative vocabulary, etc., which has had a significant if not decisive effect on official public spheres (81–2). For all of its flaws, the concept of the public sphere can also serve as a critical comparative tool. As Fraser points out, "the idea of the public sphere also functions here and now as a norm of democratic interaction we use to criticize the limitations of actually existing public spheres" (95).

Electoral guerrillas perform within this Fraserian multiplicity of competing public spheres. This terrain is filled with power inequality and discursive clashes, conjunctural agency, and contestations between strategic and tactical power. A good deal of their work is to draw attention to the fact that all candidates are not equal – that money, access to corporate media, corporate backing, race, class, and gender determine the actual "electibility" of candidates rather than any fair, objective competition in a free marketplace of ideas.[4] The excluded counterpublics and the disaffected and disillusioned members of the general populace are often the primary intended audiences to whom their ironic speech-acts are directed. Whether punks, queers, anarchists, or other "Others," they identify with one or more subaltern counterpublics, marginalized groups that, because of identity or ideology, cannot get adequate satisfaction or representation in the dominant public sphere through earnest participation in the electoral ritual.[5]

The election, a vulnerable, choice node of mainstream symbolic practice, and the focus of intense media attention, is a site of high/low distinction that is just begging, like a power plant or a railway switching station, for a guerrilla raid from the margins. Guerrilla electioneers, like de Certeau's tactical agent and Che Guevara's guerrilla fighter, do not seek to seize and hold places or territory in the lofty legislatures of bourgeois democracy. Such a goal is usually beyond their grasp. They generally lack the strategic power and resources to maintain a campaign within the electoral system as constructed by the elites. However, they are making do, seizing this predictable ritual as the ideal occasion for a tactical hit-and-run strike. They poach on the election and the usually exclusive media, using them in a way for which they were not originally designed. They invert symbols, speaking ironically through a megaphone never meant for them, to an audience rarely addressed, and withdrawing back to their base in their hopefully energized and entertained subaltern counterpublic(s) (de Certeau 1984; Guevara 1961).

These are ironic radical performance projects. They trick on Habermas's *as if*, that is to say *as if we are all equals in a capitalist society*, or *as if*, for example, *the US system, with the millions of dollars in corporate sponsorship needed for any campaign, will make room for the marginalized*. Guerrilla electioneers play along with this magic *as if*, faux-naively, and, in an "in your face" manner, declare their candidacy for office. If they can't speak truth to power, they will speak mirth to it.

## Evolving repertoires of contention and the electoral dilemma

Social movements have established techniques in their repertoire for protest, such as the demonstration, the strike, and the boycott. But they occasionally innovate/improvise new tactics that better serve or complement their contingent needs. Electoral guerrilla theatre is an innovative, disruptive, nonviolent tactic for protest that uniquely exploits modern legal and electoral systems.

Sidney Tarrow lists four different ways in which repertoires of contention can change: the institutionalization of contention; tactical interaction; paradigmatic change; and innovation at the margins (Tarrow 1998: 101). Electoral guerrilla theatre is an example of the latter. It does not radically change a whole paradigm of resistance, but rather is a parody of the typical electoral campaign.

Tarrow defines a "cycle of contention" as a period of time in which the costs for contentious collective action are lowered for various reasons, encouraging social movements to get moving across an entire society (24–5). This relates to de Certeau's concept of the "occasion," a contingent, passing opportunity in which the oppressed have the tactical agency to make oppositional or subversive moves. Tarrow's concept of political opportunity is a sociopolitically rooted version of de Certeau's tactical "occasion":

> [. . .] contentious politics is triggered when changing political opportunities and constraints create incentives for social actors who lack resources on their own [. . .] When backed by dense social networks and galvanized by culturally resonant, action-oriented symbols, contentious politics leads to sustained interaction with opponents. The result is the social movement.
>
> (Tarrow 1998: 2)

Both macroeconomic and cultural/symbolic factors are vital elements of political conflict. Social movements cannot ordain a loosening of national social policy, from the top down, in order to better facilitate their own actions, but they certainly have the agency to get more active and "seize the time" if they perceive such an opening in the chinks of the establishment's order. Satirical candidates exercise just such a tactical agency. They may not have the power to change the rules in the electoral system of their countries, nor to significantly alter the political economy in which they live. However, they can adapt their tactics to the electoral laws that regulate them, finding loopholes or unintended opportunities for satire or exposure (e.g. "equal time"-style free media coverage).

Collective contentious action takes violent, conventional, and creative-disruptive forms (Tarrow 1998: 93–100). Violence is the easiest type of action for small movements to employ, for example terrorism. However, it generally alienates the moderates in any movement, polarizes the greater society, and encourages and helps to legitimize harsh state repression. While conventional forms are often somewhat boring or passé, they have the advantage of being familiar. Movement members know what to do in order to participate safely (e.g. showing up for the next mass demonstration in the capital city, placard in hand), and the state knows how to respond according to custom (usually not too harshly due to the conventional nature of the protest).

Oppositional electoral participation is often seen as the most conventional tactic possible. In fact, it is so conventional that even calling it a social movement tactic is questionable. This presents a special dilemma for social movements who wish to influence state policy. While elections may seem like a positive opportunity, they can channel and co-opt almost unlimited amounts of activist energy and resources. Even when some headway is made, fledgling third parties, especially those representing poorer social movements, are often co-opted into the greater power structure and/or swallowed up by larger parties or coalitions as the volunteerist energy which sustains them ebbs over time. While a movement may achieve real reforms through electoral participation, even these hard-won gains can now be struck down by "free trade" agreements in the era of corporate globalization. Even the aforementioned Workers' Party of Brazil, the largest movement-based progressive political party in the world, which recently won the national election in Brazil, finds its policy-making power severely limited within the current global economic system. Electoral guerrilla theatre is a fraught response to this electoral dilemma. It is an attempt to introduce a disruptive maneuver into this most conventional tactic of all, and to use performative excess in an unexpected setting to break through the media oligopoly and call attention to a movement's grievances.

Movements with very different agendas can draw from the same tactical repertoire; note the use of nonviolent civil disobedience, innovated by Gandhi and the US civil rights movement, by elements of the conservative anti-abortion movement of today. Demonstrations and petition drives have been adopted by movements of many different ideologies and locations (Tarrow 1998: 29–42). This modularity of protest can be a great efficacy multiplier, as, for example, a large number of groups can all take the same form of action at the same time across a wide area (for example a national general strike or boycott). The one danger of modularity is that the comforting familiarity of a tactic, and the success it may initially bring, can result in the elevation of that tactic into a *strategy*. Any tactic that is relied on regardless of context can become dull in both senses – it can become boring, and it can lose its sharp, effective edge.

Disruptive forms (such as were often practised by the Yippies in the 1960s) are sometimes ludic, humorous, and unexpected by the elites. However, the surprised elites can eventually adapt to the new challenge and develop countermeasures. Disruptive forms can become routine over time, as they are adapted into the established repertoire of contention and become institutions in themselves. This dynamic parallels the process in theatre by which surprising innovations such as Brecht's become trendy, and then simply routine.

This concern applies to the guerrilla election campaign. Its shock value will likely lessen over time through repetition. While the corporate media needs to find off-beat news to cover for entertainment value, coverage may drop off as the tactic becomes less "fresh" or "newsworthy." Such a reduction in media exposure would remove one of the major incentives for this type of campaign.

## A non-taxonomy of electoral interventions

There are many categories and demi-categories of electoral guerrilla theatre. This study does not pretend to provide a hard scientific taxonomy of this phenomenon in all its phyla, kingdoms, and various subspecies. The examples listed below clearly overlap and flow into each other. However, it is important to note the variety of rhetorical and performative goals and tactics that different electoral interventions have emphasized. In line with the tendency of cultural formations to create their identity through exclusion, I note the boundaries of this study by defining what electoral guerrilla theatre is *not*.

### Representative ritual, and the political theatre of domination

The reader may be asking at this point: Don't *all* players in the electoral game perform, using humor, symbols, props, and costumes? Of course they do. Mainstream politicians and candidates wear heavily significant costumes and engage in ritualistic behavior. They kiss babies, ride in tanks, and emerge from jets on aircraft carriers. They wear ribbons, cut ribbons, and tie them around trees. They utter soundbites while chopping the air with their hands, then bite their lips in heavily rehearsed gestures of sincerity. Candidates must develop and perform their own public characters, and develop their own compelling personal "narratives." Acting and theatrical skills have been very useful in the quest for real power, exemplified by the successes of such vastly different political and artistic figures as Ronald Reagan and Vaclav Havel. Regardless of talent or critical acclaim, the face/name recognition that celebrity conveys still gives a real advantage in the electoral arena, as in the cases of Governor Schwarzenegger and the late Congressman Sonny Bono, both of California fame. But why do they repeat themselves so much on the campaign trail? Why the redundancy of language, style, behavior, form?

Electoral campaigning has ritualistic qualities. Ritual has been aptly defined as "action wrapped in a web of symbolism" that gives it more important meaning (Kertzer 1988: 9–10). Electoral speeches and other activities are repeated to the point of redundancy, but this repetition can serve as a force for "channeling emotion, guiding cognition, and organizing social groups" (ibid.). Rituals in Western political life are far from window-dressing or marginalia. They are the processes by which we form, reinforce, and transform our beliefs. These symbolic rites and trappings have a very real political power, especially since not all spectators may think of them as rituals:

> In the United States, as elsewhere, election campaigns involve the staging of [ritual] dramas by candidates as well as the attempts to get the mass media to broadcast these dramatic productions into people's homes [. . .] elections foster the illusion that American government is the result of the free, informed choice of the entire citizenry and that all are equal in deciding questions of public policy.
>
> (Kertzer 1988: 9–11)

Elections in post-industrial capitalist democracies often offer little substantial choice to the marginalized, but they are tremendously important rituals of systemic self-legitimization and perpetuation. They are the rituals of those with strategic power. The election, as a ritual of (legislative, executive, ideological) representation, is a crucial bit of thaumaturgy. These magic acts are carefully choreographed; after all, a magic trick is much harder to perform if the audience is provided hands-on access to all the gear and can view the act from all angles:

> Candidates often try to limit all contact with the public and the mass media that does not take place through carefully arranged dramatic productions, heavily laden with well-choreographed symbols [. . .] the greatest political sociodrama

> and the most elaborate competitive use of ritual in American politics come each four years with the campaign for the presidency.
>
> (Kertzer 1988: 108)

Michel de Certeau also criticizes the hollow nature of the electoral ritual:

> [. . .] membership is marked only by what is called a voice [. . .] this vestige of speech, one vote per year. Living off a semblance of "belief," the party carefully collects the relics of former convictions and, given this fiction of legitimacy, succeeds quite well in managing its affairs [. . .] all that is required is that the surveys ask not about what directly attaches its "members" to the party, but about what does not attract them elsewhere – not about the energy of convictions, but their inertia.
>
> (de Certeau 1984: 177)

While there are real issues and resources at stake in elections, the powerful influence of corporations over the electoral process and the cost of meaningful participation leave many segments of the population without reasonable hope of effective legislative representation. And so the ritual contest grinds on, continuing to legitimize the status quo with great symbolic pomp and force.

In this sense, the electoral ritual parallels Habermas's bourgeois public sphere, with its unmarked exclusion, its self-legitimization and self-perpetuation, and its failure to address the subaltern counterpublics that are waiting for a viable candidate who will speak to their agendas and needs. Or, if not a viable candidate, then *any* candidate who can express their frustration at being locked out of the electoral rituals of representation.

Earnest politicians, bent on winning the power to represent others, are tightly restricted in their behavior, body language, costume, and sense of humor. For example, in the United States, presidential candidates need to construct and disseminate compelling autobiographical narratives, and public personae, that convincingly convey initiative, strength of will, and consistency. These qualities best suit the image of the idealized bourgeois individual, as opposed to the throbbing undifferentiated mass of bodies of Bakhtinian carnival. Clothing is limited to modern corporate attire – a mandate demonstrated most sharply at one of the Bush–Gore debates of 2000, when both opponents were wearing dark blue business suits and red "power ties." As for behavior, the body of a would-be leader must be controlled and disciplined – as must the hair, using whatever chemicals are necessary. The victor's body, after all, will soon represent the health of the nation. Voices should be well modulated, though speech can be sensibly flavored with the dialect of a politically advantageous region. Quick jokes can be worked into speeches but they should be light, wry, and on point. In 2004, Howard Dean's insurgent campaign for the US Democratic nomination was conclusively torpedoed when he "lost control" while trying to rally his supporters in Iowa. He shouted the last few lines of his speech, punched the air, smiled, and gave a defiant shout. These moments of exuberance were broadcast over and over for the next few days as pundits on every station used the footage to question his statesmanship and "electability," the latter term also serving as shorthand for the amount of cash and fundraising potential a candidate seems to have (Meyer 2004).

Obviously, the performative use of props and costumes does not stop between elections. George W. Bush, in a speech which claimed that the US economy had regained its productive power thanks to his policies, stood in front of a huge stack of boxes that said "Made in the USA." However, this was just a fake backdrop, and in fact the empty boxes arranged at the foot of his podium were "Made in China," a label that had to be concealed with duct tape (Tendor 2003). G.W. Bush also made a surprise visit on Thanksgiving to the troops in Iraq in 2003 – presenting them with a massive turkey which was later revealed to be a plastic prop (Allen 2003). Such is the dramaturgy of glad-handing, sound-biting domination.

All of this, this political theatre of domination, is what electoral guerrillas mock with *candidate drag*, parodying "straight" candidates. Electoral guerrilla theatre is a low-budget response to these ritualistic behaviors. In this sense, it resembles the political theatre of domination that it parodies, using the same symbolic vocabulary with a critical twist. This study examines the behavior of "straight" candidates only as it relates to electoral guerrilla theatre, and therefore will not deconstruct the acts of tie-wearing, tank-riding, and baby-kissing in and of themselves.

### Suffragist campaigns

Suffragist campaigns were fundamentally different from electoral guerrilla theatre in that they were attempts to win the vote for women, rather than disillusioned responses to voting rights already won. However, they are real precursors to electoral guerrilla theatre in many ways. They include many strong and varied examples of disruptive, performative interventions in the electoral process. While suffragettes engaged in conventional forms of protest such as the demonstration and political parade, these actions were quite radical at the time simply because they were organized and carried out by women in defiance of the prevailing stereotypes of their sex. They also used a wide variety of creative, disruptive tactics, including civil disobedience, arson, window-smashing and other crimes against property, and even spectacular, symbolic suicide. They willfully went to jail, went on hunger strike and endured forced feedings, and other forms of state torture and repression. It has been powerfully argued that the suffragettes invented performance art in their efforts to disrupt and reform the political and electoral system (Hill: 2001).

Electoral guerrilla theatre is a post-suffragist phenomenon, reflecting disillusionment with current electoral systems. Nevertheless, this form of resistance is influenced by and owes a creative debt to the suffragist innovations that preceded it.

### Parallel elections: the "Bronzeville" campaigns

As analyzed by Susan Herbst, the "Bronzeville" elections illustrate the tactical agency of oppressed people to make do in situations where they lack the strategic power to make the rules. African-

Americans were excluded from participation in mainstream politics in racist, mid-twentieth-century Chicago. In response to this political and social segregation and marginalization, in which blacks could not win elected office on any level, the publisher of the African-American newspaper *The Defender* instituted a *symbolic* election for a *symbolic* mayor of an *invented* African-American constituency: "Bronzeville." This was an exercise in community, polity, organization and – perhaps most importantly – legitimacy and dignity. *The Defender* conducted these "elections" from the 1930s to the 1950s, providing an excellent example of a marginalized group using the highly visible (and, for the moment, exclusionary) symbols and rituals of the powerful in an unanticipated way, creating and maintaining their own "parallel discursive space" (Herbst 1994: 65–95).

The community-building aspect of these symbolic "elections" is as compelling as their directly oppositional or confrontational valences. Certainly, the practice of these shadow "elections" did expose the injustice of the "legitimate" electoral system. The very necessity of a mock-election exposed the racist nature of Chicago politics. But, more importantly, the "Bronzeville" mayoral elections, over time, effectively created the community of "Bronzeville" by soliciting *active participation* by its target audience in a loose "voting" process. The "Bronzeville Mayor" became a spokesman for his newly forged community, speaking to "Bronzeville," and to City Hall, on African–American issues and concerns of the day. However, this study will focus on satirical campaigns that take place within actual electoral systems, disrupting the state's ritual through ironic participation rather than through parallel action.

### Emergent party campaigns

Campaigns such as Ralph Nader's recurring Green Party presidential campaigns in the United States are not exactly electoral guerrilla theatre. These are earnest, movement-building engagements with the electoral system, analogous to a sports team knowing it is too weak to win the annual championship, but playing the season as a "building year." Small parties, such as the Greens, regard themselves as emergent parties that hope to gradually achieve some level of power after a generation or two of struggle.

For example, the Libertarian Party of the United States is a small party struggling to build itself in the face of the Democratic–Republican duopoly. Even though resource-poor, denied access and marginalized, it operates with the ultimate intent of building a real power base within the electoral system and not as an extended prank.

The Libertarians use their seemingly quixotic third-party campaign efforts (including the time-consuming ballot-petition signings) to build a community with social links through the internet and local activist chapters of like-minded people. Compared to other electoral systems in "Western" industrialized countries, the US system, with its two-party "First-Past-The-Post," winner-take-all electoral system, and with the immense power it yields to wealthy campaign contributors, is one of the most exclusionary towards minor, resource-poor parties. At this time, of the 535 Representatives and Senators in Washington, only three are non Republican/Democrats, and two of those were major-party politicians who dropped out of their parties while in office. This leaves the US Libertarian Party in a difficult position, with little access to the media and difficulty getting on the ballot in the states where they run. Without a system of proportional representation, it is most likely that any votes for Libertarians will be "wasted" in that they probably cannot win any seats or positions at the higher levels of government.

However, while having all of these difficulties in common with the guerrilla electioneers, the Libertarians *take themselves seriously* as candidates. They do not seem to incorporate the symbols of the mainstream into their own rhetoric in a parodic manner. They earnestly use their own symbols, or national symbols such as the Statue of Liberty and the Founding Fathers, to bolster their own legitimacy. They also have highly funded and influential think tanks at their disposal, such as the Cato Institute, to disseminate their ideas. Like the guerrilla candidate, they do not expect to win in the present campaigns, and they are trying to use the electoral system to express their opinion from the fringe. However, they do so in a straightforward way which they hope will eventually build a more powerful Libertarian Party and movement which can impose its ideology on the political system from within the legitimate avenues of electoral politics. While the Libertarians oppose the present system, they hope to increase their power and their number of adherents through a nonparodic engagement with that system. This in no way invalidates the way they build and maintain an ideological community on the margins. It merely provides a useful point of distinction between their work and electoral guerrilla theatre (Herbst 1994: 134–65).

There is no hard and fast barrier between emergent party campaigns and electoral guerrilla campaigns – the distinction must be made on a case-specific and tentative basis. Sometimes the efforts overlap, act in allegiance, or are in conflict. For example, Joel Schechter describes his own Green Party campaigns for State Senate in Connecticut as "electoral theater." Schechter created a fictional organization called "Developers for DiLieto," who made public appearances in tuxedos and with champagne glasses affixed to the top of their construction hardhats (Schechter 1994: 139). As the amused press attended these performance art events, they were entertained by the "Developers," who praised Schechter's opponents for being so helpful to wealthy developers at the expense of the local low-income inhabitants of New Haven. While noting that he did not consider his campaign a prank because he would have taken office and acted on his Green Party affiliation and principles if elected, there was a great deal of inventive, media-poaching satire in Schechter's campaign. This example straddles the line between the two types of marginal campaigns.

Sometimes electoral guerrilla theatre directly or indirectly supports emergent parties. After launching Ficus 2000, the aforementioned ironic critique of the US two-party system, Michael Moore went on to work for Ralph Nader's Green Party campaign. Punk prankster Jello Biafra also "ran" for the Green Party nomination for President in 2000, but openly stated on his website that he was only doing so to draw attention to the Party, not to compete with Ralph Nader. However, electoral guerrilla theatre can sometimes frustrate the efforts of emergent parties by distracting voter support, as in the case of the ludic Kabouter campaign, which achieved great success, arguably at the expense of the small New Left parties of the Netherlands (see Chapter 1).

## Soft satire

> A very interesting constituency this: In addition to the official Silly candidate, there is an unofficial Very Silly candidate, in the slab of concrete. And he could very well split the Silly vote.
>
> (Monty Python 1994)

"Soft satire" refers to those campaigns that are humorous send-ups of the political system that just about anyone can laugh at without feeling insulted. While satire usually has a target and a pointed critique, these efforts make fun of the political system in a more light-hearted way, without following Brecht's urging that performers must accentuate the real sociopolitical differences in the audience rather than generalize over them.

Examples of this type of satirical electoral performance are the work of the Rhinoceros Party of Canada, Will Rodgers' and Pat Paulsen's US Presidential campaigns (the former on the "Anti-Bunk" ticket), and the Monster Raving Loony Party of Great Britain. These mock-parties have sustained ongoing campaigns, though the Rhinos hastily disbanded after attracting a large chunk of the national vote in Canada. Soft satirical campaigns mock modern politics with carnivalesque exuberance and a bit of postmodern wit. While they are an important phenomenon, they are not the focus of this study. As Screaming Lord Sutch, the founder of the Monster Raving Loonies, said before his death in June 1999, these performers are just trying to "give a bit of fun for the people" (Hoge 1999).

In contrast, "sharp satire" refers to those candidates who use satire in the electoral sphere to articulate a specific, contentious ideological critique of a system that they feel marginalizes and excludes them. These guerrillas use the rituals of registration and/or canvassing, collecting ballot signatures, public speaking, or other politicians' activities to alienate and mock the whole ritual and their specific targets. Moore's "Ficus 2000" campaign is an example. Other examples are Dick Gregory's campaign for US President in 1968, Wavy Gravy's "Nobody for President" campaigns (see Gregory 1968), Christoph Schliengensief's "Chance 2000" campaign in Germany, drag king Murray Hill's campaign for Mayor of New York City, and the campaign of the Mexican professional wrestler and social activist "Superbarrio" for "President of North America."

An example of a short and simple sharp satirical action was the Yippies' public nomination of their pig, "Pigasus," for President of the United States in Chicago, 1968. In its heated context (the scene of violent conflict around the Democratic National Convention), its insulting irreverence, and its lowering of authorities to the level of the pig – echoing the contemporary derisive term for police officers – "Pigasus for President" gave a hint of more involved and extensive electoral guerrilla theatre activities to come.

Jello Biafra's electoral guerrilla campaign is an example of this kind of speaking mirth to power. Biafra, a longtime advocate of political pranksterism, helped to temporarily monkeywrench the electoral system of San Francisco with few resources besides his bitter, ironic sense of humor.

## Sharp satire: Jello Biafra puts the state in the pillories

> Jello Biafra is his name [. . .] he has used [the Dead Kennedys] as a platform to expound on his political and artistic views (he's the founder of the World Brotherhood of Peace and Anarchy and favors "creative crime," among other things). Now, Biafra has decided to go one step further – he's running for Mayor of San Francisco.
>
> (Hamsher and Murray 1979)

> People were saying to Feinstein, "What happened, Dianne? You didn't get your big win, now you have to run again against

> Kopp." Finally one of her advisors got up and said, "If people like Jello Biafra are going to get *three percent of the vote*, WHAT CAN WE DO?"
>
> (Biafra 1992)

In 1979 in San Francisco, Jello Biafra ran a campaign that used deadpan and heavy-handed humor to mock the city's corrupt power structure.

Mainstream US electioneering is a high-stakes performative ritual. It is repetitive, calculated, and rehearsed, and operates through the necessary, constant reaffirmation of established symbols and values. Biafra operated within this ritual, disrupting the election to create a moment of alienation, and revealing its theatricality.

In the San Francisco of 1979, many voters were dissatisfied with the typical US electoral choice between two evils. A year earlier, a right-wing former City Supervisor, Dan White, assassinated the liberal Mayor Moscone and the famous gay activist Supervisor, Harvey Milk, in City Hall. When White received a light sentence (part of his successful defense was his claim that eating too many Twinkies had unbalanced his emotions), there was a massive riot in the city (Ledbetter 1979; Shepard 1997: 37–56). Despite the citywide trauma, outrage, and desire for significant social change (including a groundswell of desire for police reform/review and an anti-"Manhattanization" movement decrying the increasing density of high rises), the major parties offered the electorate the usual choice: two typically tepid "realistic" candidates, centrist Dianne Feinstein and conservative Quentin Kopp. Voter apathy was noted by journalists (Liebert 1979b). This situation – the spectacular and shocking assassinations, the mild punishment by the judiciary, the outrage and powerlessness felt by many gays and leftists expressed in riot, and the routinized response from the mainstream political parties looking to fill the slots of the murdered – created a tactical occasion for radical intervention.

Biafra was the front man of the Dead Kennedys, a groundbreaking prankster-punk band as irreverent and confrontational as their name. They created outrageous and darkly ironic anti-capitalist, anti-authoritarian songs such as *Kill The Poor* (in which

Jane Fonda helps to convince the liberals that it will be okay to use the neutron bomb to wipe out the underclass and make life more pleasant for the wealthy) and *Police Truck* (a gruesome account of police brutality). Biafra alternated between whipping the crowds up with intense, frenetic, and dramatic performance and engaging them with political monologues and storytelling. He decided to run for mayor in the back seat of a cab on the way to a Pere Ubu concert. His campaign officially kicked off at a fundraising spaghetti dinner/dance at the punk club Mabuhay Gardens on 3 September 1979. Biafra saw the whole electoral run as a subversive "prank" (Liebert 1979a; Biafra 1992).

Biafra's name (and his campaign slogan, "there's always room for Jello") served to disrupt any "serious" press coverage of the election, nibbling at the assumed dignity of the process. Simply seeing a name like "Jello Biafra" in the published vote-count (he got 3.5 percent and helped to force a run-off between the two major candidates) would give pause to any bored reader flipping through the papers.

Biafra's platform included the following items: (1) in agreement with Dianne Feinstein's proposal to "clean up Market Street" and make it a nicer place, all businessmen downtown between the hours of 9 a.m. and 5 p.m. would have to wear clown suits; (2) in response to Proposition 13 and the drastic slashing of funds for education, 7,000 laid-off teachers and city workers would be rehired as panhandlers for the city, keeping 50 percent of their take; (3) a Board of Bribery would be created to set systematic standards for civic corruption; (4) Dan White statues would be erected throughout San Francisco so that the city could earn badly needed revenue selling eggs, stones, and tomatoes for people to throw at them; (5) squatting in abandoned buildings would be legalized; (6) police would be elected every four years by the people they patrol (Liebert 1979a; Biafra 1992).

There is clearly a calculated parodic effect to this platform. The setup is given first in the more absurd and attention-getting proposals. However, the serious punchlines come last as Biafra clearly tries to make a subversive political point. He ridicules the electoral process both through humor and through raising radically reformist proposals (such as items 5 and 6) that stand outside the acceptable, unacknowledged (pro-capitalistic law-and-order) limits of debate.

In any coverage of an election, a reader/viewer may be extending sympathy to the electoral system, following its limited range of debate, and the speeches of the "straight" candidates, in an engaged manner. When Biafra got on television in accordance with an "equal time" rule, and began to present his platform (at one point wearing one of his opponent's old campaign shirts which said "Quentin Kopp the Kosher Cowboy"), he was attempting to disrupt the assumed *gravitas* of the process, and to use theatricality to stimulate critical, distantiated thought.

An interview in the *Bay Guardian* gives a sense of Biafra's tone during the campaign. He was more than willing to send himself up as a frivolous countercultural public figure while he also lampooned the electoral process:

> BAY GUARDIAN: What happens to the Dead Kennedys when you're elected mayor?
>
> BIAFRA: Well, you'll have to ask them that. A lot of people have asked me if I'm just using this as a big gag to promote the Dead Kennedys, but oh no, the Dead Kennedys is a big gag to get me elected mayor. It should be obvious to everyone.
>
> BAY GUARDIAN: Well, did you have that in mind when you formed the Dead Kennedys?
>
> BIAFRA: Not at first, no. But obviously if you're going to run for political office, you have to parade all your achievements.
>
> BAY GUARDIAN: What other achievements are you parading in front of people to make your campaign look more credible?
>
> BIAFRA: Well, I'm kind of groovy.
>
> (Hamsher and Murray 1979)

Biafra straight-facedly took the US political system's vaunted openness and accessibility at face value. The system claims that "anyone can be President," that anyone in this democracy can achieve elected office. Biafra's campaign attempted to reveal the underlying, overwritten truth that, with very few exceptions, only a major-party candidate with a mainstream "narrative", "character," body language, and major corporate backing can have the funding and media attention needed to win an election in the current system. Biafra's campaign was not just absurd because of his disturbing name and bizarre platform. It was absurd because it was self-consciously but not admittedly futile. Many actors work with an *as if* to find their characters' motivation; Biafra performed *as if* the system was truly open to him in order to show that it was not. When major party candidates are introduced by their cohorts as "our next mayor" it is presumptuous; in the case of a Biafra, it is parodic.

The public's appreciation of such a guerrilla performance does not have to stop with a nod and an appreciative wink. Punks and other "fringe" folk got in on Biafra's act, carrying signs such as "If He Doesn't Win, I'll Kill Myself" and "What if He Wins?!?" And, when people actually vote for a Biafra-type candidate, they also engage in the performance, knowingly relishing in the *as if* of the parodic campaign. For alienated voters, unhappy with lame choices and sclerotic debate, Biafra offered a clear, tongue-in-cheek opportunity. Abstaining from voting only gives a vague message. Non-voters can be (and have been) analyzed as apathetic, lazy, and ignorant (implying that perhaps they don't *deserve* the franchise anyway). But when a group of voters actually motivates and mobilizes to go to the polls and vote for a candidate who plans to bedeck all capitalists in clown suits, they are knowingly playing extras in the campaign of a signifying Other. Their mass action is the true punchline of the extended joke, a sort of Boalian "rehearsal for revolution" with a smirk. In Biafra's case, enough people played along and voted for him that it stimulated public debate among the mainstream pundits ("How could this happen?") and furthered discussion of a wider range of issues.

Irony has an evaluative, critical edge. However, it also "happens" in the space between ironist and audience. The audience has creative, interpretive agency; there is never any guarantee that the audience will "get" the ironic statement/performance as intended. Irony is transideological; it can be used, on both sides of the performer–receiver relationship, by anyone of any viewpoint. An audience member may "get" the irony as intended, may not even understand it to be ironic, or may receive it in an unintended way ("God Bless America – even the kooks have free speech and can participate" or "See how ridiculous these people are? No wonder they can't get anywhere"). Irony has an edge, and it is risky for it can cut both ways (Hutcheon 1994).

The existence of discursive communities enables ironic communicative acts. Biafra could not have made the effective performance that he did without the angry, militant punk and queer groups who had just been rioting in response to an outrageous series of events that underscored their oppression. While performers have agency in the crafting of their performances and personae, the pre-existing counterpublics provide them with a core audience who are most likely to "catch" the irony as intended. It is these counterpublics who the performer hopes to entertain and energize for further struggle. However, the guerrilla electioneer often does not only want to "preach to the converted," but also hopes to disrupt sympathy with the electoral ritual among other groups as well. Biafra's campaign appealed to the grievances of the queer, left, and punk counterpublics of the Bay area, but his irony was available for interpretation by a far larger set of discursive communities. His performance was all the more effective due to its timeliness, occurring on such a ripe occasion when the establishment responded to assassinations and riot with the same old bland choices and platforms.

Sharp satire in electoral guerrilla theatre can take many forms. A recent flip on the model of the mock-candidacy is "Billionaires for Bush," who perform as a mock-support group for President George W. Bush composed exclusively of the wealthy few who benefit from his social policies. This group of progressive creative activists, with character names such as "Robin Eublind," "Ollie Gark," and "Phil T. Rich," follow Bush and his staff on the fundraising and campaign trails, "thanking" them for serving the

"Billionaires'" interests so exclusively. Using slogans such as "Tax Work Not Wealth," this intervention in the 2004 presidential elections complemented myriad street performances with original songs, videos, mass mock-posh parties, a website, and even a book. On Tax Day 2004, "Billionaires" appeared in outrageous mock-oligarchical costumes outside post offices and tax-processing storefronts where masses of people were lined up to file their taxes. The Billionaires held signs saying "Thank YOU for Paying OUR Fair Share" and thanked the "little people" profusely. The ironic approach of "Billionaires for Bush" has confused and surprised police and pro-Bush demonstrators on several occasions.

As the vehicle for maximum political agitation and contention in the public sphere, this study concentrates on campaigns that fall within the category of sharp satire, while continuing to acknowledge that these cases fall on a gradual, shifting spectrum and not a hard and fast grid of distinctions.

## Outline

This is an international comparative study, looking at cases in three nations with different electoral systems, and with varying degrees of access for minor parties and candidates to the ballot and mass media. I will examine how this varying political/structural landscape affected the maneuverability and opportunities for each electoral guerrilla. These cases were also picked to examine the effects of another major variant; whether or not the guerrilla is operating as a solo performer, or as the front-performer for a backing organization. Since irony is multivalently produced and received, there is the possibility for trouble as the candidate(s) and the backing organization make conflicting interpretations of their own ironic actions.

These case studies are also chosen for their value as *instructive disruptions*. In the first two cases, something went wrong, and internal disagreements created problems within the movement during the satirical campaign. I examine these clashes, and compare them with the relatively smooth campaign of Pauline Pantsdown, my third case study, in the hopes of determining possible causes for the conflicts.

Chapter 1, "A prank too far? The Kabouters' electoral guerrilla theatre, Amsterdam 1970–71," examines the work of a countercultural movement that achieved dangerous success as electoral guerrilla performers. The Kabouters (or "Gnomes" in English) were an anarchist, carnivalesque, grassroots group active in Amsterdam in the early 1970s. As part of their ongoing countercultural efforts, they ran for seats in several city councils as an elaborate act of ridicule of the capitalist power structure. What makes this case study unique is that, much to their bemusement and later concern, many of their candidates *won*. What can satirical candidates do in the unlikely event that they actually take power?

The Netherlands' electoral system of proportional representation, with its generous equal-time laws, helped make this unexpected success possible. However, the electoral candidates of the Kabouters soon conflicted with each other over the interpretation of their own ongoing prank and how best to continue it in office. They also experienced conflict with their backing organization, the hard-working Kabouters in the grassroots movement. These Kabouters, who were mostly against all forms of electoral power and parliamentarianism, had intended for the campaign to serve as ludic propaganda for their counter-institutions: squat-communes, crèches, organic food cooperatives, free stores, underground press, and alternative schools. While the Kabouters accomplished a great deal as a movement, their unintended success caused them perhaps as many headaches as they gave to the Dutch authorities. Drawing on archives, news sources, and interviews, the chapter examines the measures taken by the Kabouters during both the election and its surprising aftermath, the long-term effects that their campaign and tenure had on the political culture of the Netherlands, and the limits of satirical performance in the halls of political power.

Chapter 1 asks: How does a movement explicitly opposed to representative democracy cope with being "represented" by a few creative performers? Does irony help to overcome this contradiction when actual legislative power is at stake? How can guerrilla electioneering serve a grassroots movement, or backfire, when used as a media tactic?

Chapter 2, "*Sturm und Drag*: The fabulous camp-pains of Miss Joan JettBlakk" examines the campaigns of a radical leftist, working-class, African-American drag performer. JettBlakk ran for Mayor of Chicago in 1991, and for President of the United States in 1992. She was highly aware of her campy place in the history of electoral guerrilla theatre: "I've been saying since the sixties that if pigs can run for President, if bad actors can run for President, then drag queens can too." She was also aware of and influenced by Jello Biafra's 1979 campaign. JettBlakk crashed the New York Democratic National Convention in full drag in 1992, after having successfully crashed both a mainstream gay political event in Chicago and that city's St Patrick's Day Parade. The high-visibility politics of her Queer Nation Party campaign entertained and encouraged many, but caused a great deal of concern within the more assimilationist elements of the local gay community. JettBlakk faced not only this external opposition; her campaign was eventually disowned by her own activist group, Queer Nation/Chicago. This internal disruption was the result of conflicting goals for the campaign, which were reflected in the ways creative decisions were made and the changing style of her performances. Queer Nation/Chicago, as a group which intensely theorized its own work, had fundamental disagreements about what exactly the campaign was mocking and what symbolism it was using. The chapter explores the relationship between performers and social movements and theorizes possible solutions to JettBlakk's dilemma, asking: Is there something fundamentally celebrity-centered about the format, pace, and ongoing dynamic of election campaigns? If so, does that necessarily disrupt the internal processes of an egalitarian activist group that attempts to engage in electoral guerrilla theatre?

Chapter 3, "Electoral guerrilla theatre in Australia: Pauline Hanson vs. Pauline Pantsdown," examines the work of an Australian parodic political candidate and drag performer whose musical, video, and live performance work had a drastic effect on the October 1998 re-election campaign of her nemesis, far-right parliamentarian

Pauline Hanson. In a postmodern technological move that subverted the idea of authentic voice, Pantsdown digitally sampled and rearranged Hanson's own words and syllables, enlisting Hanson as the unwilling vocalist on the satirist's two hit dance singles. Hanson lost the ensuing election. Pauline Pantsdown's work is an excellent example of the transgressive introduction of the lower bodily stratum into the capitalist election's hierarchical site of high/low distinction, while simultaneously attempting to renew and invigorate subaltern counterpublics to whom the ironic, raucous humor is directed.

During her work, Pantsdown was not responsible to an activist organization (like JettBlakk was to Queer Nation/Chicago). She also had a more focused goal. Both of these factors helped her in her work. However, Chapter 3 examines Pantsdown's work as a drag performance that was partially, though not intentionally, complicit with the sexism, regionalism, and classism of the mainstream media of Australia. The chapter asks if this was necessary for the effectiveness of her anti-racist satire. Given the cartoonish nature of the performance, was such caricature avoidable?

Chapter 4, "EARTHALUJAH! The importance of being earnest with the Church of Life After Shopping" explores the project of Reverend Billy (an activist-performance artist and mock-televangelist) and his Church of Stop Shopping/Stop Bombing/Life After Shopping . . . the church's name changes with the times, as has its emotional tone and performative practice. The Church is an interesting project because it has morphed gradually from ironic anticonsumerist madcappery to increasingly earnest postmodern spirituality. As the Reverend has said recently, confronted with eco-disaster, "we are trying to put the urgency back in emergency" with work that at first seems merely absurd or titillating. The Reverend and his Church are unapologetically activist, interventionist, and spend as much time on the streets and in jail as in the "church" or the theatre. This chapter looks at the arc of the church and its tactics – from swarming "services" in Walmart, Disneyland and Starbucks, to a mayoral election campaign against Mayor Bloomberg in New York, to more calm and movement-sustaining practices such as the "sainting" of unsung and hardworking activists in celebratory church services. This chapter also compares this eco-activist work to that of the LoveArtLab of Annie Sprinkle and Beth Stephens.

Two of my four studies discuss the work of radical drag performers. Is there anything that equips and motivates drag performers for this genre of protest in particular? Radical drag performers are already experienced in demystifying the costumes and gestures of straightness as an act of defiance and personal liberation (Newton 1979). Their marginalized position in society provides them with many grievances, and the definition of the unmarked "straight" body as the national, patriotic body is one of them (Berlant 1997). Their joyous, adroit, tensive *candidate drag* exposes heteronormativity as a key component in the overall scheme of oppression.

Chapters 2 and 3 provide a necessary contrast between the identities, campaign objectives, and political contexts of JettBlakk and Pantsdown. Both were radical-left performers who operated on the cutting, critical edge of the drag genre. JettBlakk used her African-American, dress-wearing body as an ambulatory installation piece for radical queer visibility in the repressive context of Chicago in the early 1990s. Pantsdown, operating from her home base of a much more gay-friendly Sydney in the late 1990s, used her drag identity to draw attention to an anti-racist message, acknowledging her own queerness but not emphasizing it. Their local electoral systems offer stark contrasts as well. Pantsdown had little difficulty getting on the ballot in the relatively open Australian system, while Chicago's Board of Elections refused to even count JettBlakk's votes in her write-in campaign.

The concluding chapter synthesizes the lessons that these four case studies teach about electoral guerrilla theatre, paying particular attention to the variables of campaign goals, backing organizations, performative/satirical tactics, electoral systems, ethical questions, and unintended results. It analyzes electoral guerrilla theatre as a complex, tenuous intervention in the rituals of representative power and explores its limitations and advantages as a performative tactic of protest. It discusses more recent examples, including the Best Party, Die Partei, Antanas Mockus, Superbarrio, Stephen Colbert, and Einstein the Dog.

There are countless examples of electoral guerrilla theatre. In fact, when I describe this tactic to people, they often have at least a vague memory of someone who has run for office as a subversive prank. This study is not intended to provide a final closed analysis of this phenomenon, but to open the topic as a category of satirical performance and as a recent, complex, and defiant, dangerously double-edged addition to the social movement's repertoire of contention.

Chapter 1

# A prank too far?

## The Kabouters' electoral guerrilla theatre, Amsterdam 1970–71

> How does a new society grow out of the old one? Like a toad-stool on a rotting tree stump [. . .] in fact the existence of an autonomous, new community in the heart of the old order is the most effective sabotage. But whatever techniques the people's army of saboteurs may use, it will always remember that it cannot resemble the old world's armies in anything, anything, anything [. . .]
>
> (from the Proclamation of the Kabouters' Orange Free State (Plant 1992: 93))

> Well, it was all just a joke, you know?
>
> (Simen de Jong, Kabouter city council member, referring to the Kabouter electoral campaigns (De Jong 2000))

Would you vote for a gnome?

In the spring of 1970, a countercultural group called the Kabouters (Dutch for "Gnomes") launched a ludic electoral campaign that included many acts of mass absurdism and civil disobedience, nonviolent sabotage and symbolic, utopian inversion/subversion in the Netherlands. An ideologically heterogeneous, loosely organized anarchist/environmental movement, the Kabouters were unified in their opposition to the Dutch capitalist, social-democratic system and its attendant paradigms, symbols, and rituals. They referred to their counter-institutions and people's meetings as the organs of the "Orange Free State," a mythical, mystical, New Left fantasy-nation that had formed, and was meant to flourish, within the rotting body of the corrupt capitalist State. Ironically, though the movement was anti-parliamentarian, their electoral campaigns and their overall history were completely intertwined. In fact, the ebb and flow of Kabouter unity, power, and grassroots energy were reflected by their various showings at the polls. Though the Kabouters' accomplishments included the creation of an impressive array of non-electoral, grassroots, and egalitarian counter-institutions, the movement began with a municipal electoral campaign and ended with a campaign for the national parliament. This was a result of their innovative use of the electoral system as a central forum for their guerrilla theatre media strategy.

Studying this tremendous, concentrated burst of principled, talented, and confrontational activism can perhaps inform the efforts of future social movements that emphasize performative tactics. The Kabouters were marginalized, generationally and economically, by the greater society, and self-marginalized by chosen ideology and identity (Herbst 1994: 96). Their history illustrates the complexities of emergent movements' creation of new symbols and frames of action (Tarrow 1998: 106–7). To understand the Kabouters one must understand the movement from which many of their main activists sprung: the Provos. In the Provos, the Dutch authorities and police were confronted with something puzzling and even maddening: a group of anarchic and oppositional youth, artists, students, and other troublemakers with a devilish sense of humor.

## The Provos (1965–7): happeners and anarchists join in provocation

> Laugh them out of power: vote Provo!
> Laugh them out again: Ignore them, with Provo!
> Baffle them, astound them: vote Provo!
> It's a chance to save your life, idiot [. . .]
>
> – from Simon Vinkenoog's "Voting Poem: To all the Dreary People of Amsterdam" (Hamsen 1967)

> Ow! Did you see that? Come and see the violence inherent in the system! Help! Help! I'm being repressed!
>
> – Anarcho-syndicalist peasant being kicked by an exasperated King Arthur (Gilliam and Jones 1974)

The following is an example of a classic Provo action, in the Amsterdam of the mid-1960s, from a contemporary issue of the *New York Times Magazine*:

> [. . .] the riot squad is ready, but where is the riot?
>
> Abruptly [. . .] a straggling band of long-haired youths [. . .] comes running, almost dancing, in the direction of the bystanders. The lapping of leashes and growling of dogs grow more concentrated; the horses edge forward.
>
> The youths start distributing sheets of paper; as at a signal, the police move in with truncheons, evidently unaware that the sheets of paper are blank on both sides. "Make your own pamphlets tonight" the youths shout over their shoulders, laughing as they scamper off the way they came.
>
> The bystanders laugh too, attracting the attention of the frustrated and now oafish-looking police, who haven't got the joke but are somehow aware that it's on them. Just to be doing something, they move on the bystanders, roughly shoving them off the square with their truncheons and the flanks of their horses. The bystanders scatter after the youths in denim, no longer bystanders but followers in spite of themselves [. . .] the provocation has succeeded.
>
> (Lelyveld 1966)

The Provos came from the first post-scarcity generation in Dutch history, and their mission was to expose the euphemized repressive nature of the "late capitalist" society around them, a society which they claimed was headed for nuclear Armageddon and ecological suicide. They would do this by using inventive street actions, publications, and performance art to provoke the authorities into repressive action.

Robert Jasper-Grootveld, a window-washer turned "Anti-Smoking Magician," was one of the founders of the Provo movement and its ironic style of radical performance. Grootveld was an avid tobacco and pot smoker who fervently opposed the consumption-addiction society of which he was such a typical member. He was arrested for spraypainting "K" (for *Kanker*, Dutch for cancer) on cigarette ads around the city. A friend loaned him an empty building, which he immediately designated the *Kanker Kerk*, or Cancer Church. The space was also known as the Anti-Smoking Temple, and it was there that Grootveld, outrageously costumed as Black Pete, the mythical aide to the Dutch Santa Claus, would hold ironic anti-smoking rituals for the hip, "where he led 'enslaved consumers' in rites designed to cleanse them of their addiction, taking on their sins by collecting all their cigarettes and smoking them himself" (Lelyveld 1966). The faithful would chant "Image, Image" in recognition of the power of advertising and the media, and chant the "Ugge, Ugge Song," which involved coughing in unison to signify the destruction of their lungs from smoking and air pollution. The Anti-Smoking Magician would start a fire and the worshippers would dance around it. Unfortunately, Grootveld got carried away at one of these events and the Anti-Smoking Temple burned to the ground. Where were the proto-Provos to go?

The system provided an answer. A cigarette manufacturing company donated a statue called the "Lieverdje" (Little Rascal) to the city. The Lieverdje is a romanticized image of the smiling street urchin of days past, pleasant in his nostalgically charming indigence. The city erected the statue in the Spui square. Grootveld designated the Lieverdje the symbol of the "addicted consumer of tomorrow" and began to use it as the center of his performance art and happenings. Flammable materials would be wrapped around the smiling bronze boy, set afire, and "Ugge, ugge," "Image," and other chants would come forth from the dancing and improvising crowd (Kempton).

An anarchist student, Roel van Duyn,[1] first encountered a Grootveld happening in May of 1965. He saw the potential to more explicitly politicize these ironic, fun, group-improvisatory events. Van Duyn, Hans Tuynman, Robert Stolk, and other anarchist youth joined with Grootveld to form the Provos (short for *provocateur*, a label given the troublemaking youth of the time by an eminent Dutch sociologist, and proudly appropriated by the group itself). Provos began to hand out political literature at the Spui happenings, which led to arrests, beatings, dispersions, and confiscations by the police, who had been puzzled by the performance art but who knew how to deal with unlicensed political activity. At that time, all political demonstrations and distribution of political material required a permit and approval of the police department, a requirement which the Provos both opposed as authoritarian and which they chose to use as an easy trigger for highly visible repression.

The Provos were a small group, but they refused to be nailed down to a specific ideology because of their members' varied individual philosophies. Nevertheless, they left many ideological documents – including the fifteen-issue run of *Provo* magazine – and did many interviews with the press. From all this, and my more contemporary interviews, it can be generalized that the Provos were a neo-anarchist grouping who hoped to update the ideas of nineteenth-century anarchists and syndicalists to the post-industrial era.

Roel van Duyn, the pre-eminent theorist of the movement, worked out this philosophy in his pamphlets and articles in *Provo*, and in his book *Message of a Wise Kabouter* (Duijn 1972). Van Duyn argued that the working class was no longer the source of revolutionary energy, having been crushed and/or bought off on both sides of the Iron Curtain. The new revolutionary class was a non-class – the *provotariat* of intellectuals, youth, students, bums, and beatniks – the post-scarcity *raznochintzy* who felt they had no stake in the economy and to whom cultural sabotage was the only possible expression of freedom. It was up to the provotariat to provoke the authorities into showing their true repressive nature in the hopes of creating a polarized, revolutionary situation in which alliances could be made with the proletariat of the Third World. The alternative was to be passively complicit in the euphemized, consumerist, techno-bureaucratic, capitalist-communist soft slide into ecological and/or nuclear oblivion. As the first *Provo* pessimistically declaimed:

> PROVO feels it must make a choice: desperate revolt or cowering defeat. PROVO encourages rebellion wherever it can. PROVO knows it must be the loser in the end, but it cannot miss the chance to thoroughly provoke this society once more.
>
> (Mairowitz and Stansill 1971: 20)

Provo symbols included the color white (as a color of purity)[2] and the Magic Apple, a symbol which had many meanings, including the designation of the apple-shaped downtown of Amsterdam as the countercultural "Magic Centre" of Europe. This fed such actions as splashing white paint on the door of the mayor's official residence and on the monument of General Johannes van Heutsz, who the Provos saw as an icon of imperialism.

## The Provo electoral campaign

In March 1966, as their largest prank yet, the Provos chose to run for city council in the June local elections. This followed a long internal debate on whether or not anarchists should interact with capitalist power mechanisms such as the electoral process. In his book *The White Danger*, van Duyn argued that anarchists, who believed in local power over federal power, could honorably interact with a *city* government, especially if they did so only to infiltrate, subvert, and provoke. In accordance with these principles, it was decided that if a Provo was elected to the council, the four-year term would be served by four different rotating members for a year each to prevent careerism and co-optation. In addition, Provo council members would publish any secret government documents that they could get their hands on (Duijn 1967 as cited in Tasman 1996: Chapter 2). Winning a seat was only conceivable because of the Dutch system of proportional representation, in which only a small percentage of the citywide vote was necessary to elect a council member.

However, the campaign was more than just another way to tweak the noses of the authorities and their pseudo-democracy. There was a tactical innovation at play here. The Provos no longer desired the violent repression they so easily provoked. Some Provos hoped that by labeling their street speeches and actions as campaign events, and their printed material as electoral pamphlets, they might have some protection from the now-routine police arrests, beatings, and confiscation of literature (Schimmelpennink 2000). This tactic had mixed results; many Provo actions were still broken up by the police. Nevertheless, their signs still stood on several bridges and other places around town: a brightly colored, smiling mask, with the campaign slogan, "VOTE PROVO, FOR A LAUGH." Other Provo signs said "PROVOKE! (Vote list 12)," featuring a cartoon of a tiny person with a hatchet chopping at the base of an enormous jackboot, and "Vote Provo, for Better Weather," the latter a mockery of campaign promises in general (*Provo*). As part of the campaign, the Provos had unruly Friday night meetings in which they promoted their White Plans in all their reformist-utopian-ironic complexity.

**1.1 Provo election sign, 1966: "Vote Provo, For a Laugh!"**

Sourced under fair use

## The White Plans

> The Provos are not frustrated adolescents with too much time and money, relieving their boredom by acts of destruction. Rather, they are acutely concerned about and critical of society, and want their views to be heard. To assure a hearing, they are willing to use any means except violence. One of their first goals is to make Amsterdam a better place to live in, and they have several highly original ideas how to go about it [. . .]
>
> (Hamsen 1967)

The positive side of the Provo agenda was expressed in their White Plans, a combination of satirical and constructive proposals for improving the quality of life in Amsterdam. As they say in "The Technique of How to Provocate":

> The playing Provotariat must be very clever in its play [. . .] our tactic in the attack against authoritarian society must consist of a combination of reformism and provocism. Against each part of the social machine we must act by constructive White Plans as well as by negative provocations. Positive and negative, but in both extremes. On one side we must show by reformistic White Plans how society should be, and on the other hand, we must show by provocations how the society is in reality. Our provocations must create crises so that in the confusion the White Plans have more of an opportunity to be realized [. . .]
>
> (Mairowitz and Stansill 1971: 25)

These plans were meant to expose the shortcomings of the current social order of things by proposing alternatives that could be publicized through confrontational street actions.

Luud Schimmelpennink was a major figure in the Provo movement, and an engineer/inventor who hoped to make Amsterdam a more livable place in defiance of the demands of the capitalist economy. At the time, Amsterdam was plagued not only with a chronic housing shortage which hit youth the hardest, but also by industrial and automotive pollution. The Provos claimed that the cars were not only the *cause* – of cancer, unlivable streets, lack of space downtown, and traffic deaths for pedestrians and playing children – but also a *symptom* of a capitalist economy that depended on planned obsolescence, wasteful private property, destructive over-mechanization, techno-fetishism, and dehumanization at the cost of people's needs. The Provos thus proposed a new system of transport for the city, one which combined banning car traffic from downtown with a collectivized, free fleet of public bicycles:

> Amsterdammers! The asphalt terror of the motorized bourgeoisie has lasted long enough. Human sacrifices are made daily to this latest idol of the idiots: car power. Choking carbon monoxide is its incense, its image contaminates thousands of canals and streets.
>
> PROVO'S BICYCLE PLAN will liberate us from the car monster. PROVO introduces the WHITE BICYCLE, a piece of PUBLIC PROPERTY.
>
> The first white bicycle will be presented to the Press and public on Wednesday July 28 at 3 pm near the statue of the Lieverdje, the addicted consumer, on the Spui.
>
> The white bicycle is never locked. The white bicycle is the first free communal transport. The white bicycle is a provocation against capitalist private property, for the white bicycle is anarchistic.
>
> The white bicycle can be used by anyone who needs it and then must be left for someone else . . . The white bicycle is a symbol of simplicity and cleanliness in contrast to the vanity and foulness of the authoritarian car [. . .]
>
> (Mairowitz and Stansill 1971: 26–7)

The Provos proposed that the municipality buy 20,000 communal white bicycles each year to supplement public transport. This would make possible the eventual banning of auto traffic in the city centre. The Provos organized a public service and performance along these lines: every Saturday, at noon, by the Lieverdje on the Spui, they painted any volunteers' bikes white as a grassroots start of the program.

The latter component of the White Bike Plan, the public painting and distribution of white bikes, was another provocation that made the police look absurdly repressive. It was hard to depict the giving away of free bicycles to the public as a criminal act, yet Provos were arrested for painting their bicycles white, and the white bikes were confiscated for not having locks, following a minor ordinance that decreed that the lack of locks would encourage stealing. Since the white bikes were supposed to be communal property for all, they were *supposed* to be taken, by anyone who wanted to use one, and the police confiscations and arrests came across as ridiculous and petty. Nevertheless, Schimmelpennink got around the law by designing a set of locks that would open with the same key, and distributing copies of that key widely. Prominent Provo Rob Stolk and his fiancé got married dressed all in white under a triumphal arch of White Bicycles (Hamsen 1967: 37–40). Thus, the Provos successfully combined this positive-minded White Plan with public acts designed to provoke police repression.

The White Plans went far beyond bicycles. The White Car Plan used Schimmelpennink's invention and production of small, electric-powered cars and charging stations, which he was able to set up at several places around the city. For a modest fee, Amsterdammers could join the White Car system, which would enable them to drive the non-polluting cars between charging stations at will. The White Cars received a great deal of local publicity (Schimmelpennink 2000; Tasman 2000a).

The White Corpse Plan, a bitterly humorous corollary to the White Car Plan, was a proposal suggesting how the city should deal with the growing number of traffic deaths in the city:

> Provo's first contribution towards a solution of the traffic problem in Amsterdam was the White-Bicycle plan. The authorities torpedoed it by quickly confiscating all the White Bikes that Provo had presented to Amsterdam. And the traffic terrorism

> continues to increase. On the very first day of the new year the monster devoured a two-year-old child [. . .]
>
> (Hamsen 1967: 47)

This plan proposed a complicated street funeral ritual for every victim of auto accidents, to be performed and funded by the guilty driver under the supervision of a special police squad.

The White Chimney Plan, another creation of Schimmelpennink's, suggested that all roofs near chimneys should be painted white, so that polluters could easily be spotted. Schimmelpennink specifically designated a list of prohibited and heavily fined pollutants for industry, with the fines getting steeper in more heavily populated areas (Hamsen 1967: 41–2).

The White Wives Plan, written by Irene van de Weetering, was a then-provocative sexual manifesto. It called for more and earlier sex education and contraception distribution for girls and women. It also said that "Couples with two children should be warned that they will be acting irresponsibly if they have another child. The population increase is alarming" (Hamsen 1967: 44).

The White Housing Plan addressed the lack of dwellings for single people, young families, and students in the city. This plan called for the cessation of all land speculation that resulted in demolition or abandonment of housing, and for the facilitation and legalization of rent-free living in unused buildings. Rather than a new town hall being built, the Provos proposed that either the government stay in the old town hall, or "if it is necessary to expand, take back the expensively restored royal palace on the Dam (which by rights is our real Town Hall)" (Hamsen 1967: 47).

Then there was the White Chicken Plan. To understand this plan, one must understand that the word for "chicken" in Dutch is slang for "policeman." Noting that the police force had been "shaken to its foundations by new forms of art," and had shown through its brutality that it was "totally unsuited for its task," the Provos ironically called for the conversion of the repressive patrolman into a sort of social worker/outdoor party host:

The program of the Friends of the Police is as follows:

1. DISARMAMENT [. . .]

2. SOCIAL WORK
The White Chicken is the social worker of the future. He will be charged with the distribution of first-aid bandages and medicines in emergencies. He will carry matches and contraceptives, as well as Royal Dutch Oranges and chicken drumsticks for the starving provotariat.

3. REORGANIZATION
[. . .] Whenever difficulties concerning any police measures occur, individual policemen will be able to justify their actions at special teach-ins.

Every municipality will democratically elect its own chief of police. There will be a documentation center where anyone who is dissatisfied with the actions and organization of the police can look for evidence to support his claims.

4. TRAFFIC
As soon as the 'magic center' of Amsterdam is closed to all private transport, the police will be in a position to see to it that the traffic outside the center runs smoothly. The White Chicken will ride on a white bike and will be charged with the transportation of defective white bikes to repair shops where do-it-yourselvers and amateur mechanics will be able to paint and repair the bikes as part of their program of creation and recreation.

5. UNIFORM
The White Chicken is dressed in a white uniform as a symbol of his social function.

We suggest a white cap for the transitional period.

The White Chicken heralds the sweet (r)evolution of social relationships [. . .]

(Hamsen 1967: 47–8)[3]

With this last White Plan, the Provos belittled the fearsome and abusive police with merciless, playful humor.

It is interesting to note the similarity of the Provo's White Plans to Jello Biafra's electoral platform in his Mayoral race in San Francisco thirteen years later (see Introduction). In his public commentary on his electoral campaign, Biafra does not mention the Kabouters or show any awareness of their history; rather he notes an influence by an electoral guerrilla who ran for municipal office in his hometown of Boulder, Colorado (Biafra 1992). The mixture of ironic satire and earnest eco-anarchist solutions to urban problems such as police brutality and automotive/industrial pollution seems to be an attractive formula across borders.

Meanwhile, Robert Jasper-Grootveld had continued his performances, and he introduced the chant of "Come Claus, Claus Comes" into his ever-evolving anti-smoking happenings. He was ironically invoking/conjuring Santa Claus to manifest himself for the consumerist society. However, about a year later, on 10 March 1966, Crown Princess Beatrix married the German Prince Claus von Amsberg. The wedding was very unpopular in the Netherlands because Claus had been a soldier in the Nazi Wehrmacht. The counterculture took the announcement of Beatrix's engagement to "Claus" as more than a coincidence. It was proof of the prophetic power of the Anti-Smoking Magician, and the Magic Center of Amsterdam. The movement was galvanized to take action around the now anti-monarchist, anti-German mantra, "CLAUS COMES!"[4]

As the wedding procession moved through Amsterdam, smoke bombs went off all around the carriage, a spectacular act of the Provos. Though no one was hurt, they made a provocative visual picture to be broadcast around the world. Off-camera, the police went berserk and fought with street youth and Provos throughout the night. On 19 March, a photo exhibition and film of the police beatings were shown, raising concerns among the public.

Police repression escalated. On 1 April 1966, Hans Tuynman gave an anti-police brutality pamphlet to a policeman; he was arrested and sentenced to three months in prison, which inspired further Provo demonstrations for his release. On 23 April, in an amusing, multivalent but seemingly harmless gesture, one Provo activist, Koosje Koster, was giving out individual raisins to shoppers on the street; she was arrested and strip-searched. On 1 June, the day of the election, Irene van de Weetering, who was Number Two on the Provo candidate list, was arrested and abused at a "free Tuynman" demonstration. Her husband, a chess grand master, announced that he would no longer represent the Netherlands in chess competitions because of his wife's awful treatment. One Provo was even arrested for whispering "Image" in earshot of a policeman.

All of these actions, and the ensuing police over-reactions, led to the eventual fall of the local government. Both the chief of police (16 July 1966) and the mayor (9 May 1967) lost their jobs due to the massively publicized epidemic of police brutality that the Provos had provoked.

On 1 June, The Provos won 13,105 of the 510,000 votes cast, or 2.5 percent, garnering one seat in the forty-five seat Amsterdam city council. A political scientist's study revealed that Provo voters were slightly more likely to be male, unaffiliated with a church, younger than average, wealthier, and more educated than the average voter. Not surprisingly, they were also more likely to be against the marriage of Beatrix and Claus. However, over 50 percent of the Provo voters were aged over thirty-five, suggesting that they had successfully attracted a body of protest voters who were not active street Provos (*Delta* 1967).

## Provos in the city council

After all this violence and street confrontation, how would the elected Provos act? A common concern among anarchists is that participation in parliamentary democracy will result in ideological diversion, co-optation and a de-clawing of the movement. This may or may not apply to the Provos' case, but it does seem that they were for the most part "well-behaved" in the city council. They lived up to their pledge to rotate the position, and over the course of the four-year term, the seat was filled by Bernard de Vries, Irene van de Weetering, Luud Schimmelpennink, and Roel van Duyn. According to activist-historian Coen Tasman, people were not happy with de Vries after a single month. Van Duyn said he had a "star attitude" (Tasman 1996: Chapter 2). After six months, de Vries resigned, disappointed, claiming that he had had too little help from the greater Provo movement, and had met strong hostility from the Communists in the city council. This theme of the "serious" Old Left being one of the strongest enemies of the ludic New Left would continue into the Kabouter period.

In March 1967, Luud Schimmelpennink, the inventor and promoter of the White Bike and White Car Plans, took the seat and used it to promote his ideas. After a year and a half, Irene van de Weetering took the seat. She left after a year, disappointedly claiming that trying to work in the city council was "a quixotic fight against ghosts." This led to the succession of Roel van Duyn to the seat in October 1969 for the remainder of the term, though van de Weetering advised him for three months to help him adjust to the job (Tasman 1996: Chapter 3).

On 13 May 1967, four days after the Mayor had lost his job, the Provos met at Speakers Square, and with little fanfare announced the dissolution of the movement. They felt that they had accomplished as much as an unorganized band of provocateurs could hope to without being co-opted. As Luud Schimmelpennink told me over thirty-three years later, "we wanted to get rid of the Mayor and the Chief of Police, and we did" (Schimmelpennink 2000). In fact, there was fear that Provo was becoming just another cultural product to be marketed. A tourist agency was offering a "Meet the Provos" tour: for 30 guilders, tourists would be taken to Provo hangout spots to meet the local troublemakers who had received so much attention from the global press. Clearly, it was time to break it up. Individual Provos continued to be active in other local action groups, and within a few years, the counterculture regrouped to create the Orange Free State and Amsterdam Kabouter City.

## Telling fairy tales to the trolls: the parliamentary speech-acts of Roel Van Duyn

For most of the Provos, the electoral campaign was fun, but actually serving in the government was undesirable and pointless drudgery that threatened the integrity of the anarchist movement. Roel van Duyn had a different approach. His "Piggelme" speech was a key moment, introducing the kabouter as countercultural symbol and heralding a period of performative resistance from within the city council itself.

Van Duyn saw the city council as a perfect performance space, with rituals begging to be parodied and alienated:

> [. . .] from the start, van Duyn treated council procedure as pure theatre. "After all," he says, "it was a theatre. Everyone had a fixed role: all decisions were taken in advance; there was no real debate; and nobody listened to anybody else. So I decided to do consciously what the others did unconsciously. I acted a part – my own role."
>
> ("Pixie Prophet" 1971)

In this way, Van Duyn criticized the city council of Amsterdam, a body of forty-five city councilpersons who mostly acted as a rubber stamp for the eight-member College of Lawholders who, with the unelected, federally appointed Mayor, made all real decisions in committee meetings that were closed to the public.

Van Duyn's best-known performance came after the Mayor had delivered his traditional New Year Speech, when the council began deliberating on the purchase of a set of properties to facilitate the further encroachment of the city into the surrounding countryside. Van Duyn used his turn at the microphone to deliver his unauthorized, "alternative New Year's Speech." This took the form of an extremely long, rhyming fairy tale about a dwarf named Piggleme and his greedy wife. The following is an excerpt from the official council records of the 7 January 1970 meeting:

> MR. VAN DUYN, PROVO, says that he, in connection to the backgrounds of point 6d, 6e, and 6f, and also to point 7, which ideologically are in the same sphere, has to say that the Mayor and College have an insatiable appetite and they demonstrate an attitude towards the future of the environment and nature that makes the speaker think about the wife of

> Piggelme. This little woman also thought that nature was a little magical fish, and that this magical fish was endless in his gifts [. . .] to show how things end with people like the little wife of Piggleme, the speaker wants to tell the fairy tale in the edition of Van Nelle [a Dutch brand of coffee] [. . .] as a New Year's speech. The speaker will keep it shorter than the chairman.
>
> In the land of blonde dunes and not far from the sea,
> There lived a little dwarf couple named Piggelme. . . .

Van Duyn went on to read the story of Piggelme, in which a little dwarf and his wife live very poorly in an upside-down plant pot. When they hear of a magical fish who will grant all wishes, they begin to fantasize about all the things they will ask of the fish. Van Duyn's reading went on for a very long time, until interrupted by a frustrated politician from the Catholic People's Party:

> RVD: "And what would you ask him them, if you really spoke to that little fish?"
>
> "First, I think that I'll ask for a little house with a roof and a chimney."
>
> MR. ROSSEN: Chairman, can I make a proposal for order?
>
> RVD: "A little house, really? A real house, do you really dare to ask that, sweet husband? A little house with a little door, where we really can live?"
>
> THE CHAIRMAN asks how much time the gentleman Van Duyn needs for his fairy tale. MR. VD (PROVO) says that he will keep it shorter than the chairman did. He thinks that he needs approx. 5 more min. The chairman asks if MR. VD couldn't shorten the story. MR. VD says that the chairman also took the liberty to make a very long New Year's speech, and the speaker doesn't see why he can't do the same [. . .]

Van Duyn, far from being put on the defensive for reading a fairy tale into the council record, scolded the chairman for having taken so much time when it was his turn. Van Duyn thus explicitly refused to accept a hierarchy of power within the council chamber, and denied any cultural hierarchy between the rhetorics of respectable politician-talk and children's fables:

> [. . .] MR. VD says that the chairman made a New Year's speech and that he also wants to give a New Year's speech. THE CHAIR says that his New Year's speech was on the agenda. MR. VD thinks that he has more right to make a New Year's speech than the chairman because he has been elected by the people of Amsterdam, which is not the case with the Mayor.

Van Duyn used the confrontation that his fairy tale had provoked to raise the issue of the unelected status of the Mayor. Van Duyn claimed greater legitimacy to speak than the head of the chamber in which he was speaking. After this, the Mayor and Van Duyn argued about whether or not Van Duyn's fairy tale was relevant to the point currently on the agenda. In this dialogue, the Mayor was trying to preserve the dignity and proper parliamentary order of the proceedings, while Van Duyn insisted on the relevance of the poetic parallels between the fate of the greedy Piggelme and the piggish government he was critiquing, saying "it's just that people have to listen to it carefully."

Finally, Van Duyn agreed to skip to the end of the fairy tale, which revealed the connection between Piggelme's behavior and that of the city council:

> [. . .] MR. VD says that the fairy tale goes on and that the little wife of Piggelme drives the man to make bigger wishes of the magical fish, just like the Mayor and College do towards the environment in which they live. They think that they can exploit the environment constantly without end. So Piggelme asks more and more, and the little fish doesn't like that very much but he still grants the wishes. And then there comes the moment (this version of the fairy tale is published by the Van Nelle coffee company) that the wife of Piggelme wants

> better coffee than Van Nelle's coffee. Piggelme doesn't see the point, but because his wife keeps asking, he goes to the little fish, and then follows the dramatic finale that the speaker will read now:

At this point, when the Mayor and the other city councilpeople were at the end of their patience, Van Duyn's chosen text took a bizarre, commercial turn:

> "See, my wife is very content with Van Nelle's coffee, but, she would like to know of the little fish if there is any better and where. Little fish, I didn't want to come, because I thought this is going to go wrong, because there is no better coffee that Van Nelle coffee."
>
> [. . .] "Dwarf! Go to your wife immediately! And tell her she asks much too much!
>
> There is no better coffee than Van Nelle on earth.
>
> Everybody understands that who sees the name on the package.
>
> Tell her that I will punish her.
>
> I'm very sorry for you, my friend. Go home and look how the situation is there." [. . .] Piggelme then went home, and when he thought he was home, he saw that the pot was there where his house had been before. And his little wife was crying and she said "Piggelme, what a terrible fate to live again in this old pot!"

Van Duyn then hastened to explain himself:

> The analogy is that people could get into a complete ecological chaos if they go on with the making of roads, and the building of petrochemical industries which are the backgrounds of the points of the agenda [. . .] the point is about the expropriation of people out of their homes at the Haarlemer, and the purpose of the expropriation is to demolish those buildings for the building of a highway. So, what the speaker meant is that the building of highways will lead to a

situation that is comparable to the old pot – a complete chaos and a complete lack of environmental hygiene.

(Duijn 1970b: 38–42)

Van Duyn thus concluded, perhaps enjoying the additional absurdity created by his use of a commercial advertiser's version of a fairy tale that warns against greed. He went on to argue with a councilperson from the Labor Party who failed to see the connection between the Piggelme story and the city's expansion plan.

Van Duyn's action outraged the politicians who were not accustomed to such provocative behavior in the hall of power. A lowly councilperson (not even a Lawholder of the College) reading an interminable fairy tale into the official government record, and scolding the Mayor as an unelected microphone-hog who should listen patiently for the moral at the end? This was a scandalous inversion of power roles.

Later in this speech, Van Duyn named the symbol of the "culture-kabouter" as a mischievous, revolutionary, environmentally friendly creature. It was the symbol of a mass countercultural concept which would spread, if briefly, from Amsterdam across all of the Netherlands and beyond to Belgium, Scandinavia, Germany, the United States, and even Japan and the East Bloc: the Kabouters' Orange Free State.

## The Orange Free State

On 5 February 1970, a group of activists including Roel van Duyn gathered at the People's University of Sabotage (a meeting hall in the University of Amsterdam) to declare the creation of the "Orange Free State." The name of the Orange Free State, an entity conceived of by Ruud Vermeer, contained several plays on words: a free state of mind, an ironic reference to the racist Boer republic, and a state that would be free of the Dutch Royal House of Orange. The Kabouters, as a fairy-tale species positioned between humans and nature, were the denizens of this state.

In Dutch folklore, kabouters are little people (variously translating as "gnomes," "pixies," "elves," and "dwarves") who can talk to animals and even plants. They are wise, mischievous, and kind. They sit on mushrooms in caves. In some stories, for example, they will slip through the keyhole when a family is sleeping, fix and clean everything in their house, and then leave silently before anyone awakes. Van Duyn got the idea for using the kabouter as a political symbol of a new, environmentally friendly, and more hopeful movement during a brief hiatus from politics when he worked on an organic farm. The farmers there avoided the use of tractors and other heavy machinery so as not to scare the kabouters away.

The kabouter, a familiar, old-fashioned, and somewhat silly symbol, was a potent choice for the new movement. Some of the most powerful symbols for new movements are those that are familiar enough to strike a chord with the populace, yet malleable enough to sustain new meanings so they can serve an oppositional movement that seeks social change (Tarrow 1998: 106–7). Adding eco-anarchistic valences to the whimsical, non-threatening, and familiar folk symbol of the kabouter was a cultural coup that created waves of inspiration and indignation across the Netherlands for years: "A new culture with a new man – the culture kabouter who will remove the tension between nature and the old culture. Who understands animals and unites people in love, who will restore unity among everything that lives" (Mairowitz and Stansill 1971: 238).

Guy Kilian, a theorist, activist, and eventual Kabouter city council member, also noted the androgynous aspect of the kabouter. For Kilian and others, the androgyny of the kabouter symbolized the empowerment of women and the "soft man" of the New Left versus the macho, patriarchal "hard man" of the Old Left. While this feminist/progressive agenda may not have been completely fulfilled in the late 1960s and early 1970s, the kabouter was at the least a symbol of a progressive move in that direction within the movement (Kilian 2000).

The Orange Free State's proclamation inverted power roles, going so far as to declare The Hague a fantasy-state:

> A new society will steer right across the old, established order. For the provotariat the government in The Hague is only a

> shadow cabinet, its mayors but shadow mayors, its cudgelling policemen only ghostly apparitions of a fading existence. Their laws, chains of office and cudgels lose their grip on the new reality we create [. . .]
>
> (Mairowitz and Stansill 1971: 238–9)

The Orange Free State was explicitly anarchist and against parliamentary democracy:

> The new society is not governed. It governs itself because everyone is drawn into making decisions [. . .] politicians, as they now exist, will vanish. If everyone is involved in decision-making, politicians are superfluous and politics, which was always power-politics, dies. The new self-ruling society is a 'council democracy' [. . .] this socialism has nothing to do with the old bureaucratic and centralized socialism. It is decentralized and anti-authoritarian . . . It is no longer the socialism of the clenched fist, but of the entwined fingers [. . .] It is anarchism.
>
> (Mairowitz and Stansill 1971: 238–9)

The Kabouters made a clear stand on the side of the ideals of direct, participatory democracy versus those of indirect, representative democracy.

The Orange Free State, as the fantasy nation of the counterculture, had its own parodic trappings, documents, and departments. Industrious Kabouters created rubber stamps and postal stamps, passports, and a parody of the royal Seal for their documents.[5] Later, the Orange Free State would even sign an "international treaty" with other countercultural groups like the Yippies and the Hog Farm of the United States (Tasman 1996: Chapter 10).

However, their own pamphlets warned against taking their own joke too seriously:

> Of course the ALTERNATIVE SOCIETY, about which so much is spoken, is no more than a symbol, a jest. The Orange

> Free State can never compete materially with the OLD ORDER as long as they can't operate good working health insurances or provide enough unspoiled fruit to feed 13 million people [. . .] the Orange Free State will show that it could be better and in a different way than what has always gone before.
>
> ("Why One Must Vote Kabouter" 1970)

Thus, the Orange Free State was to be an enjoyable, utopian illusion that would galvanize and spread the counterculture. An article from an English underground paper agreed:

> The Orange Free State, like all important cultural freak-outs in Holland, begins as a media-hype. It's a fake. A reporter in the *Observer* last month got caught in the game, and reported that the Gnomes were a significant political force, armed with a political party, etc. But at the beginning, it was a dropped hint, a cultural rumour, a mind-fuck [. . .] a piece of pop-art. It's an image. It's keeping people busy. And it will find its own explanation [. . .] clearly intended to bring people together under a common hoax [. . .].
>
> (Mairowitz 1970)

This "hoax" seemed to make its own kind of sense to the "freak" countercultures not only in Amsterdam but also in England and elsewhere.

The Orange Free State was publicly declared in a silly and ironic ritual in downtown Amsterdam. A group of activists gathered in a square, ripped up a paving stone, and planted some grass and a dead branch with several oranges fastened to it. They then sang the Orange Free State's national anthem, the nursery rhyme "The Owl is in the Elms" (Morris).[6] It was decided that the group would have people's meetings every week on Fridays. The meetings would be open to all, and would be the ultimate authority of the movement. Eventually, smaller coordinating committees were formed to focus on separate issues and set agendas. The Orange Free State hoped

**1.2 Kabouters in the streets, protesting the housing shortage by marching with canvas walls and roofs, and signs proclaiming: "Amsterdam: Kaboutercity"**



to coordinate the activists working on all different issues in a nonbinding and loose structure, a "playful chaos" (Tasman 1996: Chapter 4).

Almost immediately after the initial people's meeting on 5 February 1970, participation in the city council elections was a major issue for the new countercultural formation. Roel van Duijn (who had changed his last name back from "van Duyn" to its original spelling) proposed that the Orange Free State participate in the elections at the second people's meeting on 12 February 1970. Coen Tasman attributes van Duijn's motivation to the desire to stay in office, as he was the last and current Provo city council member. Because the Provos had been dispersed for years, van Duijn needed to form a new movement to support his re-election, and as he had found the city council to be a great media platform for performances like his oration of "Piggelme," he felt that

**1.3 Two Kabouters and their children with gasmasks as a demonstration against environmental pollution, 15 August 1970**



a continuing presence in that body would continue to serve the "two-handed" strategy for the counterculture.

This "two-handed strategy" called for attacking the old system from within while building and publicizing the new society. Van Duijn proposed that electing an "ambassador" from the Orange Free State to the Amsterdam City Council would draw attention to the Kabouters' grassroots accomplishments and help to influence public opinion. "Furthermore, the Kabouter Party could draw attention to the fake democratic rituals and provide secret government information for activist action groups" (Tasman 1996: Chapter 9).

Many Kabouters had avidly followed van Duijn's highly publicized antics in the city council, and they enthusiastically received the proposal for a ludic electoral campaign. It was decided that the Kabouters would run on the ticket "Amsterdam Kabouter City" as the local entity of the Orange Free State. Several campaign slogans

**1.4 The little horse-drawn fruit wagon (the *Kabouter Knetter Kar*), with which the Kabouters of The Hague sold their organic food, August 1970**

© Franklin van den Berg

were thought up: "Choose Your Own Ambassador," and "Vote Only Kabouter." In Dutch, the latter is "*Stem Louter Kabouter*" which had a nice sound to it and was very popular (Coen Tasman's excellent history of the Kabouter movement is named *Louter Kabouter* for this reason).

However, a minority of more experienced Kabouters, mainly ex-Provos and more ideologically committed anarchists, had misgivings about the electoral campaign. Ruud Vermeer, who first had the idea for the Free State as a poetic and playful unifying fantasy, feared that its independent, ludic character would be lost if the Kabouter movement took the form of a political party. Hans Tuynman, the old Provo, argued that Provo participation in the city council had co-opted some of the movement's leadership and eventually became the main reason that the Provos dispersed. This faction feared for the underground character of the movement should the Kabouters be drawn into the political power games of the traditional parties. On the meeting of 9 April, Anti-Smoking

Magician Robert-Jasper Grootveld prophesied what would happen if the Kabouters did not stay in the world of "Image":

> Interviews with the over-kabouters with journalists from Tokyo, Washington, and the Soviet Union! The Provos made the same mistake! The Orange Free State is still a Utopia! Kabouters still don't exist! We are only children of middle-class people and of slaves of the consumption-society! And who will now go as an ambassador into the city council?
>
> (Tasman 1996: Chapter 9)

Nevertheless, during that people's meeting, a candidate list was hammered out. The list included popular activists from many different groups across the city. Van Duijn was the list leader, followed by Connie Bos, the only woman on the whole list. She was a theatre student and a member of Action Group Tomato, which threw tomatoes at actors in high-budget theatre productions. Frans van Bommel (number three) was an activist in the radical Union of Visual Artists. Bos and van Bommel had staged a sit-in in the Reijksmuseum at the "Night Watch" playing games and smoking hashish with friends in the shadow of the revered Rembrandt painting ("Nachtwachtzaal"). Guy Kilian, anarchist student activist, was number four on the list. The sixteen-year-old student activist Kees Hansen (number five) was the legally ineligible candidate protesting the minimum voting age of twenty-three (the voting age was eventually lowered, partly due to Kabouter pressure). Joop Peters (number six) was a leader in Action '70, a radical squatters' movement that had broken into and occupied many unused buildings in Amsterdam. Action '70 had garnered a great deal of sympathy with people across the city, as the chronic housing shortage was not only an issue for "hippie" youths. Simen de Jong (number seven) was a central figure in the activist People's Department for Education, and Peter Hakkenberg (number eight) was a radical housing architect and active member of Action '70. The rest of the list included many other activists from various sectors of the movement (Tasman 1996: Chapter 9).

One of the first acts of the Kabouters was to steal the mayor's chair from City Hall. Their demand in exchange for its return, according to one source, was the resignation of the Mayor; according to another, they demanded the establishment of ten housing communes to relieve the housing shortage. They presented a chair to the media with its legs cut off, claiming that they had cut the Mayor's power down to size (actually, it was a different chair) (Mairowitz and Stansill 1971: 233; Tasman 1996: Chapter 6). This act signaled the Kabouters' pranksterish, nonviolent irreverence for authority and the law.

The Orange Free State attempted to unify the many local activist groups in Amsterdam into one loose, anarchist federation. Wryly playing with Old Left terminology, the Kabouters assigned the role of "People's Departments" to different groups: "The Union of Squatters will be socialized into the *People's Department for People's Housing* [. . .] The People's University for Sabotage and Pseudo-Eroticism is socialized into the *People's Department for Sabotage of Power and Force*, to replace the Ministry of Defense" (Mairowitz and Stansill 1971: 240).

The metaphor/fantasy was extended into the city council, with Provo/Kabouter city council members to serve, not as politicians in the normal sense, but as ambassadors from the Orange Free State to the old and fading society: "The town hall of the old community [. . .] will act as Embassy for relations with the old society. The Provo council member [i.e. Van Duijn] is appointed ambassador" (Mairowitz and Stansill 1971: 240). Thus, according to this playful construction, Kabouters who won the elections would not be sullied by participation in parliamentary democracy; rather, they would be diplomats, spreading the good news about their gnomish utopian state to their less fortunate human neighbors.

Again, this all fitted with van Duijn's two-hands theory of countercultural struggle: with one hand, the movement would build an alternative society with its grassroots institutions, while with the other hand they would subvert and disrupt the extant, oppressive society. The Orange Free State served as the anchor for both activities, as a utopian example of a better possible future, and as a base of operation/organization for the ongoing action against the government.

There is a parallel between the White Plans of the Provos and the People's Departments of the Orange Free State. Both are utopian alternatives to the status quo. Just as the White Plans and "provocism" worked together as the yin and yang of the Provo movement, so too did the Kabouters hope to use the "two-hands" theory, simultaneously building and tearing down. However, in contrast to the doomsaying Provos, the Kabouters built a softer, more optimistic, friendly, and consciously ludic symbol-structure, centered on their playful, pointy-hat-wearing gnome character.

However, for some activists, there was a hidden price to the more friendly symbolism of the Kabouter. Schimmelpennik felt that the troublemaking, hard-core image of the Provo, while off-putting to many, at least kept away opportunists and uncommitted people. The Kabouters were far more open and less threatening, and thus a far more inviting movement for opportunists and careerists to enter and co-opt from within (Schimmelpennink 2000).

Nevertheless, the Kabouters also had a cutting side to their rhetoric, and their actions led to mass confrontations with the police (especially their break-ins and occupation of abandoned and unused buildings). They referred to the police as "hirelings," and, in the face of another wave of increasing police brutality, declared an "Eighty-Year War" on the police department, evoking the name of the Dutch guerrilla war against their Spanish occupiers centuries earlier. They also termed Kabouter activists who went to other cities to agitate for the Orange Free State "missionaries," a term sure to offend the religious Catholics and Protestants of the nation (Tasman 1996: Chapter 4).

As the campaign progressed, theoretical differences continued within the movement. Frans van Bommel and Connie Bos consistently underscored their opposition to the parliamentary system that they were playing with. Van Bommel said:

> What we want is to involve the people. Make them start thinking and not just delegate authority to the politicians

> [. . .] we don't know what form the change will take, but one of the great fallacies of democracy as we know it is [the idea] that the people, through their votes, are actively participating.
>
> (Morris 1970)

Bos agreed, saying "The political parties are dead [. . .] [The Orange Free State is] a big gimmick for the outside. We don't really believe in it" (Morris 1970).

Roel Burgler, known as the anarchist "conscience" of the movement, was quick to point out that the Kabouters were far from a unified ideological group (Burgler 2000). They especially differed in attitudes towards the election. From the beginning, the electoral effort had different meanings for different Kabouters.

In one movement pamphlet ("Why One Must Vote Kabouter"), a writer named Willemsen suggests that if any Kabouters were elected, they would publicize street actions in the motions and memoranda of the city council, discouraging the mayor from taking unlawfully repressive measures against street activists. He also argued that a low vote for the Kabouters would encourage police repression in the summer, and that the opposite was also true. He suggested that the election was actually an opportunity for an official public validation of extra-parliamentary oppositional work. In the same pamphlet, Wim Noordhoek acknowledges some ideological similarity between the Kabouters and the Pacifist-Socialist Party (PSP) and the Radical Political Party (PPR). However, he argues that the Kabouters' purpose was to undermine the parliamentary system, and that participating in that system was one method for doing so:

> The emphasis of the Orange Free State's activities is clearly not on the council members and other institutions of our oh-so-democratic governmental system [. . .] for the OFS [. . .] the council work of Roel Van Duyn [. . .] is not much more than a political follow-up of what the people on the street really start. First practical actions, which must make clear what

> is wrong, and for the public to win as much as possible for themselves, and then we pressure the city council [. . .] the Kabouter Party is the first political party in this country which has realized so logical a convergence between inner and extra-parliamentary actions [. . .].
>
> ("Why One Must Vote Kabouter")

The emphasis on non- and even anti-electoral politics was one of the key ways in which the Orange Free State distinguished itself from the other New Left groupings. However, the complex incorporation of election campaigns into the mix created a tense and possibly unstable hybridization of heretofore antithetical approaches to movement activism.

In an article from *Kabouterkrant*, the main Kabouter underground paper, some other concrete motivations are given. First, a vote for a Kabouter was a vote for a more anarchist local-council system of government:

> LOOK OUT for Bureaucrats and Suppressors! The city council of Amsterdam consists of 45 people. Most of them come from parties only seeking to enlarge their own power. Those 45 people have governmental power over the city's 830,000 inhabitants, and that has to stop. In all the neighborhoods, people should choose neighborhood councils, which would have limited authority about their own affairs. This would result in a whole network of neighborhood councils, so that all Amsterdammers can be directly involved in the government of their own neighborhoods.
>
> ("Why Vote Kabouter")

Some Kabouters thus hoped to change the system to a more directly democratic one from within.

This article goes on to argue that a vote for a Kabouter was a vote against the secret, closed method of decision-making in the present municipal government:

> City Council: Only Fake Decisions. In reality, in fact, all the decisions which are to be made in the public meetings of the city council are fixed from the start. They are made in secret meetings of the commissions that are small groups of members of the city council which talk about special things. Or in secret negotiations between the Mayor and the College with businessmen, from which people hear the results only much later. All this atmosphere of secrecy is only there to maintain the power of authorities. The Kabouters demand openness for all the commission meetings, and immediate openness of all memoranda and government papers. Openness, openness!
>
> ("Why Vote Kabouter")

The article concludes with a final condemnation of the extant political system in which the Kabouters were about to participate:

> Fairy tales Can be Realized: Real democracy is at the moment still a fairy tale. Because real democracy means that the people govern themselves, while at the moment, it is the politicians and the bosses who decide. The kabouters want the workers in the factories to form workers' councils which have the power to decide about the work and their wages. The kabouters want [. . .] a whole network of councils in which every person has the right to participate: A council-democracy [. . .] We'll have to fight hard to realize the fairy tale [. . .]
>
> ("Why Vote Kabouter")

Throughout this article, little cartoon kabouters are scattered in the margins saying things like "And remember, kabouters don't exist!" and "of course, you don't have to vote!" These cartoons suggest the ambivalence of the Kabouters towards their participation in a system that they had critiqued so radically and consistently.

In an article in a later issue, "City Council Philosophies," the desire to use the city council for street-style guerrilla theatre is made more explicit:

> Most ambassadors of the Orange Free State see the partaking in the city council as an action. Only as far as the council can be used as a permanent action-center can it function for us [. . .] the fraction strives always to the building and improvement of the neighborhood councils.
>
> ("Gemeenteraads Filosofieën" 1970)

**1.5 A Kabouter election poster. It says "There will be many gnomes on one seat!" The image of four tiny hippie-gnomes on one chair is a playful allusion to the Kabouters' pledge to share power by rotating a new Kabouter into their city council seats every year of the four-year term**

From the personal archive of the author

Some Kabouters had the idea that any proposals they put forward in the city council should be so outrageous and provocative that they could never be accepted by the rest of the city council, thus preventing the Kabouters from getting co-opted by the parliamentary process (Tasman 1996: Chapter 9). The Kabouters agreed that they would use a rotation system as the Provos did, with city council members rotating once a year as a guard against careerism and a demonstrative example of the principle of decentralization of power.

## The electoral campaign

> Holland in 1970 is a strange country. Nothing happens anymore. History has ended. Everything moves very little. People in Holland don't get anything new. Politics are in balance in Holland. The balance is divided between fifteen small parties and each party has right and left wings in balance. They need four parties [to govern], which is eight wings, and if one wing breaks off then the cabinet falls, like an airplane [. . .] and the people in Holland are uninterested. If people want to change anything, they're going onto the street.
>
> (comedian, to tourists on the VPRO video *Is it a Sin to Be Subjective?* (Coehlo and Doebloet 1970))

The Kabouters did not use every possible method of self-promotion during the campaign. In order to set themselves apart from the stuffy traditional parties, they refused to participate in electoral debates. They also made no traditional political speeches. Instead, they launched a massive, varied campaign of spectacular grassroots actions. This was a strong performative choice. Their electoral campaign proved to be a largely non-verbal series of incursions into the capitalist public sphere, e.g. decorating illegally occupied unused housing with campaign cartoons and posters. The explosion of practical and direct actions, and the lack of traditional grandstanding and policy promises, drew grassroots energy and media attention to the campaign. These joyful street actions were indivisible from the campaign. The campaign, with its specific deadline, gave urgency and energy to the street actions, which in turn promoted the anti-ticket "List Ten," the Kabouter line on the official ballots.

On 22 April, the Kabouters spraypainted "Kabouter 10" all over the city, and a week later placed election signs on twenty-six bridges. In keeping with their action-over-election principles, these boards only said "List 10" and "Amsterdam Kabouter City," leaving plenty of free space for the announcement of street actions. However, these spaces were soon occupied with election slogans and a kabouter with a pointy hat. Jan van Amerongen created large election posters on which a little kabouter on a scale outweighed a number of very fat authority figures. A progressive priest of a condemned church allowed Peter Hakkenberg and Willem de Neef to hang a banner of a kabouter and the number ten (also painted by van Amerongen) from the church steeple (Tasman 1996: Chapter 9).

On 1 June 1970, the Kabouters staged the Jericho action. A hundred Kabouters, led by Marius Ernsting in a flowing prophet's robe, marched in silence six times around the enormous Nederlandse Bank. On the seventh, they ran, shouting and playing instruments. Although, as one Kabouter wryly noted, "the walls didn't fall down," the action was captured on VPRO television cameras. This allusion to an Old Testament tale, assigning the role of the Biblical enemy to Big Capital through non-verbal, playful action, was typical of Kabouter performance technique (Coehlo and Doebloet 1970).

Ria Hazelaar had an original idea for a Kabouter action using tram line Number Ten to promote List Number Ten. She led three other Kabouters into a Number Ten tram, and, as the car traveled on its track, they poured orange paint through a funnel onto the street. The long orange trail went for many blocks on Line Number Ten before the Kabouters were arrested. This act communicated without words the Kabouters' imagination, lack of fear of arrest, and joyful disrespect for the sanctity of public and private property (Tasman 1996: Chapter 9).

Provo-style plaguing of the police continued with a collaboration with the feminist group Dolle Mina. The activists staged an action that counted on a predictable police response. They attached bunches of inflated condoms to banners with slogans written on them, and marched through town without a permit. Naturally, the police came to arrest them, so they let go of the condom-balloon-banners, which floated up into the air, creating a great image for the news cameras. According to countercultural legend, the Dutch Air Force scrambled and shot down the condom-banners for fear that they were interfering with air traffic (Hakkenberg 2000b; Tasman 2000a).

Operation Wandering Branch was an ongoing Kabouter action in which Kabouters ripped up street pavements and planted trees in the middle of urban spaces, much like their initial action in which they declared the Orange Free State. This led to the police arresting

**1.6 The condom banner action of the Kabouters and Dolle Mina, 21 March 1970**

© Coen Tasman

the nonviolent activists and their illegal trees. Naturally, the police looked a bit silly ripping up the trees and taking them away in the police wagons, and attention was called to the lack of green spaces in the city. Once again, the Kabouters highlighted a serious urban political issue through provocative and humorous action rather than speechifying (Coehlo and Doebloet 1970).

In Action Stone, the Kabouters ripped up pavements in playgrounds to make them safer for children. They advocated replacing the concrete with rubber, a reform that has since been implemented in many city playgrounds. To Guy Kilian, this was not only a microreformist action but a symbolic move to call attention to the fact that, in general, there was not enough caring for children in the urban culture (Kilian 2000).

During the last week before the elections, Frank Laufer filled his little boat full of musicians and singing Kabouters, covered it

**1.7 Policemen arresting a tree during the action "Wandelende Tak" (Wandering Branch) on 21 March 1970**

with campaign posters, and drove it through the canals of the city (Tasman 1996: Chapter 9). In addition to this aquatic carnival, the Kabouter campaign included "formal" street theatre. Dimitri Fenkelg Frank wrote a "wagonplay" for the Kabouters' Meespeeltheater (or participatory theatre) called "The Authorities and the Squatter." The Kabouters performed the play all over the city, setting up their little wagon and playing music and dancing to attract a crowd first. The play was very simple agit-prop which lightheartedly dealt with the housing shortage. In it, a woman and her children are homeless. A Kabouter shows them how to break into an abandoned building and settle into it. Enter the Authority, a generic figure wearing a cross and speaking for the general religious, economic, and political forces of repression. The Authority says that squatting is not necessary because the housing shortage is not really that bad, and anyway squatting is illegal and he will have to call the police. However, when the Policeman shows up, he has already been "turned on" by the Kabouter. He arrests the Authority and leads him away. The dancing and music resume. This somewhat escapist show drew large and enthusiastic crowds, some of whom offered empty rooms in their homes to the homeless members of the Kabouter movement (Ernsting 2000; Tasman 1996: Chapter 9).[7]

Perhaps most important were the ongoing break-ins and occupations of vacant buildings by Action '70. These mass actions led to well-publicized confrontations with the police. During some of these events, Kabouters were able to promote their election campaign. Peter Hakkenberg told the story of a particular building occupied by the Kabouters, then vacated when the police drove them out. The Kabouters managed to break in again, and the police again drove them out, barring the front door. The Kabouters broke in through a side door and managed to bore away at the front door from within. They hid the evidence of their handiwork with a large "Vote List Ten" poster on the outside of the front door. Then, during another demonstration outside the building, with a large police presence, Kabouters sneaked in and burst open the front door, ripping the poster in half and embarrassing the police once again. There were cases where squatters and police played hide-and-

**1.8 The interactive street theatre of the Kabouters, 31 May 1970**
© Coen Tasman

seek in dark, deserted complexes, and others where more direct confrontation made the police look bad to many Amsterdammers who were frustrated with the general housing shortage. The Kabouters used talcum powder bombs to defend their occupied houses in a nonviolent way. When the talcum was hit by the high-powered firehoses used by the authorities, it made the outsides of the building very slippery, causing the police assault squads to slip and fall in the middle of their attacks. This high-stakes, grim slapstick publicly connected the Kabouter campaign with nonviolent, illegal resistance to the forces of urban land speculation and police repression. No other political party engaged in such activity as part of their usual vote-getting efforts (Hakkenberg 2000a; Tasman 1996: Chapter 6).[8]

The Kabouters declared 5 May, Dutch Liberation Day, to be National Squatting Day, a move which offended some. On this day, they led the occupation of empty houses in seven major cities across the Netherlands (Kalk 1970). Thirty houses in Amsterdam and three hundred across the country were occupied.[9] As Action '70 leader, former businessman, and anti-Nazi Resistance fighter Andre Schmidt told the *New York Times*:

> We want to work harmlessly – without too much violence – but effectively within society like gnomes [. . .] we want to liberate people. At first, though, we are going to liberate the empty houses [. . .] [Speculators] have gone to the fringes of the city and left these buildings empty [. . .] the city buys some buildings and holds out on the others – but in the meantime we have all these buildings that are empty and all these students and workers and young people who need places to live. It's scandalous.
>
> (Weinraub)

Like the Provos, the Kabouters tried to use their election campaign as a shield against police repression of their street actions. Afraid that well-publicized mass arrests would result in a large sympathy vote for the Kabouters, the police backed off from several potential confrontations. On 28 May, for example, the Kabouters occupied an empty building in the Damstraat and called it the Orange Free Palace. The police, who normally would have violently evicted them, did nothing but observe. Also, Kabouters were illegally selling the *Kabouterkrant* all over town as the election approached, but they were left unmolested (Tasman 1996: Chapter 9).

When the election finally came on 3 June 1970, there was only a 61 percent turnout, surprisingly low for the Dutch electorate, which had had an 88 percent turnout in the previous election. This turnout was interpreted by some as a reflection of a widespread disillusionment with the traditional parties (Tasman 1996: Chapter 9).

The election was a stunning victory for the Kabouters, who received an astonishing 37,836 votes, or 11 percent of all votes cast. They became the fourth largest party in the city, with five seats in the council, the same as the Catholic Party. Interestingly, they gained their highest vote percentages in neighborhoods that had low overall turnouts. Class was not a constant determinant of Kabouter votes; the neighborhoods which supported them included both relatively wealthy as well as economically troubled neighborhoods. This suggests a connection between political alienation/ disillusionment and Kabouter votes. Certainly, through their campaign, which was marked by non-verbal, anti-systemic, and illegal spectacle, Amsterdam Kabouter City had proven attractive to a surprising number of voters. Coen Tasman concludes that a vote for the Kabouters was an anti-system vote (Tasman 1996: Chapter 9: Tasman 2000b).

To get a sense of the overall context, the rest of the electoral results were as follows. The dominant PvDA, or Labor Party, lost one seat, dropping from thirteen to twelve seats. The new liberal-left group, DS70, did not win a seat. The Communists (CPN) did very well, growing from six to nine seats and earning a probable claim to two seats in the College. The Catholic Party (KVP) shrank from seven to five seats. The new-left PPR (Radical Political Party) did not get a seat, but the newly formed Old People's Party won one seat. The CDU, another Christian party, lost its only seat. The unfortunate PSP (Pacifist Socialist Party) shrank from four seats to one. The far-right Farmer party lost its seat. The ARP (Protestants) kept their two seats, but the CHU (another Protestant group) shrank from three to one seat. The VVD (right-wing Liberal) gained one seat for a total of six. D'66 (left-liberals) won only three seats, and A. Martini felt that they had lost votes to the Kabouters ("Politiek" 1971).

On Election Night, hundreds of Kabouter activists gathered at the bookstore which had become their Election Center on the Spui (the square with the same Little Rascal statue that was a focal point for Provo, and then Kabouter, satiric symbolism). As the results came in they began to celebrate raucously, despite the warnings of

**1.9 The Kabouters occupied buildings in protest of the housing shortage, hardly the usual action of an electoral party. The banner on this building reads: "AMRO wants to throw the children out onto the street [the Kabouters had established a children's crèche/school in the unoccupied bank building] – children throw AMRO out onto the street! Take your money out of the bank!"**

© Coen Tasman

Roel Burgler, who was standing on a car nearby, yelling to remind them of the meaninglessness (and even distracting power) of the elections, and the importance of individual direct and local political action (Tasman 1996: Chapter 9).

Nevertheless, the Kabouters partied wildly, putting a gnomish pointy hat on the Little Rascal and dancing around it. The results included victories in other cities as well; Kabouters had won two seats in The Hague, two in Leeuwarden, and one each in Arnhem, Leiden, Alkmaar, and Amersfoort. True to their direct-action philosophy, they spontaneously initiated "Action Push-Auto" on the Spui, asking motorists to turn off their cars so that they could push them down the street "using many hands, like toy cars without smell and noise" (Morris 1970). The pushing Kabouters chanted "Auto-Cancer" during this action. Many motorists agreed and played along, but there were three scuffles with less playful drivers (Tasman 1996: Chapter 9).

The Kabouter ambivalence toward political power was reflected in their next action that night. Feeling bad for their shut-out, far-left comrades in the PPR, they tried to offer them one of their seats. When the PPR refused, they offered a seat to the PSP, who also refused. Such a seat-transfer would probably have been illegal anyway ("Politiek" 1971). Interestingly, Simen de Jong remembered this differently, reflecting an even stronger anti-parliamentarian attitude; he thought the Kabouters had offered all but one of their seats to these friendly parties (De Jong 2000).

## Unmanageable Kabouters, or Kabouters as managers? Reactions to the Kabouter victory

> June 4, 1970: In September in the Amsterdam City Council, next to 40 chairs, there will be five mushrooms.
>
> (from "Politiek Amsterdam Geschokt door Grote Winst Kabouters (Political Amsterdam is Shocked by the Great Victory of the Kabouters)," *De Tijd*)

The Kabouter victory drew a variety of responses from the surprised press corps and political elite, including outrage, depression, bemusement, and dismissal. *De Tijd* stated:

> The spectacular victory of Amsterdam Kabouter City is without any doubt the sensation of the council elections in the capital. We'll have to live in the coming four years with the knowledge that a party that is not taken seriously by many will be the fourth largest in the city council.

The Catholic daily paper also argued that the fantastic joke would have to be incorporated into the daily machinations of parliamentary power:

> The big lesson of these elections must be that extra-parliamentary action has won over parliamentary action. It is astonishing to the imagination that extra-parliamentary democracy could get such big victories over the traditional parliamentary parties. One is willing to speak about not-very-fruitful splintering, and ludic deviation, until the moment that one must actually give up seats, and until we admit that [. . .] ludic fantasies will have to be buried under mountains of very boring paper.
>
> ("Politiek" 1971)

The *Volkskrant* added that the Kabouter victory "is a writing on the wall from which one must understand that young people are especially dissatisfied with the present order, and that there is a great need for an essential and profound renewal." In a warning note, *Het Parool* noted that:

> What was appealing to the voters was the ludic style of the kabouters, which differs very much from the deadly earnest, difficult doings of the more traditional parties. Voters who supported them because of this ludic and humane aspect must not have their votes misused through aggression and/or anarchistic killjoy.
>
> ("Fairytale" 1970)

With this conclusion, *Het Parool* called for the Kabouters to show responsibility and maturity now that they had been legitimated by the popular vote.[10]

There was a perception that the ludic energy of the Kabouters drew votes not only from the stodgy center-right parties, but from the earnest, emergent parties of the New Left as well. The PvDA, PSP, PPR, D'66, and DS70 had not done well in the elections. The CPN did very well, but as the party of the Old Left, they were the most likely of the groups to feel threatened by a ludic New Left entity. While celebrating their own victory, they noted in *De Waarheid* that "A lot of voters who had voted for the (Kabouter) party should find five seats in Amsterdam much overdone" ("Fairytale" 1970). The Chairman of the Labor Party, Ed van Thijn, was disappointed with the results, and argued that the Old People's Party and the Kabouters were signs of generational polarization. He also noted that both administrative and extra-parliamentary radical action, as exemplified by the CPN and the Kabouters respectively, had found an ear with the voters. The young left-liberal D'66 party, who were disappointed with their three seats, felt they had lost many votes to the Kabouters and the Communists. Attributing their loss to the "Roel van Duyn and Harry Verhay [the leader of the CPN] effect," D'66 list-leader A. Martini said he was disappointed that

> after three years of hard work at a program that critiques the Mayor and the College, we have gained so little, while the ludic actions of the Kabouters have in a short time been so successful [. . .] the Kabouters have blocked our progress . . .
> ("Politiek" 1971)

Nevertheless, not all reaction from the Left was negative and much of it was supportive. Martini went on to say that "if they appoint good people, we are at peace with that." Han Lammers, the leader of the city's Labor Party, was initially supportive. "I see the Kabouters as allies in the struggle for a just and more humane society. I think that they should get full respect from the left-wing parties" (Lammers 1970). Even more upbeat was Eric Jurgens, list-leader of the seatless PPR. "I am no longer a list-leader because my list has vanished," he joked. He felt that the losses for the PSP, PPR, and D'66 might encourage the small Left parties to work together more. Mr. Burggraaf, the national chairman of the PSP, saw in the Kabouter phenomenon an activation of the grassroots, and therefore saw it as a positive development even if his party had lost all but one seat in Amsterdam ("Politiek" 1971).

The sharpest cut came from someone closest to the movement. Rob Stolk, the veteran Provo, had strongly opposed the participation of an anti-authoritarian movement in a capitalist election.

In an interview with the paper *Vrij Nederland* on 13 June 1970, Stolk dismissed the Kabouter victory:

> I believe that elections can't contribute much to the changing of community relations. Roel [van Duijn] thought the same way in the past, but it seems that has changed. Through the taking of a seat in the city council, he is in fact working with the status quo of the society that he said he is against [. . .] There is not much changed in the situation in the council. Five Kabouters, yes. But the PSP lost three seats. They both want something similar. So I find one more seat [after subtracting the one Provo seat] not very impressive [. . .] I believe that taking part in the election for most of the Provos was going back to the old views. And now, he does exactly what I found after the fact to be one of the silliest things we did: sitting in the city council. If he really wishes to do something, then he must do nothing. Now he contributes something to the conductors of city policy, which has nothing to do with the existence of 800,000 people.
>
> (Rogier 1970)

This harshly lucid critique of the Kabouter campaign from a veteran anarchist activist was an early salvo in an intra-counterculture struggle. Stolk voiced the concern of many Kabouters: that while a guerrilla campaign to promote the movement's counter-institutions was fine, actual participation in parliamentary politics would inevitably lead to co-optation.

Commentators from the Right tended to either dismiss the Kabouter victory as unimportant or be scandalized by it. One central question for them was whether or not the Kabouters would be responsible partners in the techno-bureaucratic management of the city as the Communists had been. Prime Minister Piet de Jong of the KVP generously called the Kabouter victory "a whiff of perfume in the onion-sprout odor of daily political life," but added immediately that there were problems in the Netherlands that the Kabouters' mentality could not solve (Tasman: Chapter 9).

The Right was asking the same question that the Kabouters were debating internally: now that the ludic anarchists had won a share of parliamentary power, would they play nicely?

H.H. Jacobs of the right-liberal VVD (Party for Freedom and Democracy) called the rise of the Kabouters "very spectacular but discouraging. I have always reflected on the Kabouter actions as a colossal joke. This phenomenon will probably lose its glitter in the coming years very quickly" ("Politiek" 1971). Haja van Someren-Downer, President of the VVD, stated coldly that "I have the feeling that the people wanted to make a joke, but they attach little importance to having a very nice City Council" (Tasman: Chapter 9). Someren-Downer is also quoted in *Trouw* as saying that the Kabouter victories were "a stupid joke of the voters" ("Fairytale" 1970).

Mr. Steenbergan of the CHU, whose fraction had shrunk drastically, was alarmed. He showed an awareness of the Kabouters' counter-institutions and the success of their symbolism, and a concern for the chaos they might bring to the city council:

> For a good forum of administration, this is an alarming setback [. . .] the influence of the Communists will increase. The growth of the Kabouter Party is a disaster for Amsterdam, infected as it is by anarchist ideas. They are trying, by the formation of councils, to undermine the whole social order. One of the reasons for their success is the disproportionately large attention of the modern media for the Kabouter phenomenon. The innocent civilian sees a ludic little Kabouter, but in fact it's life-threatening. I am concerned. If those five Kabouters behave just as destructively as that one Kabouter [van Duijn] did, I see big problems.
>
> ("Politiek" 1971)

The conservative Professor F. Duynstee, writing in the right-wing *De Telegraf*,[11] called the Kabouters "irrational and negative," arguing that "We mustn't be so naive as to see in the Kabouters no more than brownies, good-hearted kabouters [. . .] if you have profited and achieved something, you will be trapped with insults. The ludic element is unjust and insulting." Duynstee had read *Message of a Wise Kabouter* and stated that van Duijn was not a reformist who would work with the government but a radical revolutionary (Duynstee).

Steenbergen and Duynstee contrasted with Jacobs and Someren-Downer; far from dismissing them, these conservatives saw the Kabouters as a real threat to society. Mr. Sem Bonn, list-leader of DS70, the two-month-old left-liberal party that failed to win a seat, was also concerned. He called the gain of the Kabouters "very sad for Amsterdam. It's a very alarming development that will make Amsterdam more difficult to govern" ("Politiek" 1971).

The Federal Government-appointed Mayor Samkalden, who would have a series of conflicts with the Kabouters in the years to come, said that the party's new successes meant that they would have to grow up and become responsible:

> As for the outcome of the elections, it's clear that Amsterdam in general follows the national trends. There is one deviation from that – the list of Amsterdam Kabouter City. The five seats that this list has won requires the councilpeople of this party to make a very constructive contribution to decision-making. With one representative, this group could permit themselves something. But a representation of five seats brings with it responsibilities.
>
> ("Politiek" 1971)

Samkalden further noted that the CPN's victory (going from six to nine seats) was a reward for their mature and earnest participation in the city government (perhaps hoping the Kabouters would follow the Communists' example), and that D'66 had lost any potential gain to the Kabouters. Samkalden also expressed disappointment in the low voter turnout, and said it would be the responsibility of the government to awaken public interest in [parliamentary] politics ("Fairytale" 1970). While the Left was divided between those who resented the rise of the Kabouters and those who saw their gains as positive, the mainstream, conservative political class was divided on whether or not to take the Kabouters as a serious threat.

A survey of political cartoons from the major newspapers in the aftermath of the elections gives a sense of the cultural, symbolic resonance of the kabouter and the readiness with which the Dutch press latched onto and amplified the kabouter symbol. A kabouter, with a mischievous smile and pointy hat, was used to signify the Kabouter movement, whether the purpose of the cartoon was to support the Kabouters or to satirize them. As noted above, Haja van Someren-Downer, President of the VVD, had said the Kabouters were just a joke. In a cartoon after the election, she is shown tied up by a swarm of Lilliputian kabouters, one of whom, labeled "VAN DUYN," stands on her chest and says "Don't worry, this is only a joke" (Opland 1970). Another cartoon shows a little kabouter entering the city council, looking up at the huge feet of the frightened politicians, who are standing on their chairs as if he were a mouse (Untitled 1970). Then there is the strip by the famous van de Straat, whose strips always feature a generic chubby "older generation man" and his thin, more liberal son. In this strip, they are sitting next to each other silently on a bench for two frames. In the third frame, the son whispers in the ear of his father, "Five Seats." In the fourth frame, the son leans back with satisfaction, while the father fumes. The Kabouters are never mentioned in the strip, but they did not have to be explicitly named for the generational joke to resonate (Straat 1970). In another condescending but amusing cartoon, a pointy hat hangs on a bedpost. Someone is deeply buried in the bedsheets. His mother is poking her head into the room and saying, "Wake up Frans, you have to get up and go to the City Council" ("Frans . . .").

Then there are the two cartoons that mock the other parties' fears of being overthrown by the new ludic party. In one, a trio of politicians labeled "PvdA," "PSP," and "D'66," one hiding a club behind him, approach five tiny kabouters sitting on mushrooms. Their line is simple: "Can we play, too?" (Willem). In the other cartoon, the joke is similar. The grim-faced leaders of the major parties are wearing ill-fitting Kabouter outfits and fake beards and sitting uncomfortably on mushrooms. One is sadly studying a book labeled "Piggelmee" as if it were a crucial political tract. The caption reads "Maybe this will help for 1971" ("Misschien" 1970).

The Kabouter victory received international coverage from as far away as the United States. As often happens with electoral guerrilla theatre, the movement received extra coverage for its political agenda due to the media's hunger for novelty stories. The electoral victory provided the ironic twist that made the story of the Kabouters "newsworthy."

A surprisingly substantial front-page story from the *Los Angeles Times* on 9 July 1970 called "The Kabouters: Dwarf Power – Zany Politics Dazzles Dutch," details the grassroots actions, anarchist ideas, and electoral exploits of the Kabouters. "They call themselves 'ambassadors,' not city councilmen, emphasizing their role as transmitters of the people's will to the higher authority they implicitly reject." The piece extensively quotes Guy Kilian, Frans van Bommel, and Connie Bos, the most anti-parliamentary city council members who were heavily involved in squatting actions and other street protests. The piece quotes van Bommel stating that the "ambassadors" "will try to reverse the current system where eight city managers [the College] make decisions and the council rubberstamps them. They also threaten to publicize secret-council meetings." Kilian is quoted as saying "the politicians hope their words will lead to action by governments [. . .] we hope our words lead to action by the people [. . .] we don't just protest the housing shortage. We find empty ones." He sees the Orange Free State as a fantastic "platform." "It will dissolve, reform. Even the ambassadors themselves should become superfluous." Maarten Manson is aptly quoted saying "It's difficult to avoid becoming just another party." "This is the real problem," said Pastor Karel Eyckmann, one of the unsuccessful Kabouter candidates. "We are now too popular. All the Dwarfs admit it" (Morris 1970).

The Kabouters were even covered by *Time*, in an article called "Pixie Power in Amsterdam." Noting the shift in tone from the Provos to the Kabouters:

> New tactics were introduced early this year by the Kabouters, or Pixies, who decided that fun and games might be more effective than paving stones and smoke bombs [. . .] The Pixies frequently fight city hall – 140 of them were arrested last month for refusing to clear out of an abandoned building – but they also joined it, in a way, by forming a political party. Van Duijn's motto of "Sweetness, Flowers and Understanding" coupled with good deeds apparently won over many Dutch voters who had been growing impatient with youthful protesters [. . .]
>
> ("Pixie Power" 1971)

The innovative tactics and resultant electoral victory thus earned the Kabouters the respectful acknowledgement of the international press. However, that achievement came with a cost of legitimacy in the eyes of some in their own anarchist counterpublic.

### Internal debate on principles, and on the nature of the prank in progress

The narrative of electoral guerrilla gnomes now moves into the halls of parliamentary power. The internal and external conflict intensified: between Kabouters on the council and their "straight" political opponents, between Kabouter council members over issues of politics and performative tactics, and between Kabouters on the council (I will call them "council-Kabouters") and the members of the greater movement (or "street-Kabouters").

Even before the Kabouters took their seats, there was controversy between street-Kabouters and council-Kabouters. Roel van Duijn and the others had gone on the radio with many noble-sounding proposals of what the five Kabouters would do in office, including using their office to give power back to the people, but they spoke without first consulting the people's meeting. Especially controversial was the question of the fifth seat.

The fifth candidate was Kees Hansen, a purely symbolic candidate since at sixteen he was far too young to hold elected office. Nobody had expected this to be an issue, but the huge Kabouter victory meant that his slot was due a seat in the council. The people's meeting of 4 June at the Blue Teahouse in the Vondelpark decided it would be best to leave Hansen's seat demonstratively empty, and to let him shout his statements from the gallery occasionally. Melvin Visser made the innovative suggestion that a kabouter-doll should be placed on his seat, along with a tape player that could play various recorded statements or sounds during council meetings.

This was a watershed moment of performative choice for the movement. If Hansen's seat had been occupied by a little kabouter doll, it would be a powerful way to set the tone for the relationship between the Kabouter movement and the city council. The Kabouters would be giving up 20 percent of their elected power in order to show their contempt for the system. Many street-Kabouters could have expressed themselves in City Hall through the medium of the tape recorder. However, the first four council-Kabouters decided instead to appoint Joop Peters (number six) to the seat without first asking the people's meeting. This choice, while understandable, alienated many. The street-Kabouters were already worried that the electoral success would take media focus away from the movement's street actions and onto the goings-on at City Hall. Now they feared that a dynamic of representative politics was developing, and they were unwilling to be any politician's "constituents."

The Kabouters of the people's meeting felt that electoral politics was not an effort to be emphasized by the movement or even taken seriously. They still felt that the elected "ambassadors" should be answerable to the people's meeting for all their actions. On the other hand, Frans van Bommel felt that since Kabouters should not see the city council as a "higher" entity, but as just another site for disruptive and provocative pranks, the "ambassadors" should be allowed to make their own decisions and actions just like any other Kabouter group ("Gemeenteraads" 1970). Both the people's meeting, van Bommel, and Bos didn't take electoral politics seriously – but they still clashed on the issue of accountability. On the other hand, Roel van Duijn was already beginning an ideological shift from anarchism to parliamentarianism, and was taking the city council (and College) power-politics more and more seriously, despite the explicit objection of the people's meetings.

It was at the 11 June people's meeting that Frans Hoffman presented his very perceptive essay that postulated a split within the Kabouter movement between "strategic anarchists," who planned to use the city council and all other public spaces in the old society as venues to promote anarchism, and "ludic strategists," who planned to use the Kabouters' playful symbolism and style to build what was ultimately just another parliamentary political party. Hoffman identified with the former, warned the group against the latter, and argued that the electoral victory was only thanks to the extra-parliamentary actions of the base movement. Roel Burgler and Hilke Krohn, fearing co-optive "repressive tolerance" in electoral victories, proposed that the council-Kabouters should only be allowed to make proposals and notas in the city council that were so radical that they could never be accepted, but that could spark maximalist discussions (Tasman 1996: Chapter 9). Clearly, to the majority of the base, the electoral joke needed to remain just that: an extended bit of satire and provocation, not an earnest negotiation with the extant political system.

### Curtain up on the council: the swear-in

On 1 September 1970, the five Kabouters joined the rest of the council members to be sworn in at the City Hall. Unlike their "straight" colleagues, who wore the usual gray and blue blouses and jackets, the Kabouters came in full countercultural costume: van Bommel wore black leather trousers, and Connie Bos wore a halter top and a maxiskirt. There was quite a furor over the five's appearance, and Bos in particular drew a great deal of attention. Photos of her were published internationally, with headlines like "With Bare Belly in the City Council" (*Der Stern* 27 September 1970, as cited in Tasman 1996: Chapter 9). The council-Kabouters had decided to nominate Bos, a twenty-three-year-old woman, as their fraction leader, and she thus was able to raise more hell in the smaller, elite meetings of Party leaders, traditionally composed exclusively of older, male, career politicians.

Before the members could be sworn in, Kees Hansen stood up in the gallery and shouted that he wanted to be installed and that otherwise the voice of the youth wouldn't be heard. He continued to shout until the Mayor ordered the police to evict him, which resulted in a general police-Kabouter scuffle in the gallery. Joop Peters, who was to take Hansen's place, was instead sitting up in the gallery in protest (he was sworn in at a later council session) (Tasman 1996: Chapter 9).

Once order was restored, the council members were sworn in, which simply requires the politician to say "Yes" on cue. However, when it was the turn of the Kabouter faction, each one in turn said, "Yes, and I would like to add that Suharto is a murderer." Because there were four of them, they were able to wait until the previous Kabouter was finished before speaking the provocative line, despite the city council staff's attempt to interrupt and move on. In this way, they protested against both the bloody legacy of Dutch and US neo-colonialism and the planned visit of President Suharto to Amsterdam (which was later canceled) (Tasman 1996: Chapter 9). Thus, from their very first utterance as city council members, the Kabouters signaled their disruptive intentions and anti-imperialist ideology. To the sit-in and the teach-in, they had added the *swear-in*.

Once sworn in, the Kabouters took their seats and began passing around a lit hashish joint. Roel van Duijn, a non-smoker, did not partake, but the others did. A right-wing (VVD) council member apparently was the only one of the straight politicians to recognize the smell of the drug, but he did not force a confrontation on the issue. Bos and van Bommel had hoped to provoke an arrest and dispute over the illegality of soft drugs, especially since smoking tobacco was legal in the city council at the time. They came back, armed with more joints, to a later session.

The Kabouter victory had real ramifications for all the other parties: with five seats, the "freak" party had an arguable claim to one of the Lawholder seats in the College, which were usually doled out proportionately among the different parties. The College had seven seats, but the city was planning to create an eighth seat for the management of a new Department of Welfare. Roel Van Duijn wanted the powerful position of Lawholder of Welfare for himself, and very strongly lobbied both inside and outside the Kabouter movement for the appointment.

As could be expected, many Kabouters, who were philosophically against the concentration of power, did not want any of their members to take part in the College. To them, this would be unacceptable collaboration in the capitalist power structure:

> Kim wants instead of Lawholder a law-leaver or a people's commissioner [. . .] Andre Schmidt sees more in a lawbreaker. Roel [van Duijn] makes clear that the Lawholder will become a lawkeeper of the unwritten rules of the Orange Free State. He has to be a rioter. But other kabouters think a Lawholder is not alternative enough. Or even an alternative Lawholder is still too authoritarian. Democracy from the bottom-up is crucial. Begin therefore with yourself and with your children. And begin with non-authoritarian education. A gentleman in a dark suit, who is very difficult to get away from the microphone, says the game has to be played with the game players.
>
> ("Lawholder" 1970)

With the last line, the writer warns against the voice of co-opting authority, which argued that it was time for the Kabouters to grow up and play nicely, just as the Mayor and other politicians had argued.

One Kabouter cartoon not so subtly lampooned Roel van Duijn's position as the object of the majority of media attention, the apparent "leader" of a movement that wanted no leader, and an anarchist who was campaigning for the powerful position of Lawholder against the explicit and repeated opposition of the base of the movement.

The cartoon is a cut-and-paste of an old Smurf cartoon, with new text in the word-balloons. Papa Smurf stands in the middle of a crowd of smurfs, lecturing to them while they listen with consternation. Additional humor is provided by the fact that Smurfs had been used in advertisements for British Petroleum:

> PAPA SMURF: Dear Smurfs, I have always been your leader. You can't smurf me just on the same level as yourselves. I have smurfed your well-being and luxury. Have I not smurfed that BP smurfed us higher in the hierarchy? I have always smurfed you democratically. You have to smurf me some respect. There has to be peace and smurf, and if not, I will have to smurf measures. And if you have something against BP, then we can smurf for Phillips because in the end our economy has to be smurfing. I will smurf all that I possibly can, but it needs time. Everybody has to smurf understanding. But I smurf that I also will smurf the super-smurfing because everything has its smurf. But then democratically, and not according to besmurfed smurfmeasures, smurf, smurf, smurf [. . .].
>
> OTHER SMURFS: Watch out, Kabouters! He is an authoritarian smurf! [. . .]
>
> We have to sabotage him!
>
> Put a needle in his balloon [. . .]
>
> ("Maar Lieve Smurfen!" 1970)

This cartoon was another important, comedic sign of the growing suspicion from the grassroots base of the more parliamentary-minded council-Kabouter.

Van Duijn himself stated that he was very ambivalent about the Lawholder position, but he ultimately decided that he wanted it. While other Kabouters accused him of being an opportunist and a media figure, one can see in his writings a political thinker who is undergoing an ideological shift of an intense and awkward nature while under great scrutiny and pressure from his own counterpublic:

> The Kabouters demand the function of the Lawholder for Welfare for themselves. I, Roel van Duijn, am a candidate for

> it. There are people that say, that we, by that candidature, betray our own anti-authoritarian principles. And, I have to admit that I have the feeling that I am putting myself on the edge of the cliff. Because the danger of being accepted as a Lawholder by the political underworld of power-hungry job-seekers is as big as life. The danger of being corrupted and of increasing the political power that a Lawholder today still has to manipulate people, confronts you every day . . . Kabouters stand, like all other left-wing idealists, for the problem of how to struggle for a non-authoritarian society in an effective way, without becoming authoritarian themselves.
>
> (Duijn 1970a)

Van Duijn thus acknowledged the difficulties and contradictions of his and the Kabouter movement's positions: an anti-parliamentary movement now had a chance at real power. Whither the movement?

Van Duijn argued that the Kabouters had to continue to break down authoritarian structures from within, and to further democratize the city council. He wanted a continued organization of grassroots council-democracy. He acknowledged that the Lawholdership as an institution was authoritarian. Nevertheless, he argued that it was necessary for the movement to shift ideological gears at this point of unexpected opportunity in order to move for power:

> Catastrophes on a global scale that are the consequence of irresponsibility are starting to show. Only the responsibility of the masses can save us. If the use of authoritarian means can contribute to the bringing of political responsibility to the people, then the Kabouters shouldn't let that go. That is my justification for our candidature for Lawholdership of Welfare. It is a function that can help us to bring the power to the people [. . .]
>
> (Duijn 1970a)

With this, van Duijn argued that an urgent, dangerous global situation justified a cautious, reluctant maneuver of the Kabouters towards earnest seizure of parliamentary power positions. This was a clear difference in principle from the majority of the Kabouter movement.

In the end, the Communist Party of the Netherlands had the final say in the matter. The CPN had worked very hard to achieve political legitimacy and power within the extant order (to the point where they had two College seats), and they were horrified at the thought of their New Left/ludic rivals taking a seat in the College (Ernsting 2000). They felt that the non-class-based ideology and disruptive actions of the Kabouters were both "pseudo-left" and "anti-democratic." Apparently, they were more threatened by the clownish Kabouters than they were by the Right. On the first vote, they voted for an ineligible member of the right-wing VVD, and Roel van Duijn tied with a member of the Christian KVB party. On the second vote, the CPN voted for the KVB member, who took the position. Though the Lawholder issue was settled, it had clarified the division of political principles within the movement. Rob Stolk, so cynical and pessimistic about a liberation movement participating in electoral politics, had predicted the behavior of the CPN and the ultimate outcome (Rogier 1970).

The media focus on the council-Kabouters continued. Marius Ernsting, who led the Jericho action, performed in the Meespeeltheater play, and eventually rotated in as a council-Kabouter, said that "things had gotten to the point where, if one of us put a brick down on the sidewalk, the press would stand around and take pictures of it and speculate on what it meant" (Ernsting 2000).

Ernsting was not exaggerating. When Guy Kilian brought an apple into the chamber and began to eat it during session, he was photographed and those pictures were published in several papers ("Kabouterraadslid Guy Kilian" 1970). Kilian was simply hungry, and was astonished at the focus directed at his digestive act. Roel van Duijn became such a recognizable symbol of the counterculture that a statue of him was installed in Madame Tussaud's Wax Museum downtown. Such was the highly symbolized situation in which the council-Kabouters found themselves. The grassroots Kabouter movement did not get such attention in the media.

The council-Kabouters were dismayed to find that they were earning the distrust of the radical neighborhood action groups across the city, who saw the council members as part of the establishment. After all, they had five seats in the city council, were attending sessions and making speeches and one was even lobbying for a Lawholder position. This particularly dismayed Bos and van Bommel, who were very active in the squatters' movement and particularly in the massive "Operation Condemned Houses" action (Tasman 1996: Chapter 9). Again, validation via mainstream channels of power was hurting the Kabouters among their own counterpublic.

However, Roel van Duijn was in his element. Coen Tasman classified van Duijn and Guy Kilian as "kabouters of the word," and Bos and van Bommel as "kabouters of hard action" (Tasman 1996: Chapter 9). Typical of van Duijn's approach was his science-fiction-style "New Year's Speech" of 6 January 1971, during a discussion of the Mayor and Lawholders about the leasing of a property to Container Terminal "Amsterdam" Ltd. In the grimly written "letter from the future," van Duijn prophesies a dark future of social and ecological disaster, thanks to the poor decisions of the city council. Van Duijn begins his speech with an introduction reminiscent of a science fiction novel, which sets the tone for the whole "letter from the future." He says that he would not have asked to speak except that a civil servant had delivered him a mysterious letter. This letter was signed with his own name, but was dated 1 January 1981, ten years in the future; "Only thanks to the phenomenon of kabouter-years could this letter travel to us through time." Characteristically, van Duijn proceeded to read the entire letter into the record:

> 1 Jan. 1981
>
> Dearest,
>
> I am sitting here on the fourth floor of a squatted building situated exactly opposite the City Hall. I am sitting in front of the window, and under me is a cacophony of a frenzied crowd attacking the City Hall. "Water, water" they cry. It is an incredible chaos. The hysterical crowd has smashed all the

> windows of the City Hall with stones. Out of these gaping wounds point the gun barrels with which policemen under command of Mayor van Thijn defend the City Hall. Just now van Thijn has tried to give a speech to the crowd from a window, using a megaphone. But I could see how he, hit by stones, retreated [. . .]
>
> O, there I see an old woman get hit by a bullet and fall on the street. Around her people cry for revenge and furiously dig the last stones from the pavement [. . .] It seems that today all the dangers that we kabouters had already warned people about have reached their apocalyptic realization.
>
> This morning when I turned on the tap yellow foaming water streamed with a stale smell in my sink. At eight o'clock there was the news over the radio that the drinking water pollution that started in Rotterdam and all along the Rhine already last week, is now almost complete in all the industrial centers of Europe and America [. . .] Yet I am convinced that it would have been possible, if, from that first of January, we would have taken a very different course in our economy and our society [. . .] In 1971 it was still not too late to end the poisoning of the earth and the starving of millions and millions of people a year [. . .]
>
> (Duijn 1971)

Van Duijn went on to detail a series of ecological and industrial regulations in line with the Kabouter philosophy, denouncing individual council members for their earlier resistance to these proposals. With this speech, he introduced a fantastic rhetoric into a normally dry speech context, trying to raise the perceived stakes for the politicians by prophesying long-term total disaster as a result of the pattern of their small, daily decisions.

In contrast to van Duijn's performative tactic of fictional, poetic, and denunciatory speechifying was Connie Bos and Frans van Bommel's hash-smoking protest action of 16 September 1970. They had prepared a motion about the relative harmlessness of soft drugs such as hashish and marijuana, arguing for the legalization of these substances. Now, for a second time, these two city council members started smoking hash joints in the chamber.

At the start of the session, a wary Mayor Samkalden warned them, "If you start to do things which are forbidden, I shall take the necessary measures." Van Bommel immediately lit up and started smoking a joint. "Is that hash?" asked Mayor Samkalden. "Yes," van Bommel answered. Ms. Bos then announced that she had just lit up a joint. Dr. Samkalden immediately stopped the assembly, and a group of police rushed into the chamber. They confiscated the cigarettes and also searched van Duijn and Kilian. Van Duijn shouted, "I never smoke this damn stuff and I refuse to leave the chamber!" This exposed a split in tactics and politics between the council-Kabouters, who were all searched outside the chamber. Van Bommel and Ms. Bos were arrested and taken to the main office of the police for questioning and to be processed. Chief Inspector De Rhoodes, telling his own joke alluding to kabouter folklore, said "We won't hold them, we usually don't if we catch people smoking a joint. We'll send them back out into the woods" ("Wegens Roken Hasjiesj" 1970).

For the whole afternoon, De Rhoodes and five police agents from the Narcotics Division stood watch in the public gallery. In the canteen of the town hall, a force of twenty policemen waited. The Kabouters had declared in advance that they would smoke hash joints en masse in the chamber. The mass-stickie civil disobedience never happened, but Bos and van Bommel's action had generated a great deal of publicity around the issue of the legalization of soft drugs, using the media-node of the city council, and their positions as official politicians, to full advantage.

Unfortunately, this action had some other side effects beyond leaving Bos and van Bommel out on the street with the munchies. Some Kabouters felt that the soft drug issue was not one the movement should focus on, or that should be attached to them to the detriment of other social issues. Also, since van Duijn's personal ethics included anti-smoking (as opposed to the ironic anti-smoking smoking of Grootveld), he was offended and hotly denied taking part in the action. Bos and van Bommel were angered at what they saw as a break in solidarity. This public split gained a great deal of attention in the press (Hakkenberg 2000b). Van Duijn later said:

> I was searched in front of the mayor in the city council. And I didn't like it, because it gave a lot of attention to a minor thing. I think that there is certainly a right to the free consumption of drugs, but there are other more important questions: the shortage of houses in Amsterdam, the pollution, the traffic, and so on. So I didn't think that this hashish-smoking was a wise step. All the right-wing papers gave it enormous headlines and many people thought we were just doing strange things [. . .] the result was a loss of confidence in the Kabouters. It was thought that the Kabouters were too much on ego trips and were losing contact with the problems of the people.
>
> (Fox 1973)

In agreement, Coen Tasman notes that "many Kabouters were not very happy with this provocative action, which they felt damaged the image of the movement. The Kabouters could be accused now, as *De Telegraf* had already done, of making propaganda for drug use" (Tasman 1996: Chapter 9). Despite their direct-democratic and direct-action philosophies, the council-Kabouters had become symbolic stand-ins for the larger movement, and their behavior was taken to represent the Kabouters as a whole.

Guy Kilian felt that the issue was one of style and methods of provocation. He felt that he and van Duijn wanted to provoke in a way which opened people up to new ideas, and that Bos and van Bommel were provoking in a harsher way, solely for the sake of provocation (Kilian 2000). Perhaps this can also be seen as a difference in chosen audience. Van Duijn and Kilian, in their copious motions and gentler actions, treated the members of the city council as part of their intended audience, while Bos and van Bommel were disrupting the city council to galvanize and inspire the neighborhood action groups to further confrontational action. For them, the city council was part of their larger show, rather than a segment of the audience. In this sense, the authorities were meant to play the same reactionary roles as they did in the violent scenarios of the Provos.

On 3 March 1971, Bos and van Bommel performed their last action in the city council. They had been steadily involved with neighborhood action groups who were trying to fight gentrification. On this particular day, the council was deliberating about the zoning of a large office building on Bickerseiland, and the controversial zoning for the Metro in the Nieuwmarkt. After a group from Bickerseiland threw an orange smoke bomb from the gallery, Frans van Bommel threw a stinkbomb onto the floor. The expensive old rug was ruined, and the council had to adjourn because of the unbearable stench. With this action, van Bommel expressed his identification with the projectile-hurling protesters and not with his "colleagues" in the city council.

Surprisingly, the Mayor proposed only to send van Bommel out of the council for one meeting. Instead, van Bommel and Bos presented their prepared letter of resignation, Bos declaring that the council was becoming increasingly fascist (Tasman 1996: Chapter 9).

The *ROOTS* (an American anarchist journal) interview with van Duijn, conducted by Grey Fox in 1973, explores this event and the deepening split between the council-Kabouters that it illustrated:

> VAN DUIJN: [. . .] there was a difference of opinion on the tactics of opposition. The same two people who had smoked hashish threw [. . .] a stink bomb during the city council meeting. I didn't agree with this tactic, because it meant that the police were called in and the council had to adjourn for an hour [. . .]. I thought this was a bad policy, because we shouldn't use violence. We should use argument.
>
> GREY FOX: You say, we shouldn't use violence. Do you think that the throwing of a stink bomb is violence?
>
> VAN DUIJN: Yes, in this case, because it prevented people from discussing. You could call it counterviolence, but I think

> the city council in itself is not completely a bad thing. The alternative now is just a police state. So what we should do is to support at least this formal democracy while we organize informal democracies in the local communities of Amsterdam.
>
> (Fox 1973: 33)

Van Duijn's form of oppositional performance within the city council was to criticize with dystopian and utopian speeches, and to make radical policy proposals. Bos and van Bommel looked to carry the predominantly non-verbal, disruptive actions of the street directly into the city council, thus preventing "people from discussing" within that chamber. For Bos and van Bommel, this "people discussing" was merely a ritualistic process that would legitimize the inevitable displacement of the residents of the Nieuwmarkt. This ritual had to be disrupted, not participated in. While they argued that van Duijn was being co-opted, here he argues that they were being even more anti-democratic than the city council itself. Van Duijn's performance was directed to the political public sphere from a position in the Kabouter movement. Bos and van Bommel wished to continue to address their counterpublic, that of the radical direct action movement, from the media node of the city council, using the same vocabulary of symbolic, disruptive actions.

This conflict called attention to the crucial ambiguity within the visionary, oppositional metaphor of the Orange Free State. Was it a political party within the system, or a separate fantasy-nation sending gnomish ambassadors to the old State? Grey Fox pressed this point:

> GREY FOX: You said before that the Kabouters were ambassadors to the city council.
>
> VAN DUIJN: Yes.
>
> GREY FOX: This means that you didn't really recognize the city council except as a foreign government?
>
> VAN DUIJN: Yes.

> GREY FOX: But it seems that what you are saying now is that one should work in cooperation with the government.
>
> VAN DUIJN: Yes, cooperation is OK, but in the same way that ambassadors cooperate.
>
> GREY FOX: In the previous interview, you said that you didn't recognize the validity of the government, that you were only treating with the government because it existed. Is that still your attitude?
>
> VAN DUIJN: Yes, that's still my attitude. But being an ambassador, you have to represent the actual interests of the state you are representing. That has been the Orange Free State [. . .] I opposed the group that used stink bombs, because I think that you are making an ambassador's task impossible if you use bombs instead of argument. After that incident a lot of people began to disagree with the things we were doing. That was the start of the disintegration of the Orange Free State.
>
> (Fox 1973: 33–4)

With this, van Duijn still argues for an ambassador's basic protocol of behavior as the model of comportment for the council-Kabouters as they played out their roles in the staid city council. Bos and van Bommel's method extended opposition to a far wider range of physical and bodily action, and was irreconcilable with van Duijn's position.

Bos, van Bommel, and van Duijn also diverged on the symbolic importance and nature of "ambassadors" and the "Orange Free State," and of the relationship between the two. In an interview with the Communist newspaper *De Groene Amsterdammer*, Bos and van Bommel stated that they now saw the Orange Free State as no longer necessary and that they had never believed in its ludic alternative because its alternative shops, service center for the elderly, and other counter-institutions could easily be assimilated without threatening the old society. They felt that the Free State should have functioned much more as an umbrella for disruptive, confrontational, and direct actions. As for the participation in the city council elections, they both regretted it. Van Bommel stated that "we wanted to sit in the council, not to help govern the city, but to change the government, and that's not possible" (Tasman 1996: Chapter 9). Bos and van Bommel were consistently interested in being unmanageable Kabouters, not manager-Kabouters.

Naturally, all of this tumult, and the Kabouter infighting, drew a lot of attention from the media. Some grassroots action groups remained suspicious of the Kabouters because of their "establishment" status as a large political party, and because they felt that the council high jinks were drawing attention away from the street movement instead of publicizing it. Equally, many street-Kabouters (those who attended the people's meetings) were concerned that the Orange Free State was losing steam, and attention, as a result of its being partially actualized as a disorganized political force in the council.

This was a result of the hyper-symbolization that the Kabouters were experiencing in the city council. The same cultural attention that focused on Guy Kilian eating his apple, and that led to Ernsting's hypothetical jibe about the brick in the street, caused the council-Kabouters to be labeled as leaders of a movement that wanted no leaders. Indeed, Bos and van Bommel expressed no wish to be seen as leaders or even representatives, but just to be members of the collective taking creative, spectacular action on their particular site of struggle. Nevertheless, their actions were taken as representative of the movement as a whole, at the expense of the old people's service, the alternative stores, the housing movement, and the rest of the "people's departments." Perhaps some of the council-Kabouters desired that attention and assigned leader-role more than others, but the lay membership as a whole was not pleased.

## A prank too far: the national elections and the end of the Kabouters

The Kabouters' last important conflict was over the question of running for the National Parliament's Second Chamber. That election was scheduled for 28 April 1971.

Roel van Duijn repeatedly called for participation in the Federal election, but at every people's meeting at which it was discussed he was voted down. Most Kabouters were worried enough about the implications of anarchists participating in municipal power-politics, and were not too pleased with how that experiment was developing thus far. They wanted to work out what the relationship between the people's meetings and the council-Kabouters was before sending more of their activists off to the Second Chamber, where far more power was concentrated in the hands of politicians who were even further removed from the lives of average people. Perhaps some Kabouters were worried that, even as a prank, such participation in the Second Chamber would have a validating effect for the extant power structure. While van Duijn wanted to move the Kabouters further into the world of electoral politics, building on the momentum of the unexpected municipal victory, many feared this would be an opportunistic deviation from the whole concept of the Orange Free State as a fantastic, satirical, collective action project.

Hildegaard Wassenaar, a Kabouter from Utrecht, wrote an open letter to all Kabouters of the Netherlands against the election effort, following an anarchist line. "This is the last drop in the bucket. Kabouters are just not going to take part in the great deception that is called parliamentary democracy. Nobody can represent someone else. Also, *Kabouters can't represent Kabouters*" (Tasman 1996: Chapter 10, emphasis added). She felt that the money, time, and energy that such an effort would require would be better spent on the development of neighborhood councils (an idea closer to the general Kabouter platform), and that there was a danger of careerism. After all, a Second Chamber representative enjoyed a fairly high salary and a great deal of power and prestige. With so many municipal seats around the country, the Kabouters were more of a "real" party than they were at their inception, and any electoral effort that they made now could not be looked at as purely symbolic. Real parliamentary power was potentially at stake. Jealousies, ambition, and careerism were all possible plagues to which the movement was now vulnerable.

Nevertheless, Roel van Duijn argued that the electoral effort would infuse new energy into the movement, which had been slowed down by the infighting of the preceding months. He declared a "Crocus Offensive," a flower-power effort with which the Kabouters would be renewed with the spring season of 1971.

Some Kabouters felt that the Crocus Offensive was only an electorally oriented ploy. Some even felt that the Orange Free State should be dissolved, like the Provo movement, because it had lost touch with its base, the neighborhood activist groups. These included Peter Hakkenberg (who, on 7 March 1971 succeeded Connie Bos in the city council), Marius Ernsting, and others.[12] Some members of this group started what they bitterly called the Nettles Offensive, which was meant to strangle the Crocus Offensive and put an end to the Kabouters.

Coen Tasman and the rest of the *Kabouterkrant* collective took a satirical but not entirely hostile view of van Duijn's efforts, and the cover of the number ten issue reflected this. It was a gentle satire in which van Duijn willingly took part. The picture is of van Duijn, wearing an ill-fitting suit and hat, and carrying a briefcase. He is grinning, standing outside the Parliament house, and crocus flowers are drawn in as if they are sprouting up from the pavement. The image suggested that van Duijn was taking on a role for which he was ill-suited (Tasman 2000a).

This ironic image was interpreted in several contradictory ways by members of its intended audience. The Kabouters of the Nettles Offensive interpreted this cover art as a promotion of van Duijn, his Crocus Offensive, and the electoral campaign. They managed to confiscate 2,000 copies of the print run of issue number ten, and then they altered the cover to make it a satire more to their liking. They cut out Roel's face (which they felt they had seen in print far too often anyway), and wrote all over the cover "I, I, I, I, I, I, I, I, I, I, I, I, I, I, I, I, I, I, I, I, I, I, Roel van Duyn, should give it up" ("Ik. . . ." 1970). They registered their version as the legal issue number ten, and even tried to distribute it to the newsstands and bookstores where the *Kabouterkrant* was sold. One member of the *Kabouterkrant* collective even caught some Nettles-

Kabouters in the act at a bookstore, and he chased them for several blocks (Tasman 2000b). Clearly, the Kabouters were capable of using their techniques of sabotage and satire against each other as well as against external opponents.

Another manifestation of the widespread disillusionment and alienation within the movement was the Ministry of Offense, a group started by Kabouters who agreed with Rob Stolk's diagnosis that the Kabouters were "not negative enough." On 1 August 1970, these Kabouters occupied an abandoned Marine barracks in The Hague, and hung banners on it that read "Ministry of Offense." They started their own paper, the *Kabouter-Kolonel*, featuring their own cartoon character of the same name. The Kabouter-Kolonel was a pixie-anarchist-terrorist, with a helmeted head shaped like a mushroom, a dark beard and a ferocious grin. In one cartoon he is pushing the plunger on a detonator device while shouting "STOP THE PARLIAMENTARY CONFUSION!" In others, he flies into the bodies of authority figures, planting bombs in their various internal cavities and then flying back out. One particularly revealing cartoon shows the gentle, happy kabouter stereotypical of the movement looking in the mirror. He is astonished to see the Kolonel-Kabouter, holding a fuse-bomb, grinning back out at him. This cartoonish wrangling over the central symbol of the movement was not just doodling, but rather serious play around the nature and mission of the radical movement and its relationship with the greater system which it confronted (see Figures 1.10 and 1.11).

Nevertheless, van Duijn and a group of Kabouters living in a commune in Nijmegen organized an electoral effort for the Second Chamber. Above the protests of many Kabouters, particularly those based in Amsterdam, they managed to build a network of pro-election Kabouters around the country. They put forward a "round list" of national candidates, an innovative list which would feature a different list-leader in each district of the country. Four of the Nijmegen commune members justified the campaign by arguing that Kabouters elected to the national parliament would be able to possibly influence foreign affairs, voting against neo-imperialism

**1.10 Symbolic conflict within the Kabouter movement: in this cartoon, the gentle Kabouter, friendly symbol of the movement, confronts the grinning, bomb-throwing Kabouter-Kolonel in the mirror**

© Jan van Amerongen

and for material aid to developing countries. "A vote for the Kabouters was therefore a vote for humanity and against world fascism" (Tasman 1996: Chapter 10). Of course, it would be fair to point out that electoral far-left parties such as the PSP and the PPR served the same purpose in the parliament, and that there was little need for the ludic Kabouters to compete with them for votes.

The Nijmegeners called their list "Kabouter Action Center Netherlands," or 't KAN, which means "it can" in Dutch. It is significant that, though he supported the list, Roel van Duijn did not put himself on it.

**1.11 "STOP THE PARLIAMENTARY CONFUSION!" The Kabouter-Kolonel resolves the electoral dilemma with dynamite**



The conflict escalated as the National campaign proceeded. When, on 30 January 1971, the 't KAN Kabouters held a meeting in Utrecht, several local Kabouters came to protest, arguing that to partake in the elections was to become part of the system and to take part in the parliamentary deception. They also warned that the Orange Free State would lose its spirit and popular support, and would be killed by this effort. Nevertheless, the meeting went on, making radical decisions to distinguish 't KAN from the other parties. For example, it was decided that any Kabouters that were elected would keep only 25 percent of their 40,000-guilder salaries,

1.12 The Kabouter movement chained to the heavy ball of parliamentary democracy. This meeting poster by Bert Griepink reflects the conflict within the movement provoked by the prolonged engagement with the electoral system and that the rest would go to the national Kabouter fund (Tasman 1996: Chapter 10).

The Kabouters had to raise 18,000 guilders in order to register for the elections, a great sum for such an organization. Van Duijn donated some of his book royalties, and other contributions were made. This diversion of energy and money into a campaign that the majority of the movement was strongly against only intensified the antagonism between the already elected council-Kabouters in Amsterdam. Connie Bos and Frans van Bommel even called for van Duijn's resignation because he had launched the campaign against the will of the people's meetings. The people's meeting of 4 February 1971 was a very tense and aggressive one in which the Nijmegeners had to face the wrath of the Amsterdam anti-electoral majority (Tasman 1996: Chapter 10).

Caspar Schukink Kool, a Kabouter city council member from The Hague, was a leader in the electoral effort, and he was interviewed several times on the topic. He presented a very anti-systemic attitude for 't KAN. He claimed in two interviews that the Kabouters were aiming for three seats in the parliament, but on 13 March 1971 in *De Tijd* he stated that he felt the Kabouters could count on at least one seat. Regardless of the number, it was clear that 't KAN was intent on winning space in the parliament. Meanwhile in the second of these three articles, internal controversy continued to be publicly aired as Bos and van Bommel called the election campaign an insane adventure (Tasman 1996: Chapter 10).

Kool stated: "We deny both giving and accepting power. We want a community that is directed towards quality and not to quantity. 't KAN has no program, no demand list for concrete promises which could never be realized, but a philosophy." He stated that the Kabouters wanted to sit as an action group in the Chamber to infiltrate the system and to support other action groups. There would be an Ombudsman who would coordinate inner and extra-parliamentary actions, working out of a center that would be called the Sponge or the Inside/Outside Square. In the tradition of other Kabouters, 't KAN pledged to distribute to activist groups any governmental secrets to which it gained access.

On 24 April, in an interview with *De Groene Amsterdammer*, Kool stated that it would be "disastrous" if the Kabouters won five seats in the Second Chamber like they had in the Amsterdam city council. That would force them to be a constructive part of the system to which they objected. Again, Kool emphasized 't KAN's mission as one of infiltration. "We only want to be like a horsefly for the authorities, and prick and stick and be very nasty. It's to squat in the chamber, and that is our main difference with the PSP, which has a very neat party programme" (Tasman 1996: Chapter 10).

In an important divergence from the Amsterdam municipal campaign, the 't KAN Kabouters did engage in electoral speech-making, traveling the country and asking people for their vote. This performative shift suggested an underlying ideological shift, as the group began to act more like a party than an anti-party. However, they did engage in stunts and pranks as well. On 27 February, a group of twelve Kabouters "occupied" a tiny island in a pond in The Hague, using a raft and two borrowed fishing boats. They dubbed it the "Orange Free Land" and put anti-census posters on it. They were arrested for demonstrating without a permit, but not before they had distributed orange pamphlets to the onlooking crowd. On 16 March, the fifteen candidates, calling themselves the Chamber-Collective, held their initial press conference at a squatted castle estate in the country, Nieuw Amelisweerd. They were the guests of the Union of Squatters, who called the place *Groot Craekenborg* (which loosely translates as "Ye Olde Squatcastle"). During the conference, at which they were outrageously dressed, they presented the press with an ironic symbolic meal of Hague Bluff, a very light pastry that seems very large but is mostly whipped air, much like 't KAN itself. With this, 't KAN poked fun at themselves as much as the greater system and tried to maintain their identity as pranksters rather than politicians.

Thanks to equal-time media laws, the Kabouters even aired two commercials, including a 21 April broadcast of a "WANTED" notice for President Richard Nixon of the Unites States in the style of a police announcement. The commercial stated that Nixon was wanted for the murder of one and a half million people in southeast Asia, including thousands of Americans. The phone number of the right-wing newspaper *De Telegraf* was given as the number to call if the viewers had any information as to the whereabouts of this dangerous criminal at large (Tasman 1996: Chapter 10).

Nevertheless, on 28 April 1971, 't KAN received only 0.3 percent of the national vote, less than half of the 0.67 percent required to win a single seat. This was the final blow to a movement that was already falling apart. As Coen Tasman put it, "the serious play was over" (Tasman 1996: Chapter 10).

Van Duijn regretted the national campaign, acknowledging the rift it had caused:

> What happened is that the Kabouters were beset by inner troubles and inner differences of opinion [. . .] on whether to participate in the elections for the national parliament of Holland [. . .] Some [. . .] were opposed, because they said that we were adopting too much of the established system. I favored participation, because of the chance they might give us an opportunity to have a voice in parliament and to spread the message of the alternative society. But in fact our participation in the elections was a sad thing. We destroyed a lot because of the conflict that arose. So, in the final analysis, we should not have entered the elections. In fact, one of the reasons for our defeat was our inner conflict, which made us unsure of what we were doing.
>
> (Fox 1973)

This was a succinct summary of what had happened. A sort of "mission creep" had taken effect, where one success led to a divisive attempt to press a perceived advantage. By pushing the pranksterish incursion further into the realm of mainstream politics, the electoral guerrillas had strayed too far from their base of support and were dispersed.

## Back to the woods, back to the grassroots

> *(Tapping the microphone)* Hello, is this thing on? These are the jokes, folks. Is this an audience or an oil painting?
>
> (old stand-up comic lines when faced with a dead audience)

Instead of working as yet another symbolic, satirical guerrilla action against the capitalist parliamentary system, the national election proved to be an expensive demonstration of the Kabouters' lack of support. The campaigning Kabouters now made political speeches, and were riven by internal conflicts. The prank had shifted in character due to repetition in a different context. The Kabouters now had political power and could not run from "outside the system" in the same way. They entered this effort divided, without the carnivalesque energy of 1970. The audience/electorate, having heard the fairy tale joke before with better timing and delivery, acted like what some comedians call a "dead house." While the municipal campaign had mocked the stale, rehearsed theatricality of the other parties' efforts, the second campaign only succeeded in disrupting any sympathy the electorate had with the Kabouter movement, as their performance rang false. The last people's meeting was on 25 March 1971 in Amsterdam, and the few Kabouters who attended decided to disband due to obvious lack of interest from the community.

Brecht argued that theatre should intensify the political divisions within an audience rather than glossing over them. The Kabouters did this successfully with their first campaign, as shown by the radically polarized reactions they provoked across the electorate. An audience is composed of many different subcultures, and these subcultures have radically different reactions to public acts of strident irony and political critique. The division in the Dutch public that the Kabouters most successfully exploited and widened was that between disillusioned voters and voters who were still allied to traditional parties and politics. However, those disillusioned voters still had the creative agency to dismiss the Kabouters' Federal campaign as a prank too far.

The Kabouters did not seem able to sustain their carnivalesque energy and sensibility once they were elected, perhaps because carnival is very hard to sustain in the face of the realities of wielding power. When serious decisions had to be made that affected people's interests, and serious internal conflicts therefore had to be resolved, it was hard to remain ludic and keep the jester's hat on. The municipal electoral campaign had been tactically carnivalesque, with mass-participation and decentralized, multivocal creativity. However, as the council-Kabouters began to use the city council as the theatre for their individual performances, the footlights that Bakhtin denounced, signifying the hard division between actors and spectators, between politicians and constituents, were set up and turned on. The Kabouters of the parliamentary campaign completed this shift from "Sharp Satire" to "Emergent Party" modes, making proper speeches to explain their quest for legislative power. The result was the dispersal of the movement.

How does one reconcile momentary, improvised carnivalesque action with a more durable, ongoing contestation of power? Augusto Boal's experiment with Legislative Theatre shows a different way to handle these strains and contradictions. In 1992, like the Kabouters, Boal accidentally won an election, to be a *vereador* (city legislator) in Rio de Janiero. The innovator of the Theatre of the Oppressed (TO) decided to accept the office and hire TO practitioners (instead of the usual political staff) to involve the community directly in the creative drafting of legislation. Using the theatre games and exercises now called Legislative Theatre, Boal and his comrades succeeded in drawing the electorate into a more participatory and creative democratic model. Due largely to a campaign of "dirty tricks" by his opponents, Boal lost the next election in 1996. Nevertheless, this experiment continues in different forms and contexts across Brazil. Rather than condemning the representative parliamentary system as too toxic to participate in, as the more radical Kabouters did, or participating in that system as either an ambitious power-seeker (like van Duijn) or a disruptive force (like Bos and van Bommel), Boal tried to combine parliamentary and direct-democratic models using his theatre techniques. He was thus able to sustain a joyful, participatory effort during much of his work as *vereador* while continuing to contest the dominant paradigm from the streets and within the city council chamber (Boal 1998).

It seems that the council-Kabouters were engaging in a slippery symbolism, and some of them were seduced by the lure of power and individual celebrity, inspiring jealousy in some of their comrades and ideological objection in many more. The distinction between their efforts and those of "normal" politicians grayed. This final defeat was a decisive factor in the dispersion of the movement:

> GREY FOX: It seems to me that your ideas have changed somewhat over the last two years. Then you were thinking of the city council more or less as the "enemy" or something like that. Your only reason for going into elections and entering it was to get publicity and to spread your ideas.
>
> VAN DUIJN: That's still true.
>
> GREY FOX: But it seems to me that now you think of the city council as a way of getting things done.
>
> VAN DUIJN: No, that's a false impression. I do not have such illusions about the city council.
>
> (Fox 1973: 34)

Despite these words in 1973, van Duijn was on an ideological trek from anarchist to countercultural parliamentarian. As the most visible member of the Kabouter movement, a person who had been made into a symbol of that movement by the mainstream press and media, his political shift and the resultant inter-Kabouter conflict received a disproportionate amount of attention. This in turn demoralized many grassroots Kabouters as they saw the publicity which their inventive street campaigns had generated being diverted towards their infighting "ambassadors" in the city council. The Orange Free State dispersed, "the first state in history to wither away," as van Duijn himself ruefully put it (Fox 1973).

Van Duijn, who has had a long and active political career in Amsterdam, said that he had learned that satire, like any other tactic, can get old and boring with repeated use, and that one's opponents can also learn to use the trick. He now believes in clear, straightforward political communication, a balance between municipal and neighborhood councils, that the state is a necessary tool of radical change, and that a tighter organization than that of the Kabouters is necessary for a movement to be effective (Duijn 2000). Marius Ernsting, who had been such a visible Kabouter street performer and activist, went on to a political career with the Communist Party of the Netherlands, and then as a director of a major Dutch social service organization. Looking back, he stated that while the Kabouters had had a great media strategy, it took more than that to combat Capital and reaction. After making his "brick on the pavement" comment, he was quick to note that, a year after their initial splash, the Kabouters could not get press coverage nearly as easily. Eventually, argued Ernsting, even without the internal struggles, the novelty of the Kabouters' approach would have worn off.

The Kabouters rotated in and out of the city council until 1974. There were more conflicts and infighting, including arguments about when it was time for individual council-Kabouters to rotate out. Soon it was difficult for them to find activists who were willing to take a seat, as interest in the whole game had waned. As with the Provos before them, the Kabouters as a movement were outlasted by their representatives in the city council. Several ex-Kabouters whom I interviewed said that, because of the lack of tight organization, the Kabouters were like a "straw fire": bright, but quick to burn out (Ernsting 2000; De Jong 2000; Burgler 2000).

However, as with the Provos, their members continue to be active in political struggles to the present day. The experience arguably strengthened them as principled activists. The movement had many lasting effects outside of the government, with their services for the elderly, organic food shops, environmental programs, and communes taking root and spreading in the Netherlands. But even within the city council, the Kabouters left an important mark. When they entered that body, its customary role was to be merely a compliant rubber stamp for the dictates of the College. The Kabouters constantly violated this convention by initiating motions, usually formulated so radically as to be too outrageous to be co-opted. It is now standard practice for rank-and-file city council members to make proposals and motions, and for the College to react to those initiatives. Neighborhood councils, one of the main demands of the Kabouters, now exist in Amsterdam. As for the cry of "openness, openness" quoted from the *Kabouterkrant* earlier, the council and committee meetings are now far more open to the public as a result of that pressure (Tasman 1996: Chapter 11).

Hyper-symbolization of a movement can lead to initial gains, but, like irony, this phenomenon can turn on the user. Symbols and symbolic action are multivalent and open to active interpretation, leading to conflict not only between the "straights" and the "hip" but among the diverse hipsters as well. The Orange Free State was an ironic construction, a multivalent wild card for the political imagination. Its members accomplished a great deal with few resources save their enormous creative energy. But as some Kabouters began to take the Orange Free State as a serious player in the electoral sphere, they became ripe for attack from their colleagues who still saw it solely as an clever, anarchist, anti-state joke. The "friendly" kabouter image frustrated Dutch conservatives, who saw an anarchist mob hidden under the whimsical pointy hats. However, when the Kabouters started denouncing each other, their human identity was revealed, the ludic, fantastic symbol-structure was undermined, and the activist rank-and-file left the fairy tale forests for the more prosaic, tangible grassroots. Nevertheless, the brief Kabouter electoral experiment, with all its ludic joy, righteous anger and hard lessons, had long-lasting effects on the culture and politics of the Netherlands, and in the collective memory and strategic playbook of the Dutch Left.[13]

Kabouter mischief and magic managed to jump over or perhaps tunnel under the Iron Curtain, to confuse the authorities on that side of the Cold War as well. In 1970, Roel Van Duijn went to Zagreb in Slovenia to give a talk about the Kabouters. Some visiting Polish students and artists were impressed by the tales of mischievous gnomes and the Orange Free State and brought those stories home with them.

In 1981 Waldemar Maria "Major" Frydrych of Wroclaw created the Orange Alternative and declared his ideology of "socialist surrealism." As martial law was declared, and the government's crackdown on Solidarity continued, Krzysztof "Jakub" Jakubczak and other ludic artists and dissidents joined the movement with slogans such as "Dwarves Are Real!" They drew graffiti of dwarves[14] on the walls of the city – in fact, the Dwarf graffiti started as embellishments on the barely-visible remnants of Solidarity graffiti that had been painted over by the state. By adding a few dabs to these faded blobs, "dwarves" were created, a beautiful metaphor for the lingering, renewable palimpsest of resistance. These artist–activists carried out bizarre mass performances of over-identification with Communist ideology. They were able to avoid the worst of punishment by singing, dancing and their unique brand of disarming, if grotesque, over-compliance with the rhetoric of the regime.

Dwarves dressed in red pointy hats teamed up with groups such as the Society for a Merrier Present to drive around in a party bus singing Communist hymns with ironic earnestness. They stopped at the zoo and demanded that the bears be set free, perhaps in a touching gesture of friendship to the Soviets. On April Fool's Day in 1987, they held an absurdly over-loyal rally where they scrubbed the floors of a university hall furiously while one of their number delivered an archaic Leninesque speech with old-fashioned oratorical flair.

What were the Communist secret police to do? Arrest them for too much enthusiasm? At another event they called for all loyal participants to celebrate the anniversary of the Russian Revolution by wearing only red, and to bring and eat only red foods, especially ketchup. They gave away toilet paper and sanitary napkins as an act of socialist solidarity that in fact called attention to the perennial shortage of these basic items – a more pointed instance of giving out white paper than the Provos' infamous blank pamphlets. The Orange Alternative went on to help make actual strikes and factory occupations of dissident workers more festive and disarming to the authorities with costumes such as helmets made of watermelon rinds, and mock-battles with arsenals of Styrofoam weapons.

They raised the political price of repression for the authorities with their ludic and folkloric imagery, in a formula by now familiar to readers of this chapter. As with the Provos and Kabouters, but with greater danger and repression at stake, the Orange Alternative dwarves did in part disarm the authorities and throw them off balance. They were able to get away with more, and attract greater participation for resistance, than perhaps they could have with more conventional and predictable demonstrations of dissent.

The "carnivalesque" aspect of the popular resistance to Communism in Eastern Europe is well documented in Padraic Kenney's excellent book, *A Carnival of Revolution: Central Europe* (1989). In a footnote, he writes, "Frydrych enjoyed teasing journalists by inventing alternative explanations of the name [Orange Alternative]: for example, that it evoked the anarchy of *A Clockwork Orange* or had something to do with Dutch artists" (157). Understandably, with all the socialist surrealism Frydrych deployed to throw rational repressors (and researchers) off the scent, Kenney dismissed his claims of being influenced by Dutch artists as just another absurd comment. But indeed, the Kabouters' Orange Free State, in perhaps their most influential and exciting legacy outside of the Netherlands, did help to inspire the Orange Alternative. Anti-authoritarian Gnomes and Dwarves battling oppressors on either side of an Iron Curtain; a tale that J.R.R. Tolkien might appreciate, despite his conservative politics.

## Chapter 2

# *Sturm und Drag*

## The fabulous camp-pains of Miss Joan JettBlakk[1]

> It's time for this foolishness to end. It's time for some *real* foolishness to begin. If a bad actor can be President, why not a good drag queen?
>
> (Joan JettBlakk campaign slogans)

> This got away from being a caricature into being more of a real campaign. "We have to have this candidate or we're not going to be on the ballot." Well, so we're not going to be on the ballot, we're not going to be elected anyway!
>
> (Tamara Frasier, Queer Nation activist)

On 17 January 1992 drag queen Joan JettBlakk declared her campaign for the Presidency of the United States of America on the Queer Nation Party ticket with the slogan "Lick Bush in '92!" This announcement was a profoundly ironic act. An African-American drag queen? With muscular body and working-class teeth? Running for the most powerful job on Earth, in the face of all the exclusionary aspects of the US electoral system? Under a homophobic, sex-panicked dominant culture, with AIDS rampaging through the nation after twelve years of conservative administrations?

This chapter argues that the JettBlakk campaign, while accomplishing many of its external goals, sparked an intense debate within the Queer Nation/Chicago activist group. The public triumphs were the result of the inventive and clever rhetoric and performative tactics of JettBlakk and her comrades, who, with minimal resources, gained a great deal of visibility both within and beyond their own counterpublic. This gay political fantasia combined joyous, frank, and exaggerated queer sexuality with pointed ironies from a talented prankster's playbook. Drawing on original campaign materials and speeches, interviews, archived press materials, and over thirty-five hours of Gabriel Gomez and Elspeth kydd's video documentary footage, this chapter examines the tactical innovations and impact of "Lick Bush in '92."

## King versus queen: the mayoral race

Our fantasia begins when activists from Queer Nation/Chicago, an activist group of about fifty members, approached their co-founder, JettBlakk, and asked if she would run for Mayor of Chicago in 1991. After helping to start the group, Joan had tired of the constant meetings, with their lengthy debates and consensus process. However, she was missing the activist work, and was excited by the idea of the project. She agreed to run, and the last-minute, three-week campaign was on. The group intended to promote queer[2] visibility in a humorous way, and activists Elspeth kydd and Gabriel Gomez videotaped the campaign. This ultimately resulted in the short video, "Drag In' For Votes."

Joan JettBlakk is the alter-ego of Terence Smith. In fact, JettBlakk referred to Smith as her "soul brother" (Gomez and kydd 1992). Regarding his drag persona and the joy and power he got from performing, Smith said:

> Performing has always been a big part of my life. I get the same kind of charge in almost forty years [. . .] kiddie glee even as I'm putting on eyelashes. It's a lot of fun to take a character that you made and have people vote for me! [. . .] All because of this character that I created [. . .] I tell people that Joan is Terence turned up about 500 degrees. It's not that much different from me, but it's a positive side of me that I'm able to blow way out of proportion. I look like a caricature of a drag clown. Maybe more glamorous than that. Because it's so much fun and I'm the goddess of love. I'm not one of those mean bitchy drag queens by any means. I'm everybody's best girlfriend.
>
> (Gomez and kydd 1992)

Smith saw his public drag performance of Joan as a joyous, liberating political act for both himself and his community. His upbeat attitude and style as Joan would prove an effective counterpoint to his underlying, firmly confrontational cultural agenda.

Smith was raised in Detroit, and for years was the only black student in the Catholic school he attended. He began his drag performance career there, and became a spokesmodel for the Gay Liberation Front in high school, moving after graduation from home to a house run by the GLF, then to Chicago in 1977. One of his many day jobs was as a gym instructor, which is how he built up the muscular physique that would become a key part of his radical "hunky chanteuse" drag. While he had played many roles in his career, he originated "Joan JettBlakk" at a drag performance in May 1990 at Club Lower Links in Chicago. From the start, Smith was devoted to undermining performative roles and expectations, even within his own subculture. Not for Joan the lookalike lip-synching to the usual pop-divas' tunes:

> I always wanted to be a *rock 'n' roll* drag queen . . . Thanks to all the Led Zeppelin and David Bowie records I listened to, I play the best air guitar in the world. So for Joan I got a friend's guitar, and my first night I did Bonnie Raitt and Janis Joplin. Nobody had ever seen a black drag queen do Janis Joplin.
>
> (Gomez and kydd 1992)

His taste in music was not the only difference Smith explored as a critical drag queen. He never concealed his sex, all the better to alienate standard costumes and conventions of gender:

> The drag is "on the edge" [. . .] because he doesn't try to hide his masculinity. "I don't wear anything false. And I lift weights. When I wear a fish-net cat suit, well, the audience can see a bulge down there, but that's because I want them to think of sex in terms of it's not all one thing or one way of being."
>
> (DeGrane 1992)

Smith argued that this unconcealed, celebrated difference was vital for queer identity:

> One of the beauties of being queer is that we're not like everybody else. We are different, and that difference does not make us bad. I'm not trying to be a girl, but I do like the in-your-faceness of being a man in a dress, stomping on that line between male and female and erasing it.
>
> (Ford 1991)

For Smith, there was a larger purpose in this critical drag: that of modeling other possibilities for public personhood in his community:

> If you notice us, you notice that drag can be so much more than wearing a dress standing in front of a mike pretending to sing a Dionne Warwick song. There's so much more you can do with it. That's empowering to the community and to other people who do it.
>
> (Gomez and kydd 1991)

JettBlakk hoped to help create, sustain, and address a queer counterpublic, with its own values, desires, and definitions of beauty and personhood.

JettBlakk was also aware of her historical position as a drag queen of color. "Blakk dismissed suggestions that her image was inappropriate to the lesbian and gay movement. She claimed that 'Drag queens [of color] were the first people to fight back at Stonewall'" (O'Connor 1992). JettBlakk often used humorous counter-appropriation to delight her audiences. In one performance of a Madonna song, JettBlakk took a long time to set up a huge electric fan, paused for it to get to full speed, and then extended a sheet out behind her in a graceful pose; a no-budget evocation of an over-produced Madonna MTV moment. JettBlakk later quipped, "Since [Madonna]'s stolen so much black music in her career, why not steal some back?" (Gomez and kydd 1992).

For Smith, humor was a crucial aspect of what he called the "camp-pain" project ("putting in the camp, taking out the pain, honey"): "Activism doesn't always have to be angry. There is a definite place for that, there needs to be. But activism can also be complete farce. You can get the same message across with a little laughter" (Williams 1991). Smith wanted to complement the righteous, disruptive anger of many queer activists with some savvy satire.

Smith/JettBlakk also used camp humor as a survival tool in a hostile world. In fact, JettBlakk's constantly flashing smile was an integral, tensive, in-her-face element of her persona. Her upper front teeth were broken, displaying damage from some past accident or violence that she did not have the money to repair. Far from shamefully shutting up, Joan joyfully bared those teeth in an enthusiastic and delighted open smile when confronting politicians, police, or passersby. Those chipped teeth in the middle of all that jewelry and makeup undercut the usual image of drag "glamour," and showed that Joan's version of being "classy" was very consciously, confrontationally working class.

The idea of running against Richard Daley, inheritor of a virtual dynasty in the infamous Chicago political machine, was amusing in and of itself. Even with the impossible sums of money that would have been necessary to win such a campaign, Citizen Joan lacked the patronage and connections to seriously challenge Daley the Second. As Joan explained:

> Queer Nation said "we need a candidate that will admit that this election is a farce, and so we're going to take that to the extreme, and be extreme." And they asked me and I said, "Cameras? Lights? Of course!" I've got every minority group covered.
>
> (Gomez and kydd 1991)

JettBlakk campaigned on Michigan Avenue, visiting chic stores in full outrageous drag, and even kissed a cop at the request of his partner. "I said, 'He's got a gun, I'm wearing a dress, I'm not sure this is gonna work.' But before he knew what happened, I had kissed him, given him a campaign flyer, and said 'Vote for me, I'll set you free.'" A photograph of that moment was published in several local gay magazines (Gomez and kydd 1991; *Nightlines* 1991; *Outlines* 1991).

Joan's platform for this campaign was an ad hoc, queer, utopian vision addressing everyday working-class economic concerns:

> I'm going to lower the taxes. Everyone will have healthcare. I'll do away with parking tickets entirely. Commonwealth Edison might as well forget it. Electricity will cost five bucks a month, gas five, phone, everything will be cheap and wonderful, they'll have nothing to say. Gay marriage will be a thing.
>
> (Gomez and kydd 1991)

Here Joan connected her queer politics with a broad social justice agenda. She wanted to link the fight against sexual regimes of the normal to the struggle against capitalism and oppression of all kinds, in a "universalizing" effort, as opposed to a separatist, single-issue or "minoritizing" discourse of protest. In this way, Joan came into conflict with many more assimilationist, middle-class, reformist, and professional gay activists who wanted to focus their struggle solely on issues of gay rights (Sedgwick 1990: 1).

A cover article in the free weekly *New City* contrasted the Daley and JettBlakk campaigns and victory speeches, and JettBlakk was crowned the "Mayor of Queer Chicago" (Rodrich 1991).[3] The title of the article, "King & Queen: Queer and Loafing in the Victory 'Camps' of Queen Joan Jett Blackk and King Richard the Second" playfully equated JettBlakk's support with the quasi-dynastic power of Daley the Second. The campaign, as a media prank, was a small but significant success. However, Joan's campaign did not please more assimilationist gays. Moe Meyer notes that these gays ("many in editorial positions") felt that Blakk "needed to be silenced, that her Camp strategy [. . .] would do damage to the gains made by so-called legitimate caucuses" (Meyer 1994: 6). This conflict between

**2.1 The Queen of Chicago on the camp-pain trail**
From Gomez and kydd 1991

queers and assimilationist gays would only escalate in JettBlakk's next campaign.

JettBlakk was defiant and irreverent in her non-concession speech:

> Well, regardless, I've decided that I want a recount. Fuck Dick Daley, with my dick, daily. Once we get the recount and I'm elected, I'm going to change the police to the fashion police. Dye the river pink every Gay Pride Day, fuck the green![4] I don't know what else, it'll just have to come up when it *comes up*. Hopefully Queer Nation's name is out there and there will be people going "Who the fuck is that?" We can have queers running for president, for governor, for the Supremes . . . Court. And we can just scare them from stem and stern, from hither and yonder.
>
> (Gomez and kydd 1991)

In an unapologetically anti-Gulf War conclusion, she said, "You'll notice I'm not wearing a yellow ribbon." JettBlakk consistently tied her radical left politics on other issues to her queer activism. As a coalition-building, universalizing queer, she was committed to condemn the war, along with all militarism and imperialism. This speech clearly showed JettBlakk's desire to continue this symbolic contention of public power and standards of "normality" in future elections.

Dead people's votes have been known to be counted in Chicago. However, this surprisingly generous extension of the franchise beyond the river Styx did not seem to apply to queers still in the land of the living. In true City of Big Shoulders style, the Board of Elections refused to even count JettBlakk's write-in votes. Although assimilationist gays, or "homocrats" in Sarah Schulman's parlance (Shepard 2001), were beginning to be elected and appointed to positions of power around the country, this incorporation (or co-optation) did not extend to radical drag queens. Nevertheless, Queer Nation/Chicago was pleased with the performance and decided to push the prank further with a campaign for President of the United States. This was an even more wildly fantastic project, given the realities of the US political system. A successful candidate for the US Presidency needs the endorsement of one of the two major parties which exercise a duopoly over the entire system. Such an endorsement is generally only possible after a successful career as a politician within one of those parties, and even then the candidate must amass a war chest of tens of millions of dollars to hire consultants and staff and to buy enormously expensive commercial air-time. Given the lack of meaningful campaign finance reform, the (almost certainly middle- to upper-class, straight, white, Christian, center-to-right-wing male) candidate can only gather these funds through independent wealth or with the support of large corporations.

There are other systemic barriers to third-party participation in a US Presidential election. The Electoral College and the lack of proportional representation in the US system further entrench the Republican–Democrat duopoly against any third-party threat. A candidate who receives less than a plurality of the votes in a state receives none of the Electoral College votes at stake.[5] Minor-party campaigns are generally framed in the dominant discourse as illegitimate, distracting incursions into the exclusive realm of the major parties. A minor party which operates primarily in poor communities also has to face the barriers of the US's antiquated and uneven voter registration and voting process. As was shown in 2000 and 2004, voting machines in poorer districts tend to malfunction at a higher rate, and there tend to be fewer machines per capita. The voter registration process, which is automatic and universal in other industrialized countries such as Holland and Australia, serves as a barrier to the transient, the homeless, and the semiliterate and illiterate. These are all obstacles to serious alternative participation in the US electoral process. But then, of course, fantasy candidates are undeterred by such obstacles.

Like the Gay Liberation Front before it, Queer Nation was dedicated to invading straight-hegemonized public spaces. Lauren Berlant and Elizabeth Freeman write that Queer Nation opposes the implicit straightness of public spaces and the danger it poses to gays. This assumed heteronormativity must be exposed and opposed by visible queer incursions into everyday public life. In this way they could undermine heterosexist definitions of "normality":

> The queer body – as an agent of publicity, as a unit of self-defense, and finally as a spectacle of ecstasy – becomes the locus [. . .] using alternating strategies of menace and merriment, agents of Queer Nation have come to see and conquer places that present the danger of violence to gays and lesbians, to reterritorialize them [. . .] queers are thus using exhibitionism to make public space psychically unsafe for unexamined heterosexuality [. . .] [Queer Nation's] recognition of the potential for exploiting spaces of psychic and physical permeability are fundamental to its radical reconstitution of citizenship.
>
> (Berlant and Freeman 1993)

The electoral public sphere was just such a space, where a heterosexist regime of the normal was an unmarked given. While some gays had managed to be elected to office, very few defiantly anti-assimilationist queers had done so. The grim tale of elected San Francisco Supervisor and gay activist Harvey Milk's assassination still loomed over the counterpublic's history. JettBlakk's candidacy was Queer Nation/Chicago's merry, exhibitionist incursion into the assumed straights-only public space of electoral politics.

Queer Nation/Chicago had very specific cultural and political goals. They did not see the Clinton/Bush choice as one that queers could put much hope in, and wanted to expose the "grandstanding" of the US electoral process as a "big, overblown, overproduced and overpriced bit of theatre." As the promotional literature for the video *Lick Bush in '92* argues:

> If the prospect of four more years of Bush and his radical indifference to our lives seemed a terrible and dark dream then only the queerest humor could see us through [. . .] So many forgot that [Clinton's pro-gay rights] conviction was born only when he could see and smell the money of some well connected gay men.
>
> ("Lick Bush in '92")

Queer Nation/Chicago was lucid in its alienation from both major parties. They clearly saw no ally in either major candidate, and agreed with Kertzer and Edelman that modern US politics were highly theatricalized rituals of legitimization for the extant power structure. They felt the need to "show up" this grandstanding, and hoped to do so with an act of flamboyant electoral guerrilla theatre:

> This tired old beauty contest between two straight white men needed some glamour, and queers were going to provide it. So what else is new? What's new is that they wouldn't only be working backstage. Joan's campaign was an upfront, in your face queer kind of party that put some life into the most boring "we interrupt your regularly scheduled programming" stuff.
>
> (Heart of the Empire Productions 1994)

The project was one of in-your-face outrageousness and gleefully queer front-stage allure. Joan JettBlakk would complicate and complement that tone with her personal friendliness and indefatigably upbeat style.

Interviewed out of drag, Terence Smith saw himself and his campaign in a historical context of conflict between the mainstream and queers, and between assimilationist and more confrontational gays, lesbians, bisexuals, and transgendered people:

> The thing about Queer Nation is, we're not interested in assimilation. We're interested in being out, loud, and proud as much as we can. That doesn't mean standing around saying, "Oh, we're just like you." There's room for that, but there's also room for the wild side of gay life. That has always been and it will always be [. . .] Queer Nation was created for visibility and awareness. If we get press we're already doing what we said we're gonna do: let people know there are gay people – loud gay people, queers. There have always been the gay people that say, "Quiet, shhh." I'm not one of them.
>
> (Williams 1991)

JettBlakk was focused on injecting queer identity into mainstream discourse.

> You can watch the news and never hear the word "gay" mentioned ... that just unnerves me. But with this campaign, they'll have to say the word; I'll make them. I would love to hear Tom Brokaw say "Joan JettBlakk, the queer candidate for president." That would be great. It needs to be said.
>
> (Ford 1991)

JettBlakk intended to act up with maximum volume and invincible eyeshadow as a Queer Queen of the Universe, exploding any expectations of subdued or shameful public performance of gay sameness or respectability. Far from being irresponsible, this was an acknowledgement of Queer Nation's obligation to a radical queer community that could not or would not assimilate (drag queens, transsexuals, and others). The goal was to stretch, erode, or destroy the limits of respectability rather than try to be accepted within those limits. This confrontational, queer strategy would clash harshly with the agendas of assimilationist gay politicians and lobbyists.

There is a long history to this division between assimilationist, minoritizing gays and confrontational queers with a broader social critique. Very shortly after its formation in 1969, the Gay Liberation Front (GLF)'s identification of "homosexual liberation" with activist direct action and leftist social movements provoked the splitting off of a group which called itself the Gay Activists Alliance (GAA). The GAA expressly focused on legislative reform for homosexuals, and the GLF denounced them as "white, patriarchal, and assimilationist" (Shepard 2001). This split has continued to the present, between "queers, who envisioned their movements as a critique of social, sexual and economic 'regimes of the normal'" and "mainstream gay groups who sought to portray the gay community as 'just like everyone else'" as exemplified in the Millennium March on Washington of 30 April 2000 (Shepard 2001).

JettBlakk was also aware of some of the history of political pranksterism and even electoral guerrilla theatre, including the campaigns of Jello Biafra and the Yippies' Pigasus (see Introduction). In an interview after the campaign, she noted that, after an appearance at the Armory art gallery:

> A lot of people say the campaign changed, and that I became an art piece instead of a candidate, but one of the things I had in my mind the whole time I was doing it was that this was always a performance piece. It was always a prank. I was inspired by *ReSearch* magazine, they did an issue on pranks, and Jello Biafra ran for Mayor and Abbie Hoffman had some wonderful things to say about ways to fuck with the government and I really believe that running for President was a great prank to pull on everyone. So it made sense that I would appear as a candidate, which was as a[n art] piece, which was in drag, I mean there's all these extensions to it but I was quite comfortable with that.
>
> (Gomez and kydd 1992)

Although she didn't name it as such, JettBlakk was aware of the history of electoral guerrilla theatre, and was consciously innovating a queer approach to the art form.

The activists of Queer Nation/Chicago were very excited about the "camp-pain" at the outset. They saw it as an anti-assimilationist, ludic "zap" on the electoral process. Queer Nation/Chicago activist Paige Lestrude had very high hopes for the external publicity that the campaign would garner:

> What I remember of [the campaign at first] was that it was a very exciting, frivolous, satiric media blitz just to ridicule the entire campaign for '92 [. . .] behind it was a very queer identified energy [. . .] it would be as frivolous and also as pointed as it needed to be [. . .] I think what hit me was Terence's own presence at the meetings and his promise to have representation of queer women's issues as well as gay men's issues and bisexual issues. It was not going to be one big drag performance, he was going to bring up in media spots a woman's rights to her body and reproductive rights [. . .]
>
> (Gomez and kydd 1992)

Lestrude saw "Lick Bush in '92" as a ludic, anarchic campaign that would address the issues of all of Queer Nation's diverse members.

Tamara Frasier, another Queer Nation activist, stressed that this performance could be used as an egalitarian corrective for an unfortunate hegemonic, sexist, racist tendency within Queer Nation:

> Talking to Terence, he seemed very affirming of the diversity that we wanted to include for the group. One of the problems of Queer Nation is that it tends not to be inclusive of women and people of color, it tends to be a group of white gay men. We were really trying to counteract that in Chicago because we had seen Queer Nation fall apart in other cities for this reason.
>
> (Gomez and kydd 1992)

Frasier hoped that "Lick Bush in '92" would serve a positive purpose within the organization, overcoming this "boys' club" phenomenon.

These internal issues were important for an affinity group such as Queer Nation/Chicago. Affinity groups are a basic unit of organizing on the anti-authoritarian left. Ideally, affinity groups are small enough that everyone can be personally familiar with each other. Meetings are often guided by a facilitator to ensure that all voices are heard. Decisions are usually made by consensus. The group may even use predefined hand signals to ensure that communication is clear. The affinity group model of organizing is an attempt to maximize egalitarianism and direct democracy (as opposed to electoral representative democracy) within social movements. The possibility of a *de facto* hierarchy asserting itself within an affinity group is a grave threat to this ideal.

Queer Nation/Chicago sent a memo to other Queer Nation affinity groups around the country to promote the JettBlakk campaign. The memo reveals a great deal about the political desires of the Chicago local group. They hoped to use the campaign to expose and undermine heterosexism on every level. Queer Nation/Chicago pitched the campaign to their comrades in other cities as a great way to bolster queer visibility at the expense of straight politics:

> This will be a very visible and extremely noisy way to focus the nation's attention on Queer issues. It will also add a hell of a lot of camp humor to a tired and ohh-sooo-boriinngg election process [. . .] Think of it! Queers in America's living-rooms every night for months [. . .] We are all motivated by our desire for visibility and the promotion of Queer concerns as a part of the national agenda. We know the power of the mass-media. We can make it work for us and, Honey, before we are through they will be calling themselves "Miss Media"!
>
> (Queer Nation 1991b)

In a general press release that launched the campaign, Queer Nation declared the formation of "The Queer Nation Party," declaring that

> no other Party, anywhere or at anytime, has even pretended to represent the people we hope to appeal to [. . .] we will

> appeal most to those large sections of the electorate who no longer bother to vote for the white-bread, carbon-copy candidates of the Democratic and Republican Parties. Voter apathy is our strength.
>
> (Queer Nation 1991a)

The organization thus denounced the "Republicrat" system it was preparing to ridicule as a one-party system thinly disguised as a two-party system.

Clearly, there were high expectations and many ideological demands placed on this campaign by its affinity group. Because of Queer Nation's consensus-oriented, decentralized nature, JettBlakk was careful not to assume a position of power or leadership. In this sense, JettBlakk did not act like conventional candidates, who are empowered to speak for and represent their organizations and/or constituencies:

> JettBlakk is careful not to use this as *her* campaign but rather Queer Nation's [. . .] "Queer Nation isn't a political party," she explains, "so some will ask how we can have a spokesperson. That's why I call myself a spokes*model*. I don't intend to speak for all Queer Nations."
>
> (Ford 1991)

JettBlakk was walking a tenuous path between affinity and celebrity, between being a member of an egalitarian group and acting as its glamorous front woman.

On Joan JettBlakk's thirty-fifth birthday – 17 January 1992 – she announced her candidacy for President at Ann Sather's restaurant in Chicago. This was the day that she was legally old enough to run, after all, and acknowledging at least this minimal legal formality highlighted the outrageousness of the overall electoral fantasy. The audience was prepared for the Mayor of Queer Chicago's appearance by a written handout. In the text, Joan played a counter-archetypal Aunt Sam with the opening line: "I WANT YOU, HONEY!" After justifying her campaign as an attempt to drag "Queer politics out of the closet," she addressed the concern of those who felt that politics was a high-stakes, serious business with no room for such pranks:

> I have already been accused of failing to take this matter seriously and of demeaning the very Office I seek. As for serious, GET REAL! I'm a DRAG QUEEN and I think that politics should be FUN! As for demeaning the office, I keep hearing this joke. It starts out RONALD REAGAN. Then it goes on GEORGE BUSH, and the punch-line is DAN QUAYLE! Now I ask you, how can I hurt the Presidency any more than that!?
>
> (JettBlakk 1992)

With that last bit of ridicule, Joan asserted that her campaign had no less dignity and perhaps much more decency than those of her rivals for the throne of power.

When the candidate was a couple of minutes late, Gabriel Gomez climbed on the stage to apologize: "We're on QST," he explained. "That's Queer Standard Time" (Felshman 1992). JettBlakk was then introduced by three of her allies in the queer community: Rick Garcia, executive director of Catholic Advocates for Lesbian and Gay Rights, and local columnists Mother Superior and Jon-Henri Damski. Damski claimed that President James Buchanan had been a homosexual, while Garcia made a fiery statement supporting JettBlakk's in-your-face flamboyance. "While fitting in, we become more invisible [. . .] they used to call us an invisible minority – well, guess what? We ain't gonna be an invisible minority any more. And we can thank people like Joan JettBlakk for that" (Futrelle 1992). After this introduction, JettBlakk appeared in a bright pink "faux, faux Chanel" jacket and a black leather miniskirt from Frederick's of Hollywood. She accessorized with a short blonde wig, pink lipstick, and a great deal of costume jewelry (Futrelle 1992; Gomez and kydd 1992).

Her speech was a series of political jokes in which she mocked the "real" candidates, and presidents past, while reminding the audience of her underlying serious agenda. With firm disdain,

JettBlakk named the ongoing oppression of queers, women, and working people, and warned against the dangers of gay assimilation into the power structure ("If queer images are merely plugged into the old ways, then they too will function as agents of oppression. Fuck that!!"). She leavened these heavy points with hypersexual self-exaggeration of her queer persona. Joan showed good comic timing as well. She ran through the entire list of presidents since F.D.R. with a one-liner for each. She then asked everyone to take out a dollar bill, look at it, confirm that the person on the bill looked like Barbara Bush, and then, since the bills had now been extracted from their pockets, to donate them to her campaign. All politicians live off of contributions, after all.

In the climax of her speech, Joan again insisted that her campaign was no more ridiculous than the sordid and criminal

**2.2 Joan JettBlakk announces her candidacy for President, 17 January 1992**

From Gomez and kydd 1994

high jinks of those actually in power, linking queer issues with a wider leftist agenda and, again, lightening the tone with a self-sexualizing and racializing bit of humor:

> I am at this time, officially announcing my candidacy for the orifice of President of the United States. Yes, I'm throwing my wig into the ring. You might think we're joking. I'm sorry, but I think the fact that the U.S. is the only industrialized country without national health care is a joke. I think the fact that some guys with friends in high places got away with opening savings and loans that were designed to steal from hard-working people, and survived with their testicles intact, is a joke. I think the fact that a woman who accused a Supreme Court nominee of sexually harassing her was judged by a group of all men, one of them being Ted Kennedy – and he got in, in more ways than one – is a fucking joke! Are you still laughing? [. . .] well you all are gonna be laughing out of the other side of your face when we're through with you. First of all, once elected, I'm gonna fire everyone in sight. Every single soul that a president can fire, I'm gonna fire. That means that all of you have jobs in Washington. I'm taking applications, so see me later, and I do have a casting couch.
>
> But I digress, in fact I Negress [. . .]
>
> (Gomez and kydd 1992)

JettBlakk put the fool's cap on her opponents, portraying them as demented villains with a particularly evil sense of humor. In contrast, she portrayed her own *jesture* as a harmless and even benevolent exercise.

JettBlakk's campaign platform was a constantly evolving set of one-liners, ranging from camp silliness to pointed satire in a mix that other electoral guerrillas have also found useful. JettBlakk declared that if elected, the White House would become "the Lavender House – lavender and chintz [. . .] you think Jackie had it looking good – I'll have fags in there, and in no time that place will look fabulous." JettBlakk also said she would move the capital to somewhere more interesting, such as Palm Springs, and give Kennebunkport back to the Native Americans. Joan also made clear that she was for gay rights, abortion rights, universal healthcare, and an abolition of both homelessness and the military (she tied the two together, in fact, arguing that the billions spent on the military would be more than enough to build houses for all) (Gomez and kydd 1994).

The campaign did not limit its pranksterism to its own subculture. According to JettBlakk:

> We've sent letters to [anti-gay clergymen] Rev. Lez Sheldon, Rev. Donald Wildmon, and Senator Jesse Helms, saying "we want you to vote for Joan JettBlakk for president. Please give this letter to all of your constituents who are still in the closet." But we haven't heard from them yet.
>
> (Ford 1991)

Queer Nation/Chicago used JettBlakk's queer identity and camp vocabulary/sensibility to mock the straight system at every turn. The campaign issued a few comic press releases. In one, the candidate "nearly loses her wig" when hearing of the Chicago Police Chief's call for greater police powers, suggesting that he move to China where he would be more comfortable with the laws. In another press release, JettBlakk denounces the appointment of the conservative Clarence Thomas to the Supreme Court. After providing a detailed analysis and demand for full disclosure of Thomas's political views, Joan suggests that "Diana Ross would have been a better choice. She's been a Supreme since 1964, and she looks fabulous in a long black dress." A campaign flyer in which Queer Nation/Chicago endorses Joan reads "The Queer Nation Party (and we do mean PARTY, sister) Knows This Election Is Gonna Be A Drag . . . So We Decided to Make It A Real Drag . . . ELECTIONS ARE A JOKE WE'RE MAKING THIS ONE A GOOD JOKE" (Queer Nation 1991c).

Joan formed a band with some of the other activists on her campaign committee. The original songs that they played were queer anthems whose lyrics promoted both Joan's candidacy and the ideology of Queer Nation. "Queen of the City" has lyrics right out of the Queer Nation philosophy: "I learned it from TV/advertise

**2.3a Joan JettBlakk camp-pain flyer**

your sexuality." The song goes on to say "A vote for me/Is queer you see/And then we'll rule the whole country." "Drag Queen Blues" includes the lines "I got the drag queen blues/It ain't no news/It's gender I live to confuse." "Barefoot Surfer Boy" was a comic proclamation of Joan's foot fetish, again mixing camped-up and way-out-in-the-open sexuality with the politics of her campaign (Gomez and kydd 1994). This band played at many "camp-pain" events, mostly for gay clubs and demonstrations, but also at such gigs as a fundraiser for the new Museum of Contemporary Art building. These rock-celebrity musical performances usually went

***IF A BAD ACTOR CAN BE PRESIDENT WHY NOT A GOOD DRAG QUEEN?***

*Joan Jett Blakk for President, Box 14356, Chi. Il. 60614*

***IT'S TIME FOR A GLAMOUR PRESIDENT !!!***

*Joan Jett Blakk for President, Box 14356, Chi. Il. 60614*

**Lick Bush in '92**

*Joan Jett Blakk for President, Box 14356, Chi. Il. 60614*

**Let's make it amerikkka the beautiful . . . AGAIN ! ! !**

*Joan Jett Blakk for President, Box 14356, Chi. Il. 60614*

***A VOTE FOR ME IS QUEER YOU SEE !!!***

*Joan Jett Blakk for President, Box 14356, Chi. Il. 60614*

**2.3b Joan JettBlakk camp-pain stickers**

over well, but some Queer Nation activists thought they were an unfortunate diversion from Joan's more radical, disruptive interventions. One activist argued:

> I got disappointed doing only queer events as the campaign progressed onward. Queer art shows, bar appearances [. . .] that wasn't what the campaign was supposed to be for. It was supposed to be in straight people's faces who weren't used to seeing queers or drag queens.
>
> (Gomez and kydd 1992)

However, the JettBlakk campaign also made numerous forays into the straight world. Because of the notoriety that the campaign generated, Joan did a great number of radio interviews, including one with a station in Ireland. She also appeared on a Northwestern University student talk show. However, Joan's party-crashings were her most notable performances of the campaign. Her attendance at the IMPACT dinner was a prime example.

### Joan explodes on IMPACT

On 2 February 1992, Joan JettBlakk crashed the IMPACT dinner at the Hilton in Chicago. IMPACT was the only gay political lobbying organization in the city, and every year they threw a black-tie event to wine, dine, honor, and hopefully influence, local politicians. As Jon-Henri Damski, who invited JettBlakk as his date, put it:

> Last year I wore black, this time I brought Blakk. IMPACT [. . .] tries to get as many candidates and politicians and leaders and media to their event as they can. They always thought there'd be some kind of protest or direct action [from Queer Nation]. But no, when Joan comes to dinner she comes to dinner.
>
> (Gomez and kydd 1992)

JettBlakk was up to a different sort of action. Rather than sitting-in or chanting slogans, she would confront her assimilationist colleagues with queer kindness and a killer smile.

JettBlakk showed up in a black leather jacket decorated with her campaign button over a sleeveless, backless pink dress. She accessorized with a platinum blonde wig, cascades of costume jewelry, a white purse, and gloves. Her bodyguards, two stern-looking lesbians in black leather uniforms and "PROUD DYKE" patches on their jackets, accompanied her, as did the Queer Nation video crew.

Damski's date did raise a few eyebrows at the party. In video footage, JettBlakk is starkly visible in this almost entirely white, tuxedo-and-opera-dress, non-drag crowd. She worked the mostly gay-assimilationist room as a charming and unrepentant radical queer. JettBlakk presented a very friendly, funny, and kind persona throughout the event, smiling, flattering, and joking with everyone around her. The subject of conversation as she circulated included her dress, her heels, her candidacy, her platform, and her need for a good stiff cocktail ("Not bad for an old man, huh? It's gonna be a bright table, you in red, me in pink. A girl can't go anywhere without her pearls. Am I the only one in pink tonight? There better not be any other pink dresses here tonight *(laugh)*. I'm the only presidential candidate here, and the best dressed one too, *and* the only platinum blonde. Write me in, in big pink letters"). Meeting a woman who was running for a State Supreme Court judgeship, Joan said, "I'm running for President so keep your options open. I may need you in November. I'll put you in the national Supreme Court when I get there." When the woman grinned and

**2.4 Joan at the IMPACT party, with bodyguards and her date, Jon-Henri Damski**

From Gomez and kydd 1994

said "Well I have to get into this one first," Blakk just waved a hand and said "Well, maybe not, I'm changing all the rules, so I can do anything I want" (Gomez and kydd 1992).

JettBlakk was even able to shake the hand of Geraldine Δ155Ferraro, Democratic Vice Presidential candidate in 1984. The smiling JettBlakk gave her a campaign button and said, "Hi, I'm Joan JettBlakk, presidential candidate, I want to present you with this button. I supported you last time and now I want you to help me lick Bush in '92! Welcome to Chicago!" Ferraro seemed amused and wished JettBlakk good luck. Many of those immediately around her played into her act and expressed at least pleasant interest in her candidacy, but apparently many of the organizers of the event felt she was undermining the respectability of their party. While for IMPACT, having Ms. Ferraro present was a great honor and sign of their growing power and legitimacy, JettBlakk had seen it as an opportunity to test a political celebrity's sense of humor. Rick Garcia said, "I saw the Executive Director and people scowling, uncomfortable. It was a major problem for them to have Joan there" (Gomez and kydd 1994).

The conflict over gay image came to a head during the "cavalcade." During this ceremony, all the attending candidates were announced on a microphone, one by one, as they walked into a spotlight and promenaded along a high staircase looking down at the applauding crowd. This soft parade was a performance both of IMPACT's image of power, and of the visiting politician's professed solidarity with the cause of gay rights. Miss JettBlakk was not accepted into the cavalcade, and this angered Garcia:

> The Executive Director stands in a very respectable navy blue outfit, looking like a mortician, and in alphabetical order announces "our friends" [. . .] so they refused to let Joan walk down with two-bit politicans. So I guess that's good for Joan, she doesn't have to associate with those folks, but I think it sent a very bad message to our community that this organization allowed politicians who have spit in our face, who are just coming to us for votes, to get elected, who are opportunistic, are allowed to parade in front of us, but one of our

> very own, and one who has the tendency to be on the cutting edge and one who I don't think would ever sell me out, was not allowed to do that, and I found that terribly offensive.
>
> (Gomez and kydd 1994)

However, at the end of all the introductions, the spotlight operator (whom Queer Nation had enlisted to the cause) turned his light onto JettBlakk, who was sitting on the shoulders of her leather-dyke bodyguards, waving to the crowd. With a little subversive chutzpah, the Queer Nation crew was able to inject JettBlakk's unwanted queerness right into the ceremony from which she had been excluded.

The IMPACT dinner visit by Joan JettBlakk was an adroit political party-crashing. IMPACT and JettBlakk/Queer Nation were essentially battling over the image of the gay community that was to be projected to the public at large, and more specifically to the local political elite. With the crucial help of allies like Damski and Garcia, JettBlakk was able to take IMPACT on in the heart of their own territory – with smiles, small talk, and an outrageous ensemble. JettBlakk's "candidate" status gave her specific comic material to work with; it also provided the rationale for her allies to bring her as a date, introduce her around the room as a politician who belonged there, and help to hijack the cavalcade. This "candidate" status, and the help of another political ally, would enable her to make a more dangerous foray into the straights-only world of the Chicago St Patrick's Day Parade.

## St Joan's Parade

Joan's Queer Nation Party contingent was the first openly gay organization to break into the St Patrick's Day Parade in Chicago; similar groups had been banned from the march in New York and Boston despite protracted and ongoing civil disobedience and legal campaigns in the face of beatings and arrests (Cogswell 2001). Rather than petition, sue, and protest, Joan and Queer Nation stole a move from the Chicago politicos whom they were parodying; they did their thing through patronage. State Senator John Cullerton, who was friendly to their cause, was not going to march in the parade, but he assigned his slot to Joan and Queer Nation. When the police asked the festively dressed but somewhat nervous group where they thought they were going, they were able to cite the authority of a State Senator. The police backed off. Joan and her retinue marched to their space in the procession, with signs that said "JOAN JETTBLAKK FOR PRESIDENT" and "QUEER NATION PARTY."

Joan had become fabulously Irish for the event, in a faux-leopardskin coat, green skirt, and, to playfully hint at some Celtic ancestry, a bright red wig. This was a tongue-in-cheek way to adapt her costume to the specific event while calling attention to (and gently mocking) its racial and ethnic emphasis. She began waving with the poise of a celebrity and the group moved forward.

There was some nervousness among the queer contingent of forty or fifty people – would they be attacked or harassed by an angry crowd along the parade route? The Queer Nation camera crew was there not only to document the march but also hopefully to ward off any would-be attackers with the threat of being caught in the act on videotape (kydd 2001). Happily, there was no harassment of the group as they chanted and marched down the street. In fact, kydd and Gomez's footage shows a Channel Two crew walking along and interviewing Joan. As the group reached the reviewing stand, Mayor Daley was no longer there (some suggested that he had been tipped off to their approach). However, the rest of the reviewers looked suddenly solemn and aghast as a group of happy queers starting chanting at them "LICK BUSH IN '92!" repeatedly as they strolled by.

The march was an unprecedented success for queer visibility in public space. Bill Susinca of Queer Nation said:

> It was really great to have Joan as a figure to rally around. Her presence was really important. Her charisma really pulled us through. That was a perfect political use of Joan. It was what I pictured Joan's purpose, to be in people's faces outside the queer community.
>
> (Gomez and kydd 1992)

Without the political contacts that her mock-campaign had yielded, Joan and Queer Nation probably would not have gotten the political sponsorship that Senator Cullerton provided. Joan referred to this in a speech she gave at CAMP OUT, a Queer Studies Conference at Northwestern University on 11 April 1992. In speaking about the successful St Patrick's Day incursion, she said:

> So much of what we do is dangerous [. . .] because you have cops taking off their badges and their ID numbers and beating the shit out of us. Like the cops at the parade, they were like (*in a deep voice*) "where are you going" and we said (*in a high-pitched voice*) "We're in the parade, excuse me!" and we just walked on through. Now that's visibility, OK, and that's visibility in a way that is fun and harmless and there's nothing they can do about it because they can't harm you without them getting in a lot of trouble and certainly with it being on camera.
>
> (Gomez and kydd 1994)

**2.5 JettBlakk and Queer Nation/Chicago marching in the St Patrick's Day Parade**

From Gomez and kydd 1994

In referring to this event in a later interview, Terence Smith admitted the powerful effect that the documentary crew-activists had on the campaign – through their protective witnessing power, and their creative suggestion of actions that they knew would be camera-worthy:

> Every time, you guys tell me to [crash an event or location], I say no, we'll get arrested, bitch bitch bitch, and then I do it and I love it. Just like when we went to Marshall Fields. Beneton, Banana Republic. People who saw us had never seen anything like that before. That's good especially if it speaks to you, smiles and says vote for me.
>
> (Gomez and kydd 1992)

As Elspeth kydd said in an interview with the author, the JettBlakk campaign was as much a made-for-TV video creation as those of the other candidates, but in a demonstrative, subversive way. The campaign meant to reach out to the media while critically mimicking its constructedness, and without having any illusions that they would get serious or fair treatment. However, Joan did get fair coverage from the absurd tabloid, the *National Examiner*, which seemed to appreciate the humor inherent to the campaign ("A Queen In the White House"). The idea was to maximize exposure both within and outside of the gay subculture (kydd 2001). However, Joan was also happy to get her hands dirty in direct-action street confrontation with her cultural opponents.

### Abortion clinic defense

On 9 May 1992, Joan joined the pro-choice defenders of the ECDC abortion clinic in Chicago. Joan wanted to express solidarity with this feminist cause; her broad, radical approach to public health demanded that her queer activism be committed to feminism and reproductive rights.[6] As a pagan and a member of the Radical Fairies, she had an additional bone to pick with the fundamentalist Christians on the other side of the barricade. Her sign said "I KNOW THE NUMBER OF A FEW GOOD LIONS," and she explained to the Queer Nation camera crew, "It means that we know what Soldiers Field was really built for. For chewing up Christians!"

In a typical, cheerfully shameless self-promotional move, Joan put her campaign poster on the other side of the sign. For this event, she wore her blonde wig, glamorous horn-rimmed sunglasses, hoop earrings, a black biker jacket over a sleeveless T-shirt, and a pink skirt. As usual, Joan drew attention to and made humor of her costume. Gesturing to her six-inch heels, she said "I wore my special Christian-stomping heels today." As if she felt that that was too macho a joke, she then demonstrated how they could also be used to run away if things got violent on the picket line.

While taunting protestors on the other side on the street, Joan took a few verbal shots at her rivals in the campaign. "I don't see the other presidential candidates here!" When asked her view on the abortion issue, she said, "Do I LOOK like I'd be against choice?"

Only about eight anti-abortion rights protesters showed up at the clinic that day, but they did manage to yell some choice epithets at Joan while she was addressing the crowd. When introduced by one of the organizers as a "celebrity" and a presidential candidate, Joan took the mike and began to speak. "I am the only black drag queen running for President. I'm the next President of the United States so you people better get ready. They're gonna get the hell out of town, the hell out of Dodge people!" At this point some of her supporters informed Joan that her opponents were yelling "faggot" and "fairy" at her. Joan smiled and said, in a mock Yiddish accent, "This is something I don't know?!" The comeback drew laughter and applause from her supporters (Gomez and kydd 1992).

This appearance played with the gender-bending aspect of Joan's persona and politics. Terence Smith (and, therefore, I) refer consistently (and playfully) to his drag persona as a "she." However, the use of drag is problematic for many – is it mocking gender costumes or women's bodies? Carole-Anne Tyler argues, "It is important to read each instance of drag (and its interpretations) symptomatically rather than to insist it is always radical or conservative" (1991: 33).[7] When asked about her opinion on abortion rights, Joan made no bones about her biological sex, stating simply "I'm a man, so it's none of my business. That's it. How can I tell a woman what to do with her body?" Joan was a perfectly queer advocate of gender and reproductive self-determination. Just as this radical drag queen made no attempts to pass as a female, she also made no claims on the female body or female identity. However, she had shown both the playful mock-power of candidate-drag ("They're gonna get the hell out of town!") and the real power of radical, unashamed queerness ("This is something I don't know?").

Joan would make this total renunciation of puritanical shame the center of another public appearance. She used her joyous hypersexuality to mock the sexual hypocrisy of the "real" candidates and the press that devoted so much time to their alleged extra-marital affairs. On 1 August 1992, the Joan campaign came to the outdoor festival "Halsted Street Market Days" in Chicago with a parody of the puritanical sex-scandal mongering so typical of recent US electoral politics. Joan was lying on a bed on the sidewalk with a large sign that said: "CREATE YOUR OWN SCANDAL. YOUR PICTURE IN BED WITH A PRESIDENTIAL CANDIDATE." The rate for a posed picture was five dollars, money needed for airfare, rouge, and other campaign expenses. As Joan commented, "I'm the only presidential candidate that you won't have to worry about being in a scandal – 'cause it's all out in the open with me, honey" (Gomez and kydd 1994). Joan projected a queer politics of the future where the scandal-hunting media would have nowhere to go but away, with no cover-ups and no regrets. Joan had already taken this shamelessness to the very hall of power where Governor Clinton himself was ritually nominated by his party.

## The ultimate party-crash: dragging the floor of the Democratic National Convention

Joan and her documentary crew were in New York City for the Democratic National Convention of July 1992. Again, their candidate status had garnered them tactical allies: the Gay Cable Network (GCN) of New York would provide them with press passes to the floor and interview them there.

However, on 13 July, Joan was not even able to come close to Madison Square Garden, where the Convention was being held. The police were not allowing anyone who did not "belong" within a block of the Convention, and they paid particular attention to Joan in her black blouse, pink jacket and skirt, pearls, topknot, and intense, Cleopatr'esque makeup. Joan was out in the street with Glenda Orgasm, a white New York drag queen with a local-access cable show. As they walked about in the street complaining of being shut out of power-politics because of their outfits, Glenda interviewed Joan on her policies, and then the two began to interview and solicit the votes of passersby. With a light touch, Joan and Glenda connected the plight of their subculture to that of all disenfranchised people:

> JOAN: You know, we were just harassed by the police state. The whole block is cut off. This whole convention is not for everybody, it's for the select few. If it doesn't include us it doesn't include ninety-eight percent of everybody out there. The party is out here on the street.
>
> GLENDA: It was easier to get into Studio 54 during its heyday than to get into this convention!
>
> JOAN: And Andy's not here to help us!
>
> (Gomez and kydd 1992)

Joan brought out some new campaign promises in this interview:

> We're gonna take everything that's underground and bring it right out in the open. You want your FBI file? I'll bring it to you, personally! I'll be the only president who answers the White House phone herself. You'll have easy access to the people that run the country. I'll legalize marijuana, tax it, and pay for healthcare [. . .] I think we'll make suits and ties illegal, and then we'll go from there.
>
> (Gomez and kydd 1992)

The glamorous pair conversed with a few passing voters. In keeping with Joan's theme of general disenfranchisement, all of these randomly chosen people said they were disillusioned with both major parties and didn't plan to vote. Joan responded with "You're just the people I'm looking for!" The conversations usually ended with the voters agreeing to write JettBlakk's name on the ballot.

The pair then walked a few blocks over to where a large feminist demonstration was taking place and continued their interviews. Joan struck a populist tone, saying:

> The real people are out here, the people *they* should be talking to, because they can't get in *there*. We should drag them out here, oops I said that word, drag. We're the real people, look at all these fabulous people out here.

Joan denounced the DNC as elitist and exclusive, and the upcoming 500th anniversary of Columbus's cross-Atlantic expedition as a "celebration of genocide and imperialism."

While they were interviewing several demonstrators, Joan attracted the attention of the media. She was interviewed by a crew from the TV station WINS and several other camera crews as well. Joan continued to connect issues of class conflict with her queer politics and public persona:

> JOAN: If I'm elected, I'll erase everyone's college debt. If Charles Keating and Bush's son could get away with it [the savings and loan scandal], everybody else should get a break too. Forgive everybody else [. . .]
>
> WINS: What do you have to say about people shaking their heads at you?
>
> JOAN: I say they have the wrong idea about what beauty is. [They should be] shaking their heads at all these guys with suits and ties, making this an exclusive situation [. . .] at Bush being President and not doing a thing about AIDS or health-care, not at me adding some beauty to the street [. . .]
>
> WINS: What do you have that Bill Clinton doesn't have?
>
> JOAN: These shoes! (laugh) He can't wear these! I have chutzpah! 'Cause I can walk down the street in these shoes. Not Bill, he goes everywhere with bodyguards, not me, I'm out here with the people.

WINS: You have freedom that he doesn't have.

JOAN: Yes, and I intend to take that freedom and spread it all over the country.

WINS: Do you have a job when not running for President?

JOAN: (Pause) Well, let's just say I work at a restaurant. I'm a working-class Presidential candidate.

(Gomez and kydd 1992)

Joan thus spoke as a proud, cheerfully leftist black man in a skirt, combining issues of class conflict with queer cultural/aesthetic politics and definitions of beauty and freedom. She was building, speaking to, and helping to sustain a queer counterpublic, and reaching beyond that counterpublic to the greater public with a broad social justice agenda.

On 15 July, Joan arrived on the floor of the DNC in the form of Terence Smith, her "soul brother." Smith was worried about being thrown out and having his press pass pulled if he arrived in drag, and his GCN allies were afraid that that would result in all of their press passes being pulled at the same time. Smith, wearing his own hair and the social camouflage of his "male drag," a black T-shirt and black pants, was clearly angered at the situation, commenting that it was outrageous that he couldn't wear the clothing of his choice wherever he wanted. In an interview on the convention floor with Graham Ford of GCN, he said:

> I'm here to show that there's another side to family values [. . .] My outrageousness is not accepted as part of the norm of this country. I'm campaigning so that nothing is considered normal anymore [. . .] To show that the DNC is not the be-all and end-all of politics in the U.S. [. . .] and to promote visibility for a broad range of queer politics. They have made a white, patriarchal, police state of this convention [. . .] We have to keep working so that, maybe by '96 I'll be able to wear what I want to wear.
>
> (Gomez and kydd 1992)

The struggle for sartorial freedom was not over, however. After an hour or two off of the floor, a nervous Smith went into a men's room and, at the urging of Gabriel Gomez, hastily put on his makeup, seven-inch platform heels, and the tight red, white, and blue minidress he'd been saving for the occasion. Nervously warning, "This video better make me a goddamn star. I'll be really mad at you if I'm not famous," Joan JettBlakk emerged from the men's room in full glory. After a quick but nervous walk through the hallway, she entered the floor of the convention just as New York Governor Mario Cuomo was being announced – and thus, as chance would have it, Joan entered to a tremendous cheer from the crowds.

With inimitable timing, Joan instantly began to pretend that the applause was for her, dancing, waving, and blowing kisses to the thousands of adoring delegates as "I Love New York" blared from the speakers. Palpably adrenalized, Joan was in fine, defiant form while addressing the GCN and Queer Nation cameras. With sharp comic instinct, she turned a security force-defying move into a very amusing broadcast for the GCN and documentary viewers:

JOAN: Here I am, Joan JettBlakk, the only drag presidential candidate, saying hi to all of America! Hi America! [Acknowledging the fact that the convention continued to grind on around her] and they said hi back, in fact they haven't stopped talking. I'm bringing queer issues to the campaign, in a dress, OK?

GCN: Are you ready to endorse Clinton?

JOAN: No, Clinton should be ready to endorse me!

GCN: What about your platforms?

JOAN: My platforms, why tell you about them when you can see them for yourself? [pointing to her shoes] There they are, and I walk on them every day. I'd like to see Bill wear these [. . .] I'm going to ban the military, so we don't have to worry about the military banning gays.

CUOMO (in background): . . . the name of the next President . . .

**2.6 Joan declares her platform at the DNC in Stars and Stripes minidress**

From Gomez and kydd 1994

> JOAN AND SUPPORTERS: Joan JettBlakk!! JOAN JETT-BLAKK! . . .
>
> JOAN (responding to the applause for Clinton): Thank you, thank you, I'm going to take this nomination and run with it. You'll be proud of me, America!
>
> (Gomez and kydd 1992)

Thanks to daring, luck, and improvisational aplomb, JettBlakk was able to continue her playful inversion of power relations ("Clinton should endorse me, I will ban the military") into the actual hall of power of the DNC. While she only had a minimal disruptive effect on the greater convention with this act, she did provide a great show for her own counterpublic watching on television, and later on video.

## The rift in Queer Nation/Chicago

> They had selected someone [for Vice Presidential candidate] I found very pro-military, very conservative, very assimilationist

> and that went against what the whole campaign was about and that made me very angry.
>
> (Tamara Frasier, Queer Nation activist)

> It had become so much like the American mainstream politics that we were supposed to be making fun of.
>
> (Paige Lestrude, Queer Nation activist (Gomez and kydd 1992))

Despite all of these fabulous actions, some Queer Nation/Chicago activists were bitter. A split developed between Queer Nation/ Chicago and the campaign committee, the small group of people closest to JettBlakk who had been the most involved in the day-to-day operation of "Lick Bush in '92." Chief among the affinity group's complaints was that the campaign committee had become dominated by a small group of white males who were not interested in the ideas of more radical and female members of the organization who also wanted to participate. These activists felt that the campaign had merely reinscribed the "boy's club" tendency in Queer Nation.

The hectic nature of the campaign contributed to this dynamic. Members of Queer Nation who came to the campaign committee meetings were greeted not with the consensual democratic processes to which they were accustomed, but were instead assigned tasks in order to support the constant logistical needs of the campaign. As the campaign became less widely participatory, and more centered on one individual, some felt that its performances (particularly when the band played at gay events) were "stale and rehearsed," losing its wilder, carnivalesque side.

Queer Nation/Chicago activists also felt that the campaign committee was taking itself too seriously, forgetting the original goals of the campaign as a satiric cultural guerrilla action. Christina Zinnen, who had performed in some early JettBlakk performances, noted that:

> The committee was supposed to do the work but big decisions were to be made by the general meeting, but that's not how

> it worked. The committee became an elite clique of gay men. Whereas it started out very political, it became a sort of glamour thing, and it lost a lot of what the campaign was supposed to be.
>
> (Gomez and kydd 1992)

Both JettBlakk's campaign committee and the rest of Queer Nation/Chicago would accuse each other of taking the campaign too "seriously." However, as Elspeth kydd pointed out, there was always a serious purpose underlying the campaign, and the charge of "taking it too seriously" was an accusatory tactic that could be used by both factions (kydd 2001).

These dynamics – the exclusion of the larger activist group from the creative process by the campaign committee, and the perceived shifting focus of the campaign from the big-picture ideological goals to more technical/logistical aspects – came to a head in the fateful choice of a Vice-Presidential candidate to complete JettBlakk's ticket. To meet the filing deadline for the Illinois ballot, the JettBlakk campaign committee chose lesbian activist Miriam Ben-Shalom of Milwaukee without consulting Queer Nation/Chicago. Bill Susinca said that "it became maniacal, twisted, almost obsessive, to try to get on the ballot. The whole ballot issue was just a Frankenstein monster to get in the media as much as possible" (Gomez and kydd 1992). However, the members of the campaign committee felt that having Joan's name on the ballot would garner her a great deal more visibility and media coverage and was therefore worth the time, effort, and circumvention of the consensus process of Queer Nation/Chicago.

Miriam Ben-Shalom of Milwaukee was the first woman to be thrown out of the military for being homosexual. As Smith stated:

> Her issue was national in the late seventies [. . .] I saw it as taking two completely different factions of the gay community and mushing them together. I know that upset some people but they didn't understand the motive of why she was there.
>
> (Gomez and kydd 1992)

The issue of gays in the military was heating up again, making Ben-Shalom an appealing choice in some ways. Smith noted that Ben-Shalom was able to take a joke on the subject:

> When I went to the Gay Pride parade in Milwaukee, I said on stage with Miriam that I was going to completely abolish the military when I was elected and she would have to get another job. They cheered, she laughed, she thought it was really funny.
>
> (Gomez and kydd 1992)

Smith went on to note the difficulties of bringing specific difficult issues into a guerrilla theatre campaign:

> I never expected to be up on stage with Miriam, not in a red, white, and blue miniskirt. Well of course, it's real politics. That's what we wanted to do is get some real politics into this outrageous fantasy of a drag queen being President of the United States. And of course where the real politics comes in is where the dissension comes in because real politics breeds dissension anyway.
>
> (Gomez and kydd 1992)

There always seems to be a danger in electoral guerrilla theatre that the theatre-makers will get more "hung up" on their own fantastic symbolism than the powerful targets of their satire do. To some extent, this happened with the Kabouters, and this seems to be the problem that Queer Nation/Chicago faced at this time. The JettBlakk campaign committee felt that the actual choice of Vice-Presidential candidate was symbolically of lesser import and a matter of expediency for ballot access, while many members of the rest of Queer Nation/Chicago felt that ballot access was less important that the identity of the chosen candidate. Neither faction actually thought this campaign was a "serious" one, but they nevertheless had urgent, irreconcilable symbolic agendas for it.

Some members of Queer Nation/Chicago had felt disenfranchised by the JettBlakk campaign committee. While chafing at the undemocratic process of V.P. selection, members of Queer Nation/Chicago also disagreed with the choice itself on ideological grounds, seeing it as an assimilationist move. Ben-Shalom, after all, was trying to get gays accepted into the military, an institution which many Queer Nation members opposed on principle. They wanted a radical Vice-Presidential candidate, ideally a leather dyke, from another region so as to appeal to non-Midwestern Queer Nation members.

While Smith respected the opinions of his co-activists, he did not seem to think that the choice of Ben-Shalom was as destructive or unfortunate as they did. He felt that this kind of internal argument was endemic to highly motivated and ideologically sophisticated activist groups, and probably unavoidable. He also did not think it was that serious a problem:

> I don't think that Miriam undermined what was going on. It was just a misunderstanding because the campaign went on and we used each other's names but we weren't in the same place at the same time. Miriam and I were more like Salt'N'Pepa than like any Presidential team you can think of. More like Jerry Lewis and Dean Martin.
>
> (Gomez and kydd 1992)

Nevertheless, the stakes were high enough in the eyes of the larger Queer Nation/Chicago group to provoke a split.

The controversy was the result of the different interpretations that the various factions of Queer Nation had made of their own ironic campaign. The campaign committee wished to maximally appropriate the trappings of the electoral system for national and statewide visibility. Queer Nation/Chicago preferred to reject all trappings of the electoral system – including the need for ballot access or a consistent political platform – while artfully and outrageously mocking the mainstream methods of gender and candidate construction. As Paige Lestrude said:

> My objections were like, look [. . .] this is for publicity. We are trying to present a wake-up call in our own way with

> this campaign and we know that it might not reach a whole lot of acceptance in mainstream hetero culture, but what the fuck do we care? We want the queer cultures all over the country to wake up and have this be a galvanizing force for them [. . .] and I just felt that Miriam would not be focused on that, it would be focused on her military career [. . .] it would be let's just assimilate into mainstream culture as best we can [. . .]
>
> (Gomez and kydd 1992)

These activists expected the campaign to be run by Queer Nation's consensus process, and that it would remain open to the creativity and opinions of all its members. Instead, the actual decisions of the JettBlakk campaign left many of these activists feeling excluded.

After many rumors, confrontations, and negotiations, the two entities publicly separated on 11 August 1992, with a Queer Nation press release making it official. This release was far less playful in tone than the early "Lick Bush in '92" releases had been. Stating flatly that "the Joan JettBlakk Committee became male-dominated [. . .] These issues came to a head in the selection of the vice-presidential candidate," this press release added that "This separation is mutual and non-hostile. Members of both groups continue to work together on other issues" (Queer Nation 1992). On this note, the campaign split from the activist group which had launched it.

It is important to note that this happened in the context of Queer Nation chapters breaking apart due to political infighting all over the country. In fact, the Chicago chapter lasted longer than some others. There was an inherent tension between the group's desire to unify all queers regardless of identity, and its actual practice:

> As a partial replacement for "lesbian and gay," the term "queer" attempted to separate questions of sexuality from those of gender. But in terms of practice, this separation was incomplete. The new coexistence of gay men and women was often uneasy; ACT UP and Queer Nation chapters in many cities

> were marred by gender (and racial) conflicts. The new "co-sexual" queer culture could not compensate for real, persistent structural differences in style, ideology, and access to resources among men and women. This recurring problem suggested that while the new queer politics represented the assertion of a sexual difference which could not be assimilated into feminism, neither could gender be completely subsumed under sexuality. Despite their apparent commonalities, lesbians and gay men were often divided along much the same lines as heterosexual women and men.
>
> (Stein 1998: 561)

Fraser's critique about Habermas's bourgeois public sphere (see Introduction) applies here. Even in an avowedly safe space such as a Queer Nation meeting, divisions such as gender, race, and class cannot be overcome or erased simply by desire or declaration. Some of the white women in the group felt excluded by the white men around Joan. On the other hand, Joan, the jet black diva candidate on a roll, was not to be held back by anyone; Joan was as charismatic, confrontational, and controversial as fellow radical working-class transgender activist of color Sylvia Rivera herself (Shepard 2004).

JettBlakk continued to campaign, and even gave a speech at an IMPACT celebration on Election Night; apparently IMPACT was able to have a sense of humor about Joan once it was clear that Bill Clinton had defeated George Bush. Her speech was unapologetic and forward-looking. She continued to use sexual humor and encouraged youths in the closet to come out and prepare to continue the battle against the religious Right:

> Well here we are, the day we've been waiting for, the day of elections. Now obviously you all voted right? Well I have to tell you this is not really a concession speech because queers concede nothing [. . .] With the help of fabulous people in this room, we took our message to people who never expected to see a drag queen at all much less one who was running for President. It's true along the way we opened a few minds,

> hearts and more than a few zippers [. . .] Now just because George Bush is no longer in the White House it doesn't mean that our fight is over. We must arm ourselves. I think we should arm ourselves at the jewelry store. Boys, wear more makeup. Girls, get shorter haircuts. Subvert the norm at every opportunity you can. Cause I gotta tell you the religious Right is out to get us and they are not gonna stop.
>
> (Gomez and kydd 1994)

In essence, JettBlakk was urging her supporters to continue to do in everyday life what she had been doing on the campaign trail, as a queer "spokesmodel" of behavior.

In an interview with Gomez and kydd, JettBlakk's final thoughts on the campaigns were upbeat:

> I got my skinny little black ass on every TV station that I possibly could, which is all that running for President really is [. . .] People now know that black drag queens can run for president. And I've been saying since the sixties that if pigs can run for President, if bad actors can run for President, then drag queens can too [. . .] It meant fun. It's meant fun from the beginning and it's fun now [. . .] If it wasn't for us, what would you have, football?
>
> (Gomez and kydd 1992)

With minimal resources, the Joan JettBlakk campaign made some significant splashes for queer visibility in local and national politics. This visibility continued with kydd and Gomez's video "Lick Bush in '92," which was released in 1994 and was very well received on the festival circuit. With the use of sharp, ribald humor, JettBlakk and company poached on the media node of electoral politics in the United States to galvanize their own queer counterpublic, to light a bit of a fire under the larger gay assimilationist community, and to communicate their grievances and alternative political fantasies to the larger straight majority.

However, this impressive accomplishment had come at the expense of the affinity group which had launched the campaign.

As "Lick Bush in '92" took on a momentum of its own, its fast pace caused the committee to act as a central command center, leaving the larger group out of many decisions and eroding their own process. They began to operate more along the lines of a representative politics than a consensual politics, which is exactly what the affinity group mode of activist organizing is supposed to prevent. The fight over the Vice-Presidential nomination, and ballot access, was only the most extreme and final example of this.

There is something inherent to electoral politics that encouraged this dynamic. Elections center on individual personalities – the candidates – surrounded by support staff who, like extras in films, fade out of focus behind them. "Lick Bush in '92" was a parody of a straight campaign, but as it imitated that format, it became more about its central celebrity and less about its affinity group. JettBlakk made great use of Brechtian drag to make the familiar strange, and the strange a little more familiar, in elections and other public rituals. Her inventive work was personally liberating for her, and disruptive of its targets. However, as the campaign continued, its spect-actorship decreased, and anti-participatory, non-Bakhtinian footlights increasingly widened the gaps between her and both comrades and audiences. This affected the nature of the performances themselves; hence the critique by one activist of them as "stale and rehearsed." However, there was nothing stale or rehearsed about the major party-crashing interventions of the campaign, from the IMPACT dinner to the St Patrick's Day Parade to the Democratic National Convention.

The relationship between JettBlakk and Queer Nation/Chicago had not been worked out clearly enough from the start. JettBlakk was a charismatic performer who had little patience for long consensus meetings in the first place; given the chance to be a diva candidate, it was perhaps naive to expect her to stop and get permission for each move from the larger group. Had the campaign operated in a more consensual way, fewer appearances and performances might have been organized, but Queer Nation/Chicago might have thrived on the project. Alternatively, JettBlakk might have started from the beginning as an independent performer, in solidarity with but not bearing the label of Queer Nation. Clearly, the symbols of electoral power and contestation are potent ones, and playing with them can be a dangerous, Faustian game. However, as kydd noted, the campaign never fully became what it was satirizing, because a "real" campaign would probably have attempted to suppress or cover-up any such internal controversy (kydd 2001).

In the next chapter, I will examine another critical drag performer and electoral guerrilla, Pauline Pantsdown. Pantsdown used digital technology and ribald humor in her electoral campaign, sabotaging the political career of Australia's pre-eminent racist politician. With a more focused campaign goal and no ideologically demanding backing organization to answer to, Pantsdown had far fewer homefront distractions as she crafted her guerrilla performance.

Chapter 3

# Electoral guerrilla theatre in Australia

## Pauline Hanson vs. Pauline Pantsdown

Sydney: 3 October 1998. Election night for the Australian Parliament. Pauline Pantsdown, candidate for the Federal Senate and drag persona of performance artist Simon Hunt, hobbles in high heels down a dark street in Marrickville – a working-class, multicultural, immigrant, inner suburb of Sydney – headed for the headquarters of Anthony Albanese, local Member of Parliament for the Australian Labor Party (ALP). Although ostensibly an Independent rival to the ALP, Pantsdown is the entertainment on this critical evening. Present are scores of the local electorate and several local leaders of the left faction of the ALP. Pantsdown is in her full campaign costume, a cartoon-drag version of far-right MP and founder of the One Nation Party, Pauline Hanson: a bright red frizzy wig, outrageous lopsided makeup, and an inexpensive bright red dress (the same brand that Hanson wears). Pantsdown is no traditional drag queen, but a radical, critical,[1] candidate drag queen, who apes grotesque politics with mask and mimetic excess.

When Pantsdown arrives, Albanese, a shoo-in for re-election, tells her that Hanson has lost her seat in Parliament. The mood in the hall is festive as Albanese introduces Pantsdown to the audience as "the person who has done the best job of exposing the fascism that Pauline Hanson represents." Pantsdown immediately launches into a performance of her anti-Hanson, chart-topping hit, "I Don't Like It." The crowd cheers as Pantsdown bobs about like a puppet on a string, lip-synching to Hanson's voice, digitally remastered and rearranged to form the anti-Hanson lyrics of Pantsdown's creation. These lyrics mock both Hanson's cultural racism and her taste in music.

A bit of Pantsdown political stand-up comedy follows: The candidate mocks Hanson's cultivated image as a working-class "battler" by detailing the huge profits she made and tiny wages she paid as the owner of a fish and chip shop. Pantsdown then recounts buying the same brand dresses at the same warehouse where Hanson does her shopping. Those dresses cost only $39 apiece, "so where is the money going?"

The performer then details her current legal troubles. Her first song, "Backdoor Man" has been banned as a result of a lawsuit by Hanson's One Nation Party against JJJ, the youth radio station of the Australian Broadcasting Corporation (ABC). Hanson's lawyers claimed that the song, an earlier cut-and-paste satirical reworking of the parliamentarian's words, is defamatory.

As the set-up for her closing song, Pantsdown pulls the deputy premier of New South Wales, the local state-level representative, and Albanese up in front of the blue-collar Vietnamese/Turkish/Greek/Anglo audience of about 300. The politicians are each assigned a part, which they awkwardly but good-naturedly struggle through. They play lawyers and judges, reciting actual transcripts of Pantsdown's day in court, which ended with "I'm a Backdoor Man" being banned from airplay. A good, beery, left-wing time is had by all and Pantsdown shakes many hands on her way out the door.

After the show, Pantsdown is whisked by her campaign staff (a couple of friends) to Sleaze Ball '98, the huge, annual gay performance event which, in 1998, happened to fall on the same night as the election.[2] Pantsdown, the main event for the 16,000 people in the hall, performs her second song, "I Don't Like It." The grand scale of the Sleaze Ball contrasts sharply with the labor hall. There is a huge, frightening, papier mâché Hanson head on stage. Laser lights beam; a powerful sound system booms. A dozen "Dancing Hansons" back up Pantsdown in an earthy, bawdy, and tightly choreographed routine. At the end of the song, the massive Hanson head explodes and the Dancing Hansons collapse to the floor. Pantsdown steps to the mike and announces Hanson's electoral defeat. The place goes wild and the party escalates (Hunt and Regan 1998).

## The target: Pauline Hanson

Sometimes electoral guerrillas mock liberal democracy and its unacknowledged exclusionary devices and structures. Simon Hunt, a gay, left-wing composer, lecturer, and film critic from Sydney, had a more specific target in his sights: far-right parliamentarian Pauline Hanson. Hunt proclaimed, "There will be either two Paulines or no Paulines." Hunt felt that his drag persona's sole function was to ridicule Hanson's public presence; once the latter retired, so by necessity would the former. To understand Pantsdown we need to know Hanson.

In 1996, to the surprise of pundits and politicians, Pauline Hanson won the traditionally Labor, blue-collar, and rural Queensland seat of Oxley. Hanson, from a small town in Queensland, was a fish and chip shop owner, and a single mother twice divorced with three children. She fit the popular Aussie image of a working- to lower-middle-class "battler" struggling to make ends meet. Hanson had accepted the seemingly hopeless job as the right-wing Liberal Party's candidate for Oxley, but was expelled from the party for anti-Aboriginal comments printed in a local paper. Her expulsion happened too late for Hanson to be removed from the ballot as the Liberal party candidate. She thus won the votes of both habitual Liberal voters and economically disaffected Labor voters because of her newfound credentials as an independent given the boot by the Establishment.

Within a year of her upset victory, with the help of far-right political adviser John Pasquarelli, Hanson solidified her anti-Asian-immigrant and anti-Aboriginal politics into her own party, a new magnet for the far-right called "Pauline Hanson's One Nation Party." Having Hanson's name in the actual name of the party reflected the desire to use her newfound, controversy-driven fame and celebrity to promote One Nation and its agenda. One Nation's policies included: the withdrawal of Australia from the United Nations; a halt to all immigration (and a zero-net-gain immigration policy from then on); the cessation of all foreign aid; the abolition of the Aboriginal and Torres Strait Islanders Commission; a halt to

**3.1 Pauline Hanson at the Mortdale Bowling Club, 24 September 1998**

From footage for *Send in the Clown: The Pauline Pantsdown Story*, an unfinished documentary video (directed by Sally Regan and Simon Hunt; produced by Sally Regan)

all subsidies of any kind for Aborigines; and a subsidy for medical care for elderly rural whites, the party's power base. One Nation opposed Aboriginal reconciliation, a difficult, fraught process of cultural, legal, economic, and political reparation which the cultural left-center has been pursuing for decades. While Hanson insists that she is not racist, Jon Stratton notes that her racism takes the form of cultural racism, in which cultural behavior is immutably equated with racial identity (Stratton 1998). Thus, according to One Nation, Asians as an undifferentiated, homogenous group will act in ways culturally inimical to "mainstream Australia." Therefore, they will never assimilate. And of course, according to this world-view, assimilation is the only way in which mainstream (read "white, Anglo-Celtic") Australia can accept any newcomers.

Hanson had enough support in her home district to win the election, but how was she received by the mainstream media?

**3.2 In the early morning of 4 October 1998, Pantsdown sat onstage at the big Sleaze Ball, next to the huge papier-mâché Hanson head**

From footage for *Send in the Clown: The Pauline Pantsdown Story*, an unfinished documentary video (directed by Sally Regan and Simon Hunt; produced by Sally Regan)

Journalist Tracey Curro's interview on Australian *60 Minutes* on 20 October 1996 is a good example. Hanson's racist politics were thoroughly critiqued, as were the vast inconsistencies and illogic within her party's ideology and platforms. However, there was often a classist and regionalist bias in the media. In the *60 Minutes* piece, Hanson is shown misreading her speeches and confusing her syntax – the unpolished, uneducated Deep Northerner with a Queensland accent from the perspective of the cosmopolitan, southern, and multicultural urban centers:

> CURRO: [. . .] Well, let's look at some actual numbers then. There are 866,224 Asian-born Australians out of a population of over 18 million. Now, is that "in danger of being swamped"

[referring to Hanson's public claim that "we are in danger of being swamped by Asians."]?

HANSON: I don't believe those figures.

CURRO: Well, these are from the Department of Immigration.

HANSON: That's, they're as far as I'm concerned they're booked figures. I don't believe those figures.

CURRO: Are you xenophobic?

HANSON: (Pause) Please explain?

CURRO: (Pause) Xenophobia means a fear of all things foreign.

HANSON: No, I don't think I am. No, I'm not. Is there a problem? Just because I might be . . . (Pause) I find this very hard because I have to sort of clarify all my, what I think and how I feel about things, isn't it?

CURRO: Precisely, because you are a federal politician. We're not just sitting around in a pub, talking about things [. . .]

(Wilkinson 1996)

For months, "Please Explain?" resonated as a favorite quote throughout Australia. Many amused viewers saw Hanson as a xenophobe who didn't even know what the word meant. But this sort of condescending coverage angered Hanson's supporters, further galvanizing them against what they perceived as an elitist, intellectual media. Naturally, Simon Hunt/Pauline Pantsdown acted within this Australian battle of stereotypes. In crafting his drag performance, Hunt drew on Hanson's public persona as reflected in the mainstream media's coverage – her slogans, phrases, accent, and dress.

## The guerrilla's art

The electoral guerrilla's art is improvised. Electoral guerrillas have what de Certeau would call tactical agency as opposed to strategic power. Low on resources and wherewithal, the guerrillas do not make the laws or strategic frameworks in which they operate and have little hope of changing them. The guerrillas make do by using the tools and refuse of the strategic power, in a way not originally intended, to gain media exposure and access to audiences that would otherwise be beyond their reach.

Electoral guerrillas, like their military counterparts, are greatly aided by the pre-existence of "base communities" of support (Guevara 1961). These communities are both the social groups from which electoral guerrillas draw support, and the targets of the positive, galvanizing aspect of their performances. They are counterpublics located in a world of polyglot, internally fractious, rival, overlapping, and conflicting sub-publics with their own rhetorics, positionalities, and worldviews (Fraser 1997). Both Hanson and Pantsdown were operating in this complicated terrain, where a public performance that entertained or satisfied one group was sure to enrage, alienate, or simply confuse another.

Hanson and One Nation met a great deal of enraged opposition from the Left. A youth group called Resistance (which One Nation labeled a Red Front of foreigner-manipulated youths) constantly confronted One Nation with counter-demonstrations. Hanson was definitely successful in polarizing the country and bringing race to the forefront of political debate.

### Simon Hunt (the guerrilla behind the makeup)

Simon Hunt, a.k.a. Pauline Pantsdown, teaches digital sound editing at the College of Fine Arts in Sydney. In 1989, he used this skill to satirical effect against the anti-gay, right-wing, Christian Democratic Party leader Fred Nile: he recut Nile's voice into an absurd speech which he played at full blast while Nile and his Christian fundamentalist followers marched through the gay neighborhood of Sydney on a "moral crusade" (Hunt 1999b).

When Hanson appeared on the national political scene, Hunt decided to answer her racist nationalism with digital sampling, lip-synching, and satirical, gender-critical live performance. These satirical elements came from what he had always seen as the less serious side of his work, having placed a higher premium on his original musical composition and film work.

Hunt's research into both Nazi propaganda and anti-Nazi cabaret satire for the uncompleted film project *Risk* were of great use in this "low artistic" enterprise. Hunt drew parallels between Hanson/One Nation's rhetoric and that of the Nazi Party. While acknowledging that there was a vast difference in degree between the two, Hunt stated that both used the rhetoric of internal and external enemies as threatening to the racially constructed nation. The Nazis depicted the Jews as a subhuman ethnic minority eroding and corrupting the nation from within. One Nation assigned that role to the Aboriginals. The Nazis used the French as the external threat (as well as, I would add, the Soviets). One Nation positioned Asia – a racial mass undifferentiated by nation, politics, or economics – as the "swamping" threat. Hunt decided that:

> [Hanson] was the next candidate for my cut-up technique, that I could get my ideas out in that way [. . .] the Pauline Pantsdown project [. . .] seemed to be the project that pulled in all the different bits and pieces I'd been doing before that – performance, music, humor, politics [. . .]
>
> (Hunt 1999c)

## "I'm a Backdoor Man": the Pantsdown project begins

Hunt composed his first anti-Hanson song, "I'm a Backdoor Man," as a satirical cut-up of Hanson's words, mocking her politics. The piece was originally written in August 1997 to accompany a dance piece for his drag queen friend Vanessa Wagner's dance party. In the piece, Pauline Pantsdown threatened the survival of a bizarre 1950s Australian family, but was exposed in the end as a space alien (with antennas hidden under her wig) and banished. The name "Pauline Pantsdown" was chosen because it played on Hanson's name and went well with the song's title. Like any tactical player, Hunt had to work with the "castoffs" of the target – the words and phrases that Hanson had publicly spoken – and he worked to rearrange them to maximum satirical effect.

**"I'm a Backdoor Man"**
By Pauline Pantsdown

*Unless otherwise specified, all lyrics are spoken in Pauline Hanson's re-edited voice.*

JAUNTY MALE CHORUS (*sampled from the American musical movie* The Perils of Pauline):
I'm as worried as can be, Pauline
I wonder what the end will be, Pauline

HANSON:
Yes
Here I am
I find this very hard3
But I look at it this way
I'm a backdoor man, I'm very proud of it
I'm a backdoor man, I'm homosexual
I'm a backdoor man, yes I am, I'm very proud of it
I'm a backdoor man, I'm homosexual *(giggles)*
Backdoor, clean up our own backdoor
We need to get behind, and we'll do trade with you
Backdoor, all our fears will be realized
But I'm a happy person
Because I'm a backdoor man, yes I am *(giggles)*
What I've called for is a homosexual government, yeah
Join us, be one of us
Come out, be one of us, yeah
I'm very proud, that I'm not straight
I'm very proud, that I'm not natural
You know, I'm not human
Someone hit me on the head one day, yeah
You know, I'm not human
Someone hit me on the head one day and,
I don't know I don't know I don't know

MALE CHORUS:
Poor Pauline, Poor Pauline, Poor Pauline, Pauline and her peril

On a rope they dangle her, then they choke and strangle her
With an axe they mangle her, always something new

HANSON:
I like trees, and I like shrubs and plants
And trees and shrubs and plants
But I've put the fence up now so they can't get in, yeah
Please explain, Me, me, me *(3 times)*
Please explain

MALE CHORUS:
Poor Pauline, Poor Pauline, I'm a worried as can be Pauline and her peril

HANSON:
I'm a backdoor man
I'm very proud of it
I'm a backdoor man
I'm homosexual
And back here, this is a circular driveway
I still work it, I worked the other night
I'm rostered on, I think for next week
Now a gentleman came up and told me, he said that
"Other people don't receive"
They've got to accept it here inside
Or I'm saying that they up and leave
Yes, it's a little bit country, it's a little bit country, country, country

VANESSA WAGNER:
It's a little bit rock and roll if you ask me

HANSON:
Yes, it's a little bit country, of course, of course

MALE CHORUs:
Of course, her horse, will neigh, neigh, neigh, Pauline

HANSON:
I'm very proud that I'm not straight
I'm very proud that I'm not natural

*I'm a backdoor man for the Ku Klux Klan*
*with very horrendous plans*
I'm a very caring potato.
We will never have the chance *(repeat)*
Please explain, ME
Me me
Please explain
Please explain, Me *(repeat)*
Thank you
Please explain, please explain, thank you
(Hunt 1997, emphasis added)

In his construction of "I'm a Backdoor Man," Pantsdown was inspired by the cabaret performers who satirized Hitler. These satirists faced the challenge that Hitler's views were so extreme that they could not be mocked through exaggeration. Instead, Hitler's Austrian accent, his quirky speaking style, and his erratic logic were mocked by portraying him discussing something innocuous like grocery shopping with the same insane fervor and hatred with which he ranted against the Jews. Hunt says he drew on this tradition. Instead of dealing directly with Hanson's white supremacism, he used her argumentative methods and her actual (digitized and rearranged) voice to advocate for gay supremacy in rhythmic rhyme (Hunt 1999a).

A close reading of these lyrics reveals how the song operates on several levels, through both direct and indirect satire. Lines like "I find this very hard," "clean up our own backdoor," "We need to get behind/And we'll do trade with you," and "This is a circular driveway" were matched to appropriate sexual gestures in the original stage performance. These lines can also be seen as the "way in" for listeners through entertaining, silly, slightly titillating lyrics.

The male chorus' lines, sampled from an old American film, are perhaps a bit disturbing in their violence, especially as they are sung in a jaunty Broadway musical style. However, they are also a parody of Hanson's self-portrayal as the victim of invisible and powerful forces: the media, the foreign-sponsored Left, and other persecutors.

Of course, Pantsdown makes hay of Hanson's famous "Please Explain" gaffe, while only implicitly referring to Curro's question, "Are you xenophobic?" Pantsdown's answer is, "Yes, of course, and ridiculous as well." Pantsdown depicts Hanson as a loopy xenophobe with such lines as, "I like trees and shrubs and plants [. . .] but I've put up the fence now so they can't get in." Pantsdown gives "Please Explain" an added twist by changing it to "Please Explain Me"; Hanson is forced to ask the Australian people for an explanation for her own bizarre politics, character, and, by implication, her incarnation as Pantsdown.

Pantsdown makes ironic use of anti-gay rhetoric in the song. "I'm very glad that I'm not natural," coming after "I'm very glad that I'm not straight," mocks the reactionary construction of queerness as "unnatural." "You know I'm not human/Someone hit me on the head one day" refers to gay bashing in a way that is both flip and chilling.

"What I've called for is a homosexual government." With this line Hunt casts his new persona, Pantsdown, as a gay supremacist. The threat, "[. . .] other people don't receive/They've got to accept it here inside/Or I'm saying that they up and leave," parallels One Nation's Anglo-Celtic cultural supremacist ultimatum to all immigrants, whether Asian or Southern European "wogs": assimilate or evacuate. With the line, "All our fears will be realized/But I'm a happy person," Pantsdown deftly summarizes, alienates, and debunks the rhetorical strategy of the modern friendly fascist who combines an approachable, down-home, grassroots persona with the worst of scare tactics and dark prophecy.

Forgive the usage in this context, but the ironic anti-gay rhetoric and the gay-supremacist bits rub up against each other in a slippery way. It fascinates to hear these "both sides of the backdoor" rhetorics juxtaposed to a bouncy beat, and orated by the voice of a known homophobe. The joyful contradictions and multivalent, multileveled ironies make "I'm a Backdoor Man" still engaging after multiple listenings.

The payoff line, of course, is "I'm a backdoor man for the Ku Klux Klan with very horrendous plans." Here, Pantsdown ties together the strands of the satire: the direct mockery of Hanson's voice, accent, and speech patterns; her argumentative tactics; her rhetorical and grammatical confusion; and her cultural racism and xenophobia.

### "Backdoor" censored

Hunt never intended for this song to be a big hit on the radio, or to achieve escape velocity from his own subculture, the gay performance scene of Sydney. However, when a friend managed to get it played on JJJ, the Australian Broadcasting Corporation's national youth radio station, it received countless call-in requests for airplay and was heard over and over again for eleven days, until One Nation filed a defamation suit against JJJ. The court imposed an injunction against its further play on that station until the case could be resolved. This injunction was imposed despite the fact that the song was prefaced before each playing by a disclamatory note saying it was satire and not to be taken seriously. One Nation leader David Oldfield, the top adviser for Hanson, went so far as to call "I'm a Backdoor Man," "the biggest sex scandal of the last decade" (Hunt 1999c). The injunction had a chilling effect; no other radio station was willing to risk a suit by playing the song.

Hanson and One Nation played right into the satirist's hands. When accused of racism, Hanson had consistently claimed that she was merely exercising her right of free speech and that the Labor governments of the past had stifled honest discussion about race:

> As a citizen, the right of free speech under the law is fundamental to our nation and way of life. As a democratically elected parliamentarian, it is vital. Stopping free speech will lead in the end to a totalitarian society, ruled by dictators, where no one will have the right to disagree [. . .] I respect the right of people to disagree with me [. . .] Instead of attacking me [. . .] they should consider the end result of this attempt to silence me.
>
> (*Weekly House Hansard* 1996)

Waving the free-speech banner cost Hanson once she sued for the censorship of Pantsdown's work. In fact, once censored, Pantsdown drew on this quote, saying, "now we know that Hanson's statement was not a warning but a wishful fantasy." One Nation appeared to be for free speech only in some cases. Hanson played the straight woman to Pantsdown's comedic queerness, showing that she couldn't take a joke.

One Nation's legal argument was remarkable. In order to keep the injunction in place, One Nation had to show that there was actual defamation in broadcasting "Backdoor Man." Hunt and JJJ argued that no one would ever think that this song was actually written by Hanson or that it expressed her beliefs or sexual preferences. One Nation claimed that because it used Hanson's voice, listeners would assume it was her speaking. This claim was astoundingly literal-minded, providing Hunt with tremendous Pantsdown material. However, the courts upheld the injunction.

One Nation's leaders and lawyers played the role of Steven Dubin's *homo censorus* perfectly (Dubin 1999). They declared only one possible interpretation of a multivalent piece of art. They argued that Hanson, and the public at large, would be deceived and harmed by the song. They also failed to silence "Backdoor Man." As Dubin notes, censorship rarely truly censors. The song was made widely available on the internet. To evade One Nation lawyers, offshore websites were set up. A whole subculture formed around the song's distribution. Little kids were singing it in the schoolyards, including the children of outraged One Nation members. Even though it was only played for eleven days, at the end of the year listeners voted it number five of the top hundred songs played on that station. It even made it onto the listener's list of "Top 100 Songs of All Time." Clearly, the injunction had only helped create more attention for the song.

Hunt had hoped that the "drag" novelty aspect of his work would provide him with a way into the news as a cartoonish bit of fun, enabling him to make his greater political critiques (Hunt 1999c). On 29 August 1997, Pauline Pantsdown and Vanessa Wagner were interviewed on the *TODAY* show (Hunt had not yet legally changed his name but did hope to keep his real name secret for both satirical and personal safety reasons).

On the *TODAY* show, Pantsdown was in an early form of Hanson-drag: a tight wig, heavy but not absurd makeup, and a red dress suit that included fascistic jodhpurs and boots. She wore a band of tiny, impaled koala bears pinned to her chest as medals. In later appearances, Pantsdown would be in her second and final costume: a frizzier wig, more outrageous and lopsided makeup (Hanson's lipstick was often crooked), and two dresses of the same brand as Hanson's:

> Visually, I tried to replicate her as closely as possible. I began to wear the same brand of clothing as her. I think the replication worked two ways. I was sending up her actual construction as a so-called "non-politician," the idea being that I was no less real than she was. Secondly, replicating her media presence isolated the absurdity of her politics, because they were the only difference between us.
>
> (Hunt 1999b)

However, for conservative viewers, the main difference between the two was their *gender and sexuality*, as traditionally defined: a difference that was emphasized by Hunt's drag-replication. Hunt's visually driven critique probably resonated more clearly for audiences who were already open to the genre of drag.

But on this particular day, the host of *TODAY* was wearing a red dress very similar to Pantsdown's, providing an extra, unintended visual joke. In the ensuing interview, Pantsdown and Wagner played off each other as a comedy duo, with host Tracey Grimshaw playing the obliging straight woman. One of Pantsdown's priorities was to undercut Hanson's use of "mainstream Australia" as a euphemism for Anglo-Celtic Australians, her usual claim being that "a majority of mainstream Australia will back me on these issues":

> *(Headshot of Grimshaw)*
>
> GRIMSHAW: Now how is it that two shy, retiring boys like yourselves find yourselves in the middle of political controversy?

PANTSDOWN: *(In a loose Hansonian accent)* Well, I think obviously the point is that Pauline Hanson has no sense of humor. I mean she talks about freedom of speech and you know we're just having a bit of fun, Vanessa and I, and she doesn't seem to quite understand it. But I think that mainstream Australia, when they listen to this song, they'll realize that her words make much more sense when arranged this way [. . .]

WAGNER: Really, it's funny because, she's upset a lot of people with her comments, and I think it's very hypocritical that she's become upset about this rather small and humorous thing. She's very un-Australian if she doesn't have a sense of humor.

PANTSDOWN: Yehs, and I think mainstream Australia will back me and Vanessa on that as well, yehs.

GRIMSHAW: What is it about her that rankles you two so much?

PANTSDOWN: Oh, that she's a racist really, people talk about the reputation of Australia overseas, which of course she's damaging, but it's more of what she's doing to Aboriginal Australians and Asian Australians. It's absolutely appalling, very un-Australian and un-patriotic.

*(Camera zooms in on Vanessa Wagner's bracelet, then pans back to a close-up on her and her costume.)*

WAGNER: *(Big smiles throughout)* Yes, and she does have appalling dress sense, and she really does need some makeup tips! *(Bar appears: "'VANESSA WAGNER' Song Producer")*[4] And we thought we'd bring some color and movement to this whole poisoned debate!

GRIMSHAW: So that's what bothers you the most then, the dress sense and the makeup?

WAGNER: *(mock-earnest)* It does me personally, yes.

PANTSDOWN: That's right, the racism, the dress sense, and the makeup, perhaps in that order, yehs.

WAGNER: A nasty combo, actually.

GRIMSHAW: *(laughs)* But you agree that you've probably – just a little – misrepresented her in the song?

PANTSDOWN: Well, see her lawyers say that people will think it's her. But now, if people believe that it's really Ms. Hanson saying things like "I'm a caring potato" and things like that then, well they must be even sillier than Ms. Hanson herself, and there's not many of those around, let's face it. Yehs [. . .]

GRIMSHAW: Did you expect that she would sue? Did you think in the back of your mind, as you were doing this – 'cause I know you spent weeks and weeks working on this in the sound studio –

PANTSDOWN: Oh, yehs yehs yehs listening to her voice for quite some weeks, in the studio working with it, some people say it's had a permanent effect, I can't see it myself.

WAGNER: You almost wanted to sue her for the effect that it's had on you, right?

PANTSDOWN: Oh I know, that's right, emotional distress actually, yehs. Well the legal advice was always that she might sue for defamation, but when something is so obviously satire, it'll just be laughed out of court.

WAGNER: Do you think so?

PANTSDOWN: Oh yehs, and I think 102 percent of mainstream Australians will back me on that.

WAGNER: Oh, most definitely, Pauline!

(Palmer 1997)

In this appearance, Pantsdown and Wagner accept (and even play up) their role as queer novelty items, while asserting their agenda on race, satire, and their alternative definition of patriotism and Australian identity.

The Australian Broadcasting Corporation decided to fight the injunction in court. To keep it in place, One Nation had to show that there was actual defamation in the act of broadcasting "Backdoor Man." It took them thirteen months to formulate their argument; in fact, One Nation only put forth its Statement of Claim five days before the court date, long after the injunction had been put in place. While Hunt and JJJ argued that no one would ever think "Backdoor Man" was actually written by Hanson, One Nation again claimed that the use of Hanson's voice would convince listeners it was her speaking, and that they would take her words literally.

Below is an excerpt from Hanson's legal Statement of Claim:

> 11. The song, when given its normal and ordinary meaning would, or could, be taken by the ordinary person to mean, [. . .]
> (g) that the Plaintiff is a homosexual;
> (h) that the Plaintiff is proud to be a homosexual;
> (i) that the Plaintiff is a homosexual (gay) activist;
> (j) that the Plaintiff is proud to be a homosexual (gay) activist;
> (k) that the Plaintiff is a prostitute;
> (l) that the Plaintiff is proud to be a prostitute;
> (m) that the Plaintiff engages in unnatural sexual practices including anal sex;
> (n) that the Plaintiff is proud to engage in unnatural sexual practices including anal sex;
> (n) [*sic*] that the Plaintiff engages in unnatural sexual practices including anal sex with the Klu Klux Klan [*sic*];
> (o) that the Plaintiff is proud to engage in unnatural sexual practices including anal sex with members of the Klu Klux Klan [. . .];
> (r) that the Plaintiff is a "potato" (which is understood to be a word associated with a male engaged in sexual acts with another male who has had the genitalia of the other male voluntarily inserted in his anal passage)[5];
> (s) that the Plaintiff is engaged in illegal and immoral acts;
> 12. The Plaintiff has not been associated with or involved with any of the assertions or imputations referred to in the last preceding paragraph [. . .]
> 22. As a result of the publication of the song the Plaintiff has suffered;

> (a) mental anguish;
> (b) social embarrassment;
> (c) damage to her political image as a Federal Parliamentarian;
> (d) likely damage to her chances of re-election as a Federal Parliamentarian, or an election in any other political capacity in which she may choose to stand in the future [. . .]
>
> (Hanson 1998)

Hanson's lawyers made this starkly literal reading of Hunt's text in order to win their case, and they succeeded. On 1 September 1997, the court replaced the temporary injunction with a permanent injunction against any further playing of "Backdoor Man" on JJJ. No other radio station has since dared to tempt a similar suit.[6]

The One Nation suit provided Pantsdown with a cornucopia of comedic material. Several Australian legal scholars published articles opposing the court's decisions and arguing for the merits of satire such

**3.3 Pauline Pantsdown, in a dress representing the diversity of Australia, flees a huge Hanson puppet chasing her with a legal summons. At the annual Sydney Gay and Lesbian Mardi Gras parade, Saturday 28 February 1998**

Photo by Garry Convery

as Pantsdown's, an unexpected expression of support from the mainstream (see, for example, Fitzgerald 1998). The Australian Broadcasting Corporation appealed this decision, and the Supreme Court of Queensland in Brisbane set the court date for 28 September 1998. Pantsdown immediately starting mocking the absurdity of Hanson's "Statement of Claim" in the media, soliciting the public to verify One Nation's creative definition of the word "potato," and handing out autographed potatoes to her fans. Pantsdown's act was integrally tied to the public statements of One Nation and Hanson, and the latter had just provided her with a great routine.

In this context, de Certeau's tactical agent/strategic power binary parallels the vaudeville relationship of the "straight man" and the "funny man." The straight man was traditionally paid more and had top billing over the funny man (that's Abbot over Costello, or, in this case, Hanson over Pantsdown). Hanson had more power and resources (personnel, advisers, followers, media attention, money, etc.). But by performing as a public politician, she unwittingly and unwillingly provided set-up lines for Pantsdown's tactically and contingently improvised punchlines. In responding to Pantsdown, Hanson did not have a free range of motion. Her own visibility restricted her. Even as an "anti-politician," she still had to establish and maintain some kind of legitimacy in the public eye and in the national legislature. She could be penalized for excess and inconsistency, the very staples of an electoral guerrilla's performative repertoire.

Hanson had to repeat sound bites. It is the job of a politician to utter simple, catchy, and reductive phrases over and over, e.g. "Mainstream Australia," "fringe dwellers," "ordinary Australians," "we are being swamped by Asians," "Asians form ghettoes and do not assimilate." In this necessary act of redundant "message-drilling," Hanson fed Pantsdown her straight lines. Pantsdown completed the routine by improvising punch lines to close the jokes. During the election campaign, Hunt read newspapers looking for Hanson quotes, then prepared himself in character for the inevitable calls from journalists for his in-character reactions.

The electoral guerrilla usually has neither the capacity nor the desire to take parliamentary territory. The guerrilla aims only to

**3.4 Pauline Pantsdown campaign flyer**

Courtesy of Simon Hunt and Kate Gilroy

drain the resources and the legitimacy of the greater power through harassing tactics and spectacular "zaps" and "hits," mimetic excess, and the use of the enemy's weapons against them, in this case endlessly repeated sound bites that are flipped, inverted, and fired back as frequently as possible.

However, this also limits electoral guerrillas to making do with the cast-offs and "lost" or "surrendered" material of the more powerful enemy. Writing his speeches or preparing for press phone calls, Hunt was dependent on what Hanson and her party officials said the day before. Pantsdown's songs were also limited to the syllables actually uttered publicly by Hanson.

## The campaign

During the 1998 Federal Election, Hanson ran for re-election in the seat of Blair (Oxley had been reshaped). Simon Hunt legally changed his name to Pauline Pantsdown and declared his candidacy for the Senate in his home state of New South Wales. One of his opponents was the number two man in One Nation and Hanson's alleged "Svengali," David Oldfield. Pantsdown felt that he could escalate his battle against Hanson by appearing on the same ballot as her party. He hoped that this would merge their images even further in the media, helping to show that Hanson was no less a public construction than Pantsdown. He also felt that as a candidate he would move from "novelty" press coverage to "news" coverage, a tactic that proved successful.

To elect senators, Australia uses a proportional-representational electoral system with preferences. This means that voters rank candidates in order of preference. The result is a more open system than that of the United States. In Australia, citizens can vote for minor candidates without "wasting their vote"; a vote will simply go to the second choice if the first choice is not elected.

More importantly for the electoral guerrilla, who hopes for visibility over viability, getting on the ballot is much easier than in the United States In 1998, candidates could get on the ballot "below the line," as minor-party candidates, for A$700, and "over the line" for A$7,000. Conservatives in Australia have expressed alarm at the openness of this system, claiming that it allows for too many "trivial candidates." In addition, all citizens have to vote or pay a fine, and voting is much more convenient in terms of work hours and registration than in the United States. Expensive voter registration and election-day mobilization campaigns are not necessary or even possible. Voter turnout tends to be at 96 percent, an incredible figure compared to the United States (Australian Electoral Commission Website 2000). All this limits the impact of major-party financial resources on elections.

There were sixty-nine New South Wales candidates running for six open senate seats. Pauline Pantsdown urged her supporters to "do a sixty-nine" on David Oldfield by ranking him last on their ballot.

### "I Don't Like It"

Pantsdown's campaign launch was contingent on the success of her second anti-Hanson song called "I Don't Like It." In "I Don't Like It" Pantsdown attempted to create an embarrassing sound bite – a bite-back, one indicative of Hanson's overall negative world-view – and attach it to her with a catchy beat.

Pantsdown was warned by her lawyer/agent/friend not to try satire by analogy as she had with "Backdoor Man" because this was likely to result in another injunction. Pantsdown couldn't call Hanson a male homosexual sex partner of the Ku Klux Klan and prove that in court. But she could call her a racist, and she did. While its satirical method is simpler, "I Don't Like It" is more technically complicated than "Backdoor Man." It actually creates new words from different Hanson syllables; for example, "San Francisco" was pieced together from four different words.

Unlike "Backdoor Man," which was meant for one subculture and unexpectedly spread to a wider audience, "I Don't Like It" was designed to break on radio. The song was released on a single CD, along with a dance remix to be played at clubs, and an original Simon Hunt composition, "Pauline's Nightmare," featuring Asian wind and string instrumentation complemented by electronic sound effects. In her "I Don't Like It" lyrics, Pantsdown wanted to walk the line between satire and novelty song. If "I Don't Like It" came across as a "fun, bouncy, silly little song," it wouldn't frighten DJs and might be played every couple of hours. Thus for every "racist rubbish, racist hate" there is a "my shopping trolley murdered, my groceries just gone" (Hunt 1999c).

In fact, "IDLI" is the audio equivalent of the "Hitler Jig" film put together by Allied propagandists during World War II. These filmmakers wished to ridicule Hitler just at the moment when he seemed undefeatable – after France had capitulated to the Wehrmacht. Using a brief film clip of Hitler raising and slapping his own knee upon hearing of France's defeat, the filmmakers spliced, reversed, and respliced Hitler's gesture until it appeared that the Nazi dictator was performing an ugly, jerky, and ridiculous little jig. Thus a frightened or demoralized populace was empowered to laugh in the face of their enemy – thereby diffusing their fear, at least temporarily.

In "I Don't Like It," Hanson's words, down to the very syllable, are spliced and respliced to make her appear ridiculous as she voices both surprising non sequiturs and jokes at the expense of her own politics. Pantsdown even wanted to make Hanson say, "Hey hey, ho, ho, Pauline Hanson's got to go," but the satirist couldn't configure the syllables quite right (Hunt 1999c).

**"I Don't Like It"**

I don't like it, when you turn my voice about.
I don't like it, when you vote One Nation out.
My language has been murdered, my language has been
    murdered,
My shopping trolley murdered, my groceries just gone.
1-2-3-4-5-6-7-8, racist rubbish, racist hate,
1-2-3-4-5-6-7-8, racist rubbish, racist, feel the heat.
I don't like it, when railway lines are white,
I don't like it, when day becomes night.
My language has been murdered, my language has been
    murdered,
My shopping trolley murdered, my groceries just gone.
I don't like it, no, no, no I don't, never did,
I don't like it, I don't like anything.
I don't like it, no, no, no I don't, nowhere near,
I don't like it, I don't like anything.
Please explain, why can't my blood be coloured white,

I should talk to some medical doctors,
Coloured blood, it's just not right.
I don't like anything, I can't do anything about it.
But I like dancing, and I like the disco,
'Cause I left my heart in San Francisco.
Feel the heat, on the street,
Dance to the beat, out of your seat.
Feel the heat, on the street,
Dance to the beat, out of your seat.
Get down, get down, down, down.
I don't like anything,
Except I like Neil Diamond, yeah?
Disco dance, disco dance,
Disco nation? Not a chance.
Disco dance, disco dance,
Out of my tree, out of my branch.
[. . .]
I don't like a puppet without strings,
There's a muppet in the wings,
And it's saying racist things,
I won't cop that, no way.
I don't like anything! I can't do anything about it.
Video killed the racist star.
Howard[7] wonders what you are,
But he is on the scrap heap too – bit of a Downer.[8]
I don't like anything, I can't do anything about it,
But I like dancing [etc.]
Feel the heat [etc.]
I don't like it [etc.]
No, the whole thing is wrong, and it stinks, and
I DON'T LIKE IT!

(Hunt 1998)

Pantsdown opens her second song with an immediate and cheeky reference to her first song and its attendant controversy. "I don't like it, when you turn my voice about/I don't like it, when

**3.5 "Racist rubbish, racist hate." Pauline trashes Pauline**

From the music video for "I Don't Like It" (produced and directed by Greg Ferris and Justin Ball; courtesy of Simon Hunt)

you vote One Nation out." With these lines, Hanson's voice is manipulated to say, "Stop manipulating my voice!" The irony, of course, is that even this line, the only one that Hanson might actually agree with, is digitally constructed. This complaint is immediately connected to Pantsdown's ultimate goal: encouraging the listeners to defy Hanson's whining and "vote One Nation out." The rhyme completes the joke and connects Pantsdown's digital manipulations to Hanson's electoral defeat, a connection already made familiar to Pantsdown's fans and the mainstream Australian public by Hanson's well-publicized suit over "Backdoor Man."

"My language has been murdered, my language has been murdered/My shopping trolley murdered, my groceries just gone." Here Pantsdown makes Hanson push her original complaint about the authenticity of her own voice, and the diversifying landscape in Australian conversation and cuisine, into the realm of bathos and absurdity. This is an attempt to end the first stanza on a note of "safe novelty song," not "controversial political song," for the disc jockeys.

"1-2-3-4-5-6-7-8, racist rubbish, racist hate" opens up a new front of anti-Hansonism: direct, blatant, and denunciatory. This is followed by two whole stanzas of silliness, perhaps to ensure a lyrical balance, and to characterize Hanson as a useless, ridiculous "whinger" (Aussie for "whiner"). In a sense, the lyrical tactics of this song are similar to Pantsdown's entire electoral campaign: an attempt to balance a trenchant anti-Hanson critique with humor, sugar-coating the pill to ensure that the message gets through to the maximum number of people.

"Please explain, why can't my blood be coloured white/I should talk to some medical doctors/Coloured blood is just not right." With these lines, we return again to direct ridicule of Hanson's racism, set to rhyme.

This is followed by a lighter series of lines detailing, absurdly, what exactly it is that Hanson does like. This shift in tone and content is accompanied by a musical change. This is the "bridge" in the song, a bouncy break. Hanson's likes are an absurd list: dancing, disco, San Francisco, Neil Diamond. These lines, and the "feel the heat, dance to the beat" lines, are as much directed toward encouraging a club crowd to shake and grind as they are towards directly ridiculing Hanson, all the better for the popularity and ultimate effectiveness of the song.

After this break, "Out of my tree, out of my branch" returns to a direct mockery of Hanson, which is pushed even further and more explicitly in the "puppet without strings" stanza.

The next stanza, now that the audience is hopefully hooked on the beat and/or dancing, starts with a clever twist on a famous Buggles hit with "Video killed the racist star." One of Pantsdown's ultimate goals was to connect John Howard, the conservative Prime Minister, with Hanson in his anti-immigrant and anti-Aboriginal policies. Pantsdown follows through with this in the next lines, even going so far as to suggest that Howard will sink with Hanson.

The song then returns to the upbeat "break" lyrics and music, followed by a final ultra-whinge from Hanson as the song ends.

"I Don't Like It," as a phrase summarizing all of Hanson's political outlook and philosophy, had been attached to her voice and public persona; "I Don't Like It" turned out to be a chart-topping single.

Because One Nation did not sue, Pantsdown was able to make a low-budget music video for "I Don't Like It." Pantsdown drew on every favor owed her, and also received a great many voluntary contributions of skill and materials from politically sympathetic Sydneyites. The video was shot and edited in two days. To parody Hanson's "swamped by Asians" line, everyone in the video, except for Pantsdown and a David Oldfield lookalike, is Asian. The "plot" of the video features Pantsdown hurting her finger while stamping "NO" on a stack of forms, passing out, then waking up in an all-Asian-staffed hospital. Overwhelmed, she succumbs to her injury and is welcomed into an all-Asian, queer, disco-dancing Heaven. So, one could argue, the video has a happy ending of sorts.

The song did remarkably well on the national charts, and media coverage of Pantsdown's campaign increased. "I Don't Like It" received two nominations for the 1999 ARIA national music awards, the Australian counterpart to the American Grammys.

"I Don't Like It" also came in handy for protestors. As Hanson arrived in one town, a local DJ dedicated the song to her before he played it. On another visit to a shopping mall, the workers in a music store blasted it at full volume as her entourage walked by.

### Live performance on the campaign trail

During her campaign, Pantsdown performed live for a wide range of communities: Aborigines, university students, political youth, immigrant/left-labor groups, queer demonstrations, at record stores and drag events, culminating in the huge performance on Election Night, Sleaze Ball '98. Pantsdown's format – the two songs sandwiching a stand-up routine – worked well. People were usually eager to hear the banned "Backdoor Man" followed by the big hit, "I Don't Like It." Pantsdown inserted her spoken political humor between the two. She rewrote her between-song patter for each specific audience and event, often arming the audience with humorous rebuttals of Hansonite rhetoric to try on their workmates and neighbors. It was particularly important to her in these speeches to undermine Hanson's image as a "battler" by documenting and joking about the politician's actual substantial wealth and the paltry (government-subsidized, at that) wages she paid her workers. Sometimes Pantsdown would present her nine-point "Ten Point Platform" which was a parody of One Nation's vague, incomplete, and contradictory policies. At one performance, she ripped up her speech in an apparently spontaneous move, and then explained that she was coached to do so by her advisers in order to seem more "'natural," a mockery of such stagey gestures.

It appears from video footage of these performances that Pantsdown intended to motivate her audiences to vote for anti-racist candidates, or at least to put One Nation last on their ballots and to continue organizing progressive alternatives to Hansonism. For example, on 22 September 1998, Pantsdown performed at the University of New South Wales in Sydney, and brought Jason Yat-Sen Li, the leader of the newly formed Unity – Say No To Hanson Party – onto the stage during a dance moment as an endorsement. These performances differed from Pantsdown's appearances in the mass media where she had much less control over how her material was edited and broadcast. Far from being limited to a few sound bites chosen by newspersons, Pantsdown had the power to present her message in full for a friendly audience. She could thus take the time to instruct the crowds in the finer art of Hanson-mockery and how to convert their fellow Australians from the ideology of Hansonism. Pantsdown was both mass-mediated queer novelty item and popular, live-performance, grassroots-based, anti-racist activist. The two incarnations complemented each other.

Pantsdown also had an ally on another front, Garry Convery, who formed a Pauline Pantsdown Fan Club Website on the internet (http://pantsdown.wild.net.au). Using tactics similar to Pantsdown's, Convery took the texts of One Nation publications and changed some of the words and names in order to ridicule them. The website was also filled with show dates, related events, and late-breaking news about the Pantsdown campaign and her biography; for example, did you know that Pantsdown is really Pauline Hanson's long-lost sister?

## The last week of the campaign: the Paulines merge

Timing is crucial both in comedy and elections, perhaps even more so when the two are intertwined. The timing for the 1998 election worked in Pantsdown's favor. In the crucial last week of the campaign, the public personae of Hanson and Pantsdown, if they did not actually merge, were fastened tightly together, much to Hanson's dismay. Pantsdown's goal was to force people to choose, not between Hanson and other "serious" candidates, but to bring Hanson down to her level and force people to choose "between Paulines."

The drag-guerrilla's campaign distracted Hanson and drained her political energy. At least once she fled from Pantsdown to avoid being in the same picture. Yet their images were conflated on several occasions at this most critical time. By the final week, the mass media spliced pictures of Pantsdown and Hanson together to form the graphic headers for news stories.

On 24 September 1998 outside the Mortdale Bowling Club, where Hanson announced her party's healthcare policy (and where her supporters roughed up some of the journalists covering the event), Pantsdown confronted Hanson and David Oldfield, maneuvering into the same photographic frame. These photographs made the national press.

The date for the final appeal against the injunction for "I'm A Backdoor Man," 28 September, turned out to be also during the final week of the campaign. While Pantsdown never imagined that Hanson would waste one of her precious last days of campaigning on this, she showed up in court and then made a brief public statement of vindication after the appeal was denied.

Pantsdown arrived just a few minutes after Hanson left. Pantsdown's denunciation of Hanson was broadcast on TV and

**3.6 Personae juxtaposed: "Seeing double" news shot with Pantsdown and Hanson heads**

Videotaped from television for *Send in the Clown: The Pauline Pantsdown Story*, an unfinished documentary video (directed by Sally Regan and Simon Hunt; produced by Sally Regan)

printed in major newspapers. When asked if she regretted the grief she'd caused Hanson, she replied:

> I regret the grief that she has caused to the many thousands of Australian people who she has divided with her views. I regret that Mrs. Hanson has caused a rising tide of violence against Asian people in this country. I regret that Mrs Hanson has caused unimaginable pain to the Aboriginal people who were so close to finding some sense of justice in this country. My action, my song, was trivial. It was a joke.
>
> (Hunt 1999c)

It may seem surprising that Hanson made such a politically costly appearance at this time. Her appearance was testimony to the effectiveness of Pantsdown's electoral guerrilla attack. Hanson's lawyers argued that if the injunction were lifted at this tactically crucial time, then JJJ and many other radio stations would probably play "Backdoor Man" nonstop for the last week of the campaign, which could have had a lethal effect on One Nation and Hanson at the time when so many swing voters make up their minds. In a sense, Pantsdown left Hanson with only bad options: either look petty, censorious, litigious, and easily distracted from the home voters by appearing in court, or don't show up and increase the chance of losing the injunction, leading to a blaze of airplay of a very electorally damaging song. Hanson chose her day in court, triggering yet another news item linking her public persona to that of her queer, multi-culti doppelganger. On the other hand, of course, she may have been hoping to galvanize her base by showing herself once again doing battle with a radical drag queen from the big city.

There was also the matter of the Grand Final Breakfast in Melbourne, a traditional politicians' roast tied to the Australian football finals. Pantsdown was invited to the breakfast in Hanson's place as a joke. But because this was a mainstream event where the leaders of the major parties were present, Pantsdown was not allowed a mike. Also, Hanson was not the only politician worried about being caught in the same frame as Pantsdown. Pantsdown glad-handed the leaders of the various parties, but when she came to shake the hand of Prime Minister John Howard, a pair of secret service agents twisted the video-documentarian's aim away from the scene for a few seconds to prevent that moment from being filmed. This performance was followed by a more conventional drag performer, dressed as Monica Lewinsky, who performed a long, bawdy (and miked) monologue interacting with all of the candidates including the Prime Minister. The act's final line: "Well, you will have to tell me who of you wins the election, so I know who gets the *head job*" (Hunt and Regan 1998). This event served as a reminder that there are many kinds of drag, some subversive and some reactionary, some threatening to the mainstream and some tailored to its gender-hierarchical agenda. It also is indicative of the complexities and limitations of collaborating with the mainstream against, for example, the extreme Right.

In the end, Hanson lost her seat to the conservative candidate, Cameron Thompson, who stated, "I focused on doing something for the local people while she was doing battle with Pauline Pantsdown and running a three-ring circus with the media" (Convery 1998). Since this defeat, the One Nation Party has imploded due to internal factional strife and legal/funding troubles; of course, this may be only a temporary setback for the far Right. In keeping with the "two Paulines or no Paulines" axiom, Hanson's relatively low-key public presence meant that Pantsdown was largely inactive though still occasionally invited to perform at countercultural events. However, Pauline Hanson was later convicted of defrauding the government out of election funds, and served eleven weeks in prison before being acquitted on appeal. Hanson also announced that, after six years, she will finally sue the Australian Broadcasting Corporation for damages for playing "I'm A Backdoor Man." In a bizarre twist, she also declared plans to record her own country music song (Letton 2003). Perhaps Hanson and Pantsdown will make amends for the good of the family and collaborate on a new song, touring the country as the Pauline Sisters.

## Below-the-belt hits?

So, who was this character, "an alternative Ronald McDonald" for the multicultural generation, as Pantsdown described herself (Hunt 1999c)? A radical drag pop star to answer and hopefully irrevocably blend with Pauline Hanson's image, to reveal the latter as an equally constructed, rehearsed, and costumed glamour queen of the grassroots far Right? I believe that Pantsdown was more consistently successful in mocking Hanson's politics and appearance than in exposing her constructed nature. To some audiences, in contrast to Pantsdown's obvious drag, Hanson seemed more "natural," more of a "normal" and battling, hardworking, and straightforward rural northerner. Also, Pantsdown's stated desire to replicate or "merge" with Hanson was limited by their bodily differences – differences that clearly made a difference. The use of male-to-female drag as an entertaining, queer attention-getting device precluded any actual confusion of Hanson and Pantsdown, and actually heightened the differences between them for some audiences. Nevertheless, Pantsdown certainly haunted Hanson, pursuing her both physically and as a sort of radical queer spectre that effectively latched on to her media image.

Jon Stratton (1999) considers Pantsdown's work to be a radical, anti-racist performance that nevertheless – because it is drag – is socially conservative, aimed against females who show stereotypically male traits of assertiveness, independence, and political power. In the music video, for example, we see Pantsdown-as-Hanson in the fish and chip shop hurling fries while ranting and later riding in a shopping cart through the aisles of a supermarket. Pantsdown/Hanson might thus be read as a grotesque female figure, a woman tied to food, images of domesticity, and excessive behavior; in short, a woman, out of control, who does not know her place. Perhaps the Pantsdown drag act carried the classist/regionalist baggage of the *60 Minutes* coverage into the realm of live-cartoon satire, buying into the mainstream media's method of attack, debunking Hanson's racism while also mocking her lack of polish and education and her "cheapness" in clothing, hair, and makeup. While this depiction galvanized the anti-Hanson forces, it may also have activated One Nation supporters, polarizing the North, stereotypically constructed as white, rural, and homophobic, against the stereotype of the urbane, queer-friendly, cosmopolitan South.

Such is the risk with any political cartoon, an art form that is by definition unfair. Irony's critical edge is double-sided and multivalent (Hutcheon 1994). Audiences do the work of interpreting or ironizing. Depending on which counterpublic is consuming the irony, there is always room for backfire, misfire, or return fire.

In August of 1999, I asked Simon Hunt about these issues (he had changed his name back by then). While acknowledging that Stratton's interpretation was plausible, Hunt argued that he was using Hanson's individual characteristics as a way of critiquing her politics, her dangerous and willful ignorance, and most importantly her lack of justification for her extreme and harmful racist statements. He had to do drag to imitate her, and that helped him to be a novelty item in the mainstream entertainment news. Drag was a way "in" for his satire (Hunt 1999c). Pantsdown focused his punch lines on Hanson's values and ideology much more than her background/class/education. In this sense, Pantsdown's drag follows in the radical traditions of Church Ladies for Choice (Cohen-Cruz 1998), Ladies Against Women (Schechter 1985: 180–3; Burbank 1998), or the Gulf-War-era Overkill Brigade in Philadelphia. Pantsdown's choice of Hanson as a target, instead of a male figure in One Nation, was necessary. Hanson really was the main publicly recognized face of the party; again, the full title of the party was "Pauline Hanson's One Nation Party" in order to draw on Hanson's familiarity to the public. Also, Pantsdown was better able to control the emphasis of her own satirical work when performing live in front of friendly, countercultural audiences; when her work was mediated, as edited snippets appearing on mainstream, national television, the more regressive elements of the work were more often brought to the forefront.

Some cultural theorists, such as David Kertzer and Murray Edelman, analyze and call attention to the ritual and symbolic nature of politics in modern democracies. Pantsdown's project paralleled their work, using *Verfremdungseffekt* as an absurd participant-performer in the electoral process. By making her costume and makeup just a little more obvious than those of the other politicians on TV, she attempted to demonstrate the constructed nature of all political leaders. It is impossible to tell if Hanson would have won the election without Pantsdown's counter-campaign. However, the "Pantsdown Phenomenon" was certainly a factor in Hanson's defeat, creating a parodic performer-symbol around which the Australian cultural Left continues to rally on occasion.

## "Little Johnny Coward": a revealing failure

How would Hunt's techniques work against a male, center-Right, more powerful and polished politician? Simon Hunt attempted to answer that question with his Little Johnny Coward project.

Hunt was angered by Prime Minister John Howard's success at denigrating Hanson while sponsoring immigration and Aboriginal policies only somewhat less draconian than those of One Nation. He found a subject for a song about Howard when the Prime Minister refused to apologize officially for the Australian government policy (recently depicted in the film *Rabbit Proof Fence*) of kidnapping "half-caste" Aboriginal children and raising them in camps and with white families, a practice which was only discontinued completely in 1970. Howard's position was essentially that the past was past, and it wasn't the place of the government to apologize. Hoping to avoid any reparations lawsuits that an official apology might trigger, Howard eventually issued a tepid and vague "expression of regret." Hunt digitized the Prime Minister's voice and did the same sort of cut-up job as with Pauline Hanson. In the song, "I'm Sorry," his character Little Johnny Coward apologizes for a list of absurd things, and finally, as the music shifts to a more serious tone, apologizes for the "Stolen Generations." The music video shows Hunt as "Little Johnny," in very convincing male-conservative drag and a comb-over hairdo.

Despite its virtuosity in editing, composition, lyric-writing, costume, and videography, "I'm Sorry" failed. No radio station would play it. Perhaps this was because Hunt's cut-up technique had lost its novelty, and no longer seemed funny to the disc jockeys. The very real power of a sitting Prime Minister may have deterred the public radio stations. Or maybe "Little Johnny" simply fell flat in a heterosexist society where "straight white male conservative" drag fails to titillate as much as a more traditional idea of "cross dressing." The more regressive elements of Pantsdown's satire – mocking a woman on the political fringe who lacked polish and whose accent was marked as a sign of ignorance – did not apply against Howard. The mainstream media laughed along with Pauline Pantsdown, but perhaps Little Johnny was a little too close to home. The failure of "I'm Sorry" is as instructive as the relative success of the Pantsdown songs. It provides a lesson about the limits of tactical agency, and of drag as a satiric tool within the greater context of a gender-hierarchical culture.

Pantsdown was often asked, "What if you *win*?"[9] Her first response was, "Well, I only have two dresses, so I'd have to wear each one for three years straight." But, on second thought, she ventured, "Well, I guess I'd just hang the wig and the dress up by my seat in Parliament and everyone can take a turn putting them on and being Pauline" (Hunt 1999c). With this, Hunt put forward his costume as an ironic dig at the far Right, as a more generally absurd symbol of the constructed nature of public political personae, and, perhaps, as an expression of a felt need for a more equal-access, participatory, and creative democracy. After all, Pantsdown could only have been elected in the context of an energized and satirically activist electorate, the kind of citizenry who would be happy to skip work and take their turns wearing a cheap dress and "playing Pauline" in the halls of power. Pantsdown's fantasia would have been actualized, and her political-pedagogical project completed: from an electoral guerrilla to an electorate of guerrillas, or, to paraphrase Che Guevara, "two, three, many Pantsdowns."

However, the electorate would not have received training for such performances from Pantsdown's campaign itself; it was not mass-participatory. While its bawdy and earthy humor evoked the carnivalesque, the performer–audience divide was very much in place during the staged and rehearsed performances. This campaign's actions centered on the energy and talent of a creative solo artist, manifested in the monologue, the media interview, and the lip-synching dance of that artist's own digital music. What spect-actorship there was did not take the form of spectators actually intervening in or contributing to Pantsdown performances; rather, some viewers took the modular tools Pantsdown provided, the songs and the jokes, and used them in other contexts. This campaign relied far more on Brechtian *Verfrumdungseffekt*, alienating and calling into question many assumptions about Hanson's persona and party, than on an interactive, creative mass dynamic.

There were some advantages to this approach. Pantsdown's target was specific, and she was able to focus on it relentlessly throughout the campaign. Pantsdown's relationship with the multicultural coalition movement of Australia was as an individual artist who was invited to perform, not as a member of an affinity group. Sometimes a live social movement performer, sometimes a mediated culture-jammer, she was always a free agent. Pantsdown was able to hone her drag act and digital editing skills as the campaign escalated without needing the approval of a larger group, and could react quickly to exploit the gaffes and missteps of One Nation. She also was in no danger of "representing" an activist group, with all of the potential pitfalls and resentment that that can entail. The Pantsdown project, with its focused, tactical critique, its galvanization of a diverse, live-audience base, and its fraught, tensive interventions into the mainstream, provides a strong example of the potential of electoral guerrilla theatre to sabotage an opponent, galvanize a counterpublic, and, perhaps, further polarize an electorate.

Since these events took place, Pauline Hanson has appeared several times on reality TV shows, once in court for campaign finance fraud (convicted, imprisoned, found not guilty on appeal, and released), and several times on the campaign trail trying to be re-elected. As Hunt said self-deprecatingly, "she's the consummate B-grade celebrity, she stole the career that was rightfully mine!" Hanson came very close in 2015 to winning a seat in Parliament but fell just short. Simon Hunt has continued to lecture and participate in human rights campaigns as an artist–activist. In the past 15 years he has only put on the Pantsdown drag a couple of times; he has mostly moved on to using graphic art and social media to help mobilize mass direct actions for women's rights and queer rights.

Reflecting upon his techniques and inspiration, Hunt noted how things had changed since his actions with Pantsdown in the late 1990s. He noted his own inspiration by ACT UP and Gran Fury, their powerful interventions that got real policy results due to relentless action and striking graphics. In the 1990s,

> when I did my thing, there was still a big monolithic media to break into; the Murdoch-owned media, and a government radio and TV station. Getting on the charts, getting onto mainstream TV, because there was only one media at that time, it had to be an intervention in that way. Whereas now

> it's a completely different media landscape. But I'm also completely fascinated with social media. The structure of the way that it works and the viral. When to be serious and when to be funny.

Hunt has been successful in his transition to a social media activist. His Pauline Pantsdown Facebook page uses the image of Pantsdown to attract fans, and then enlists them into mass actions to help successfully disrupt the operations of misogynistic or homophobic public figures, and of homophobic far-right churches and the politicians who support them.

As for Hanson, "it was never about hurting her or 'getting her,'" said Hunt in a recent interview. "It was always about the politics. If there was a risk of her getting into power and doing harm, then I would get involved." In other words, it was never personal, except in the sense that the personal is always political and vice versa.[10]

Chapter 4

# EARTHALUJAH!

## The importance of being earnest with the Church of Life After Shopping

> ... there is a type of constructive, nonviolent tension which is necessary for growth. Just as Socrates felt that it was necessary to create a tension in the mind so that individuals could rise from the bondage of myths and half-truths to the unfettered realm of creative analysis and objective appraisal, so must we see the need for nonviolent gadflies to create the kind of tension in society that will help men rise from the dark depths.
>
> (Dr. Martin Luther King, Jr., from "Letter From Birmingham Jail")

> Start spreading the wealth, I'm hoping to stay
> I came to live my life here, New York, New York
> Those neighborhood shops, they call out my name
> Don't need no supermall, in old New York
> I want a city made of 500 neighborhoods
> Where we can pay decent rent, buy a home if we should
> Those billionaire blues, they cannot compete
> The greatness of this town, it's on my street
> I made it here, ain't moving anywhere
> It's up to us, New York, New York
>
> (Reworked lyrics for "New York, New York," Reverend Billy's campaign song)

Commuters fill a subway car on the F Line in New York City. They focus on their own internal and intimate mental space as a coping mechanism in the crowded space – reading the paper, staring at the floor, listening to iPods .... Suddenly, as the doors open at the next stop, a tall man in a dazzlingly bright blue suit and minister's collar, with the voice, cadence, and pompadour of a televangelist, jumps into the car, followed by a dozen disciples in flowing choir robes.

This man is running for Mayor of New York. He wants to represent the hopes and aspirations of the beleaguered neighborhoods – ordinary working (and unemployed) people, shopkeepers, straphangers, artists, and everyone threatened by gentrification, the oligarchy, and the current economic crisis.

And he has 45 seconds to speak before the train reaches the next stop.

> People, I'm Reverend Billy. I'm running for Mayor on the Green Party ticket. What's happened to our city? All this corruption! Michael Bloomberg is spending $300,000 a day on his own re-election. What is that doing to democracy? Well, THIS is democracy! We've got it right HERE. We're talking and listening right NOW! Please, take our literature!

The choir starts to sing a populist reworking of the old favorite, "New York, New York" and give out campaign literature. The train tops, the doors open, and the Reverend and his flock exit, enter the next car on the train, and do it again.

They do this at every stop on the F line. Miles of campaigning, in a no-budget whistlestop ride, as an attempt to interrupt the hegemonologue of Mayor Bloomberg's inevitability – not only the inevitability of billionaire Bloomie's bought-and-paid for election victory, but the perceived inevitability of his ideology and everything he stands for: technocratic oligarchy, the corporate approach to running this city as a financial fiefdom.

Bill Talen is the performance artist-activist who created the character of Reverend Billy and the anticonsumerist Church of Stop Shopping in the late 1990s. The Church, which has changed its name to the Church of Life After Shopping in the current economic crisis, has made many dramatic, disruptive interventions in Starbucks, Walmart, Disneyland, the Disney Store, and other chain stores around the world.[1] While the project began more ironically, as a progressive parody of the bouffanted buffoonery of televangelists – it quickly morphed into a playful but heartfelt and earnest life-performance. Talen has essentially evolved into his character, the Reverend.[2] Talen's director and partner, Savitri D, co-conspires equally in the dramatic conception and shaping of Bill and the Church's actions and interventions.

In the depth of the economic crisis, in a city where Mayor Bloomberg proved almost omnipotent (including his successful end-run around the term-limits law to wrest the right to run for a third term), the Reverend and his Church ran for Mayor in 2009.

The subway's whistlestop tours served as a metaphor for the overall Reverend Billy campaign: how its members envisioned their role, and what they hoped to achieve. With no TV cameras present, this may hardly seem a practical strategy for reaching and preaching to as many people as possible in an effort to win office. However, it fit perfectly with this group's poetic approach to politics. They embraced the personally transformative value of such a grueling effort, and what they themselves learned by engaging with so many different New Yorkers:

> SAVITRI D: The subways have been a highlight. We did a marathon. I appreciate the drama of the effort, doing the entire length of the F line, Jamaica to Coney Island. Really transformational. It was hard. We saw so many different kinds of people at so many times of day. That was educational. It's liminal space. People are used to being interrupted there, but they're surprised when people don't ask for money – unless they're proselytizers. It's very intimate, no police, no ads interrupting, a strangely unmediated place.
>
> BILL TALEN: We're interrupting dream states. It may be their only time to be alone, between home and work, sitting on the F train. I feel grateful to be permitted to share that.
>
> SAVITRI D: It's a closed space, you can't get out. Our action is framed by the opening and closing of the train doors. No cops. It's so democratic. It's just us. A bunch of humans, no way out. You have to work it out. If someone were to say "quiet," we'd have to work it out.

Talen and Savitri D clearly appreciated the quotidian sacredness of the subway space in the rhythm of ordinary people's lives, and did not take lightly their own intervention into that space. But they aspired to create, both in the form and content of their own electoral performance, a kind of direct democratic engagement that would stand in stark contrast with the "real" election, a lopsided and purchased affair, occurring at great distance from the lives and agency of the average city voter.

This chapter will examine the ways in which the Reverend Billy campaign theorized and strategized itself, as a wholly different performative phenomenon from the conventional political campaign. It was a campaign that sought emotional and dramatic effect upon its own members and the inhabitants of New York in an immediate, unmediated sense, defying conventional strategy, embracing the ineffable, and engaging the imagination with sincere, personal connection/confrontation and dialogue as the ultimate form of, and hope for, democracy.

## Billy versus Bloomie: archetypes collide in Gotham

Like Batman and the Joker in Gotham City, Reverend Billy and Mayor Bloomberg seem custom-made to clash symbolically in New York's swirling world of politics, especially in that particular moment of economic crisis. As Mark Read, long-time New York activist and Action Engineer-in-Chief for the campaign, observed:

> This campaign takes place in a moment of a collapse and crisis of capitalism. Reverend Billy and the Church have always been about questioning the inevitability of this system and calling people to reimagine their own role in it and to question the legitimacy of it. Bloomberg, a billionaire, is a kind of champion of Wall Street, the only billionaire that has not lost money in this crisis. He is the cheerleader for hyperdevelopment, hypercapitalism, hyperconsumption. The idea of the campaign would be to pit these two characters in opposition to each other, thereby questioning the authority of the story that we're told about how things work, the inevitability of markets,

> of infinite growth, and of Bloomberg's third term. The inevitability of all this, what's possible and what's not possible.
>
> The architecture of that metanarrative needs always to be reinforced. So if we are talking about gay marriage, or gas drilling, or whatever, we need to come back to that clash of archetypes. The archetype of that smug, "everything's under control, everything's working fine, there is no crisis," Bloomberg, versus the archetype of Billy saying "hold on, this whole system is ruinous on every level, to our souls (which is why he is a televangelist preacher), ruinous to the planet, to relationships, it is just a tragedy." The best way to call attention to that tragedy is in this case comedy. We need to keep that story in mind. And keep in mind that right now this economic crisis provides the perfect backdrop for that story, and that conflict, to play out.[3]

Bloomberg's successful maneuver to get around term-limiting laws so that he could run for a third term was unpopular, even though most New Yorkers accepted his victory as inevitable. Meanwhile, Bill, Savitri D, and the Church of Life After Shopping had built, in the preceding ten years of nonstop performance and activism in the city, and with the release of their film *What would Jesus buy?* a reputation and a profile in alternative performance and community organizing, as reflected in their coverage by the neighborhood and alternative city press, and even the *New York Times* and the *Wall Street Journal*.[4] This suggested that a campaign that played on the great meeting of archetypal opposites, which portrayed "Billy" and "Bloomie" as matter and anti-matter, could provide a compelling narrative that would motivate many New Yorkers.

However, there was an incredible disparity in resources between the two – imagine the Joker with the Pentagon backing him, and Batman with a great costume but no gadgets. Bloomberg the billionaire spent scores of millions of dollars of his own fortune on his re-election campaign. But the media market in New York City was so expensive that it precluded any purchasing of airtime on radio or TV by the Reverend:

> SAVITRI D: This is a city where unless you have a lot of money you can't do marketing and advertising – so we're talking, basic analog kinds of communication. Mark Read set up our own radio station, in which we talk and have regular New Yorkers talk about what's happening in their neighborhoods. We need a community telling their stories, to get people into a room together talking and amplifying those voices. That's the great hope.

The danger remained that the whole Reverend Billy Campaign could remain invisible to most New Yorkers, even if the intrepid team exhausted themselves completely on the effort.

There was also the difficulty of running for office as insurgent, rebel artists. The entire structure of electoral campaigns seems custom-designed to absorb and co-opt as much radical energy as activists can muster. And it is a format ill-suited to the exuberant, visionary energy and style of the Church of Life After Shopping. Billy explained:

> The theatrical conventions of this political campaign, of politics period, are very conservative, very narrow, very repetitive, it's just a series of five or six gestures, five or six poses, it's absolutely conservative and so we're ignoring that. I'm saying no to candidates' forums, because you can spend all your time trying to keep up with the demands of a traditional campaign. We want to blow this [format] up.

Indeed, as mentioned in the Introduction, the conventional candidate's body is so regulated that Presidential candidate Howard Dean was delegitimized by whooping to his supporters at a rally in 2004. With that one expression of excitement, his entire heretofore viable campaign collapsed. Billy was experiencing that restriction himself and it simply could not contain his performing body – jittering, pouncing and shouting, possessed by the anti-consumerist spirit.

Savitri D voiced her own frustration about the challenges of doing election work as opposed to community organizing and agitation:

> Activism and being inside a candidacy are totally different things. When you're an activist you're in an oppositional stance. You're generating things, of course, but essentially you're pressing on the law, pushing laws, advocating. When you're running for office, you are inside the law, inside an arcane system of rules. The brittleness of that position cannot be overstated. How it affects the imagination, the vision of the candidate and the team, the community. You need to make sure there's a couple of people taking care of that and then ignore it altogether because it is really damaging.

The reader may begin to wonder why the Reverend, Savitri D, and all their organizers, volunteers, and professors of tactical performance were bothering with this campaign. Why not just continue to do their usual performance activism? Why engage with such a problematic format as the election campaign? What was at risk, and what was to be gained?

**4.1 Election postcard for Reverend Billy**

From the personal archive of the author

### Keeping score: what are the goals?

Like with other electoral guerrilla campaigns this was an attempt to use the trappings and dramatic structure/infrastructure of the election campaign, not to win office, but to leverage a radical socio-political critique to a wider audience. Talen argued that the election, at this historical moment, offered a special opening to engage with people who might otherwise ignore the Church: "The horserace narrative of politics is a strong, compelling motivator, and I think that Obama's victory brought that possibility to life even though he has been such a disappointment." Savitri D and Talen went on to talk about what they hoped they could accomplish with the campaign:

> SAVITRI D: We hope to leave a communication network in place, a channel for future activism. And knowledge, deep education for ourselves. That's one of the ways that we can win every day, as we're *losing*, losing all our money and energy . . . [laughing] falling apart piece by piece . . . we hope we can break open the democratic process in New York a little bit, although that's harder to evaluate. We're doing this as a promise to the future – that we defended democracy now. And that's the kind of story making that is kind of ineffable, but that when history looks back at this time in New York City, and it will not look favorably, they will see that there was a group of people that were trying.

> BILL TALEN: This is a Tammany Hall kind of period that history will not regard favorably. We are making images and texts, bringing many different kinds of people into public space together singing and saying things together. The media that is closest to political change is *embodied* media, people in public space where they exercise their First Amendment rights together. We've settled into a groove now where we have a series of events in public parks every Sunday, and local activists from around that park come and we introduce them and they talk about their work, we sing and everybody brings food and people meet each other, strengthening relationships within that neighborhood.

So, in part, the artist–candidate team wanted to use this format to engage with New Yorkers across the whole city, people they had not reached before in their years of agitating. They were leveraging the campaign format to get new people involved and make denser local activist networks and human connections for future action. They also hoped to transform themselves by learning more, through direct experience and interaction, about the city where they lived. They were writing a story with their campaign, an exemplary tale of radical defiance in a Gilded Age gone sour, that will perhaps be written about in some future iteration of the *People's History of the United States*. This is a sort of *destemporalizarse*, a Zapatista concept that the struggle should be "detemporalized", not made about winning today or this week, but if necessary through slow and steady change over the course of centuries.[5] These are hardly traditional campaign goals, but they line up very well with those of electoral guerrilla antecedents such as the Kabouters, Joan JettBlakk, Jello Biafra, and many others.

Mark Read expressed a similar desire for the campaign, one of encouraging people to reimagine their very lives outside of neoliberal capitalism and with more local autonomy and agency:

> "The Rise of the Fabulous Five Hundred Neighborhoods" is the campaign motto. There's some hope to construct or encourage an ethos of local control where neighborhoods and local communities begin to assert their own decision making power. Systems for that actually are in place already and they just need to be grasped by local communities. This campaign isn't a community organizing effort but it is an idea that people can have agency, take control and have some say in how their lives are managed. If that idea gets in there, that this sort of top-down politics is not the way out of this problem. The way to solve this crisis is not more top-down solutions. The way to solve these problems is locally, looking to one another. Figuring out the best way to support each other, to create a fabric of life, a web of life. That's the real base note of the campaign – it's about local control, autonomy, decision-making. If that gets into people's heads and it begins to activate

> or take root in some way then the campaign has done a real service.

With these goals in mind, what complications and challenges occur? Cutting straight to the chase, Savitri D voiced a clear problem:

> We're trying to figure out how to explode the election because we know what it is to enter a structure and explode it. That's what we've been doing for years. But to do that with a candidacy, that's hard. It's much harder than doing it with corporations. I'm not sure why.

Indeed, this task does seem much harder. There are several reasons for this. When the Church of Life After Shopping goes into a Starbucks and conducts a joyous, disruptive, anti-chainstore religious service, there is a clear action that provokes a clear reaction. The staff ask them to leave, the police arrive, the church members leave and/or arrests are made. A mono-cultural corporate space like Starbucks, or Disneyland, is a place for consumption. It is not built around dialog, there is no pretense of this, nor our First Amendment rights protected on private property. It is a place for consumption and "appropriate" behavior.

However, an election campaign is a process with dialogical pretensions. It is not one place or a space with a built in counter-reaction that builds an engaging narrative of opposition. It invites participation but then, without enormous financial resources or legitimacy, one's efforts are dropped into an apparently bottomless well. It is the conundrum of Marcuse's "repressive tolerance." It is the challenge of simultaneously operating inside and outside of the system.

As we have seen in the earlier case studies in this book, another central challenge of electoral guerrilla theatre is that the very format of the election is top-down. To win, a cult of personality must be built around the central figure – the candidate. This was challenging to a group that hopes to embrace, enhance, and demonstrate an egalitarian, communitarian ethos. The challenge was to tie an almost fictional campaign to a compelling narrative. Essentially, electoral guerrillas such as Reverend Billy must pick and choose, taking some aspects of the election seriously (the issues at stake, the opportunity for contact with new communities, the drama and dramatic arc of the race), and other aspects (the need to be "realistic," "respectable," "efficient") not seriously at all. It was a complicated, exhausting dance (as the Reverend Billy wrote in his blog, the nonstop campaign actions gave him heart palpitations and required a brief period of rest). But the goal was to push the boundaries of what is possible in the imaginations of New Yorkers, to culture jam the hegemonologue with moments of defiant and joyous dialogue, to exalt the everyday talk and public spaces of a city under siege by corporatism. As Reverend Billy says:

> Ordinary talk in the neighborhoods, that's what's really fascinating. We're refugees from the theatre world, and yet we're finding that the clearest statement of inventive American radicalism right now is in the casual vernacular of the street corner, the bodega, the stoop, the bus stop. The people have been confronted by such an obvious collapse of the corrupt economy and the flamboyant clowns who fell from Olympus. We all watched that happen together and now we're talking about it and talking about it in a much different way than government spokespersons and commercial media, with their carefully constructed and lawyer-vetted language.

Yes, but what about *spectacle?* Is not spectacular action vital for a Quixotic performance art campaign?

It seems that there were three different kinds of action to be taken: a) conventional electoral events such as candidates' forums, which the Reverend and Savitri D ruled out and from which he was largely excluded anyway; b) grassroots, communitarian, direct dialogue events and campaign tactics such as the subway whistlestop tour and the neighborhood park barbeques and gatherings, which became the mainstay of this campaign; and c) outrageous, disruptive, artful interventions in public/corporate/governmental events and spaces that could leverage a great deal of (outraged, amused, bemused) media coverage for the campaign. The latter type of interventions have been at the heart of the Church of Life After Shopping's activist work in its many years before the election. However, that disruptive flame was turned way down to "simmer" during the election itself.

Full disclosure: I was a creative consultant for this campaign, and participated in an artist–activist brainstorming session in June 2009, at which we thought of more outrageous actions and political policy positions. We came up with a fun, ten-point platform much like the platform of electoral guerrilla Jello Biafra when he ran for Mayor of San Francisco in 1979 – a mixture of earnest, progressive policies leavened with great heapings of radical ridicule. When it was proposed that the Ten Points should be written up like Martin Luther's Ninety Five Theses in acknowledgment of Billy's clerical persona, I suggested that he actively dramatize that parallel by nailing the document to the door of City Hall. Such a clear allusion to the historical act of Luther, an act of wry nonviolent civil disobedience, would certainly draw a legal and police reaction that might yield major media coverage for the campaign and a public discussion of the issues at stake.

I do not know if this idea would have worked or not, but I do know why, for the first time, the Reverend and the Church backed off from such "arrestable" spectacular action. Billy was certainly not afraid of such an act; he has been arrested countless times in chainstores and city streets around the nation and beyond. Nevertheless, he told me that he had considered the whimsical–serious Ten Points, and being more outrageous in general, but that he was conflicted because he felt a responsibility to deeply engage with the new communities he had connected with during the campaign, and did not want to ruin that by acting so outrageously that it might alienate or embarrass those groups. Mark Read, acknowledging the Jello Biafra platform, noted both the need for, and problems with, the spectacular, mischievous option:

> "Interesting" is the only card Billy has, the only asset. We have to use outrageous street action to draw attention to our sincere, earnest, straightforward and thoughtful website [www.

> voterevbilly.org/], which shows our platform to make the city liveable, healthy, vibrant. We only need the media for an initial burst of interest – to get people to our website so they can learn what we stand for. So that should free us to be goofy out on the street – because once we get people to see the website, they will see that we are serious and thoughtful.
>
> However, this kind of onerous burden of "being taken seriously" has felt like a straitjacket. There are still a lot of people in the campaign that will resist getting really wacky. I do not know what Jello's campaign was like but I imagine it was mostly Jello, and his fans and friends helping him out. Billy is not beholden to, but is *accountable* to a community of activists who have really profound concerns about the way the city is being run, about the way the world is, and they do not want it to be all laughs and jokes. Even though the laughs and the jokes can be the most effective way of getting the message out.

This is a classic dilemma for electoral guerrilla theatre: how to find the right balance between whimsical and earnest engagement with a grimly serious ritual contest by which power is assigned and legitimized. Naturally, any campaign will have a coalition of different interests, ideologies, and styles. But the need to be "taken seriously" sometimes trumps the need to be noticed in the first place, yielding poor results. Savitri D also acknowledged this problem, noting that there were "pragmatists" in the campaign who urged the Reverend and the Church to be "realistic" in their tactics, making Savitri D think, "Wow, your imagination just collapsed and you didn't even notice."

Savitri D's advice for future electoral guerrilla artists:

> Make peace with who you are and remember that the professional politician did not always exist. Stop trying to fit into the shape and size of what a politician is. You need to come to terms with that before running. Even for us it's been incredibly difficult to break through the restraint. Be free of that really narrow idea of what is realistic that's just based on neoliberal democracy, this really shallow narrow idea of "real."

> I see it sometimes in radicals, they dismiss things that are not "realistic." Well, where does the "real" come from? What's the "real?" Where's this neutral zero place where there is "real?" Is it Wall Street? Is it Mike Bloomberg? He has 60 billion dollars. Is that "realistic?" Is running New York City like a corporation "realistic?" So be clear, disciplined, and "realistic" about separating yourself from all that.

The Reverend Billy campaign struggled to balance the different kinds of actions to meet its goals, deepen its alliances and networks, and tell a radical story for the future history of this city. In the last phase of the campaign, the team made a deliberate push towards the whimsical, confrontational, and spectacular.

On Halloween in New York City, there is a tremendous parade that marches through the Village. Tens of thousands of spectators line up to watch the brilliant floats and costumes (and the occasional participation of creative activists, such as the glamorous Perms for Permawar in 2003). This time, spectators saw Reverend Billy walking backwards, screaming for his life, and backing away from a swarm of about ninety "Zombergs," zombies wearing Bloomberg masks. The Zombergs pursued him for the length of the parade, moaning, staggering, and trying to eat him. Savitri D created the masks for the Zombie–Bloombergs. Occasionally Reverend Billy would be pushed into the crowd, and he would shout at the police, "You have to do something! Help us! These people have been mayor for *centuries*! They won't *die*!" According to Billy the police got the joke and laughed, as did many in the crowd. The idea of an undead politician, immortal but feeding off the people, resonated in an absurd way, and perhaps was also a swipe at the zombie-like acceptance of many voters towards Bloomberg's victory.

But before then, on October 13, an intervention that made a large splash in regional media was Billy's interruption of Bloomie at the one and only candidate's debate in front of a public audience, between Democratic candidate Bill Thompson and Bloomberg (as a minor-party candidate, Talen was not invited to participate in the debate). The debate was held in El Museo del Barrio, and there were a few hundred mostly working-class protestors outside, herded by the police into the confining "protest pens" that have become the unfortunate custom in the city.

Savitri D and Talen brought with them a nine-foot-tall, plywood facsimile of Bloomberg. They had created it for this event. Savitri D held it up by its handles in the back, taking up a position outside of the permitted protest pens. The pair then invited the protestors to dare leaving the pens so that they could come up to "Bloomberg," tell him why they were upset with him, and throw a shoe at him in protest. Talen and Savitri D thoughtfully provided a large heap of shoes for the protesters to use so they would not end up barefoot. Many people took them up on their offer. As Talen said:

> People made wonderful speeches before throwing their shoes. About losing their homes, about being unable to afford day-care for their children, heart-breaking and angry speeches. Many really made exaggerated throws, too, lifting their legs in the air like baseball pitchers.
>
> It felt good to offer to people the option to leave the pen. You had to step outside to participate. And then they would get into it. New York One, Channel 9, all carried this image.[6]

This participatory performance, an edgy reference to the Iraqi man who threw his shoes at President Bush, turned a somewhat dreary and overregulated-as-usual protest into an opportunity for people to express their personal dissent, anger, and creativity.

Reverend Billy then went into the Museo building. Police officers who had arrested him in Starbucks asked him why he was there, and he showed them his ticket. His full neon-blue suited, pompadoured televangelist drag attracted the attention of earset-wearing private security, who shadowed him as he took a seat in the fifth row.

Billy's first plan had been, once inside, to throw his shoes at the Mayor. However, to avoid jail or worse (who knows if those Blackwater-type private bodyguards would open fire?), that idea transformed into the outdoor shoe-throwing event. Billy watched as about six hundred people gathered, and he prepared himself:

> I got to watch how the elite gather, people on the inside, they were so excited to be allowed in, in their very expensive clothes, [former Mayor] Koch was there . . . the political ruling class is gathering. I'm this glowing, out of place, televangelist with my own contingent of Blackwater guys hovering over me . . . but the theatre of democracy is being satisfied.
>
> My heart is beating ferociously, and I've got my heart medicine. I've finally realized that I'm 59 years old . . . I've got my heart pills, I've been inside the world of heart medicine now . . . our hearts are supposed to be on a reggae beat, but for ten days last summer [due to all the strain of the campaign], my heart was on a rock and roll beat . . .

Mayor Bloomberg won the picking of straws, and was about to speak. Reverend Billy stood up and said, as can be heard on YouTube to this day (www.youtube.com/watch?v=nh5RZZL6DIQ): "Mike, what are you doing here? We voted for . . . term limits! Democracy is important! Eight is enough! Eight is enough!" Quickly, Billy was escorted out of the room by security, along with a couple of activists he did not know who had spotted him, sat behind him, and joined in when he started.

If you listen closely, there is a brief pause in his interruption. According to Billy, he stood up, said "We voted for—" and then paused, frozen, drawing a blank as sometimes happens to performers under pressure. People around him immediately rose to the occasion, and said "term limits!" The public served as prompter, helping Billy out in a tough moment. Everyone knew how to fill in *that* blank; it was on everyone's mind. This was a subtle but revealing moment – everyone knew what Bloomie was doing, but Billy prompted them to say it out loud in the hall of power.

This interruption was heard around the world, but Bill was not satisfied, and it was in fact a troubling moment for him. He wondered why he did not jump on stage, interrupting the visuals of the live feed with the spectacle of Billy and Bloomie in the same TV frame. Part of the hesitation was a fear of being shot, of course, especially as a soon-to-be father. However, there was more to it than that, according to Billy:

> I agree that change never comes in our society without some people risking their lives. That's standard Howard Zinn. I wasn't able to do that. Why? Because Savitri's pregnant? I was sort of lifted away from the rigor of my own radicalism by nine months among political people – constantly compromised, hedging. Savitri and I became taken away from ourselves, our own game, and that manifested on that night.
>
> I should have risked the famously nervous trigger fingers of the New York Police Department (NYPD). I'm older. I'm about to be a father. But I've always made my theatre out of doing things that other people wouldn't do, like Abbie Hoffman. But on that occasion, I tiptoed on the edge. I interrupted from the fifth row.

Even here, by invoking radical historian Howard Zinn while contemplating if he should have jumped in front of the Mayor at risk to his own safety, Billy continues to think of his entire mayoral campaign, and perhaps the history of the whole Church, in terms of future history, of how the story will be told by the next generations of activists, as much as what the action will accomplish in the moment. When asked how he felt about the fact that his great cathedral in Barcelona would take over a hundred years to complete, the architect Gaudi replied "My client is not in a hurry." Gaudi built, slowly, meticulously, for his God, and Billy performs wildly, recklessly, for the future historians of social movements.

Missed opportunities for martyrdom not withstanding, Billy did manage to interrupt the "$108 million man – what every New Yorker would have wanted to do" [Bloomberg ultimately spent that sum on his own re-election]. But it is interesting that as a radical performance activist, he analyzed his own hesitation and relative moderation as the by-product of being immersed in electoral politics for nine months.

The final score? In conventional terms, the campaign's achievements were significant but modest. They collected 18,000 signatures in order to get on the ballot, the result of months of enormous effort by staff and volunteers, and well over the number needed.

They collected $50,000 in campaign donations, with the average gift being about $50 each from about 1,000 donors.

Finally, on election day, Reverend Billy received about one percent of the vote.

Of course, these are not the only measures by which the campaign would evaluate itself. Talen said:

> Mostly, we were glad it was over. We were taken out of our game, and by about halfway through the campaign both Savitri and I got very sick. We don't regret it – we were in the neighborhoods all the time, in the subways. Savitri saw a real improvement in my speeches – just through speaking to people so often – I've been getting to the point sooner. I trained with an opera singer so I could speak to large crowds without the need for a bullhorn.
>
> (Talen 2010)

The Church of Life After Shopping carries on, leaving the electoral game behind and setting up their mobile pulpit in a chain store near you. Savitiri D and Bill Talen are turning their attention to issues such as gay marriage and mountaintop removal mining. They came out of the campaign with a new affinity group of very dedicated activists. "The Church has become larger. We feel brave, we feel the callouses from the campaign. We're still fundamentally all about keeping public space public. We will continue to resist militarism and consumerism."

Amen?

When I asked the Reverend and Savitri D more recently about this election project, they both spoke of it as a distant and unpleasant memory or bad dream. Bill said "Running for mayor was not a good application of the Reverend Billy idea."[7]

Perhaps this election campaign was like trying to pound in a nail with a violin – you do serious damage to your own precious instrument without making commensurate progress. In fact, the nail is better designed to poke holes in the violin than the violin is to drive the nail further into its plank. The Church was a finely tuned and specific tool of disruptive, earnest and soulfully outrageous intervention. The election system was perfectly designed to drain the Church's energy and leave it tired and in need of repair. And yet, the Church lives and moves on.

### Making saints: the Church as social movement sustainer and place of solace

We are inside St. Mark's, a combination church and theatre space in the East Village. The Reverend and the Church are holding one of their weekly "services," a song and sermon filled performance that draws a capacity crowd of enthused agnostics. Indeed, the Church of Life After Shopping preaches many values – anticonsumerism, a reverence for the labor history of commodities, the elevation and celebration of the Odd. It creates a warm communal and nurturing space for the "god for people who do not believe in god." This may seem a contradictory phrase, but it shows a savvy understanding that all communities need nurturing, affirmation, and sustaining myths and storytelling, even if they do not embrace any religious doctrine.

These services are one of the sustaining events of the Church, just like the routine incursions into Starbucks, which they complement in function. It is not enough to constantly disrupt the chain-store, to tilt at the windmill of the Billionaire Mayor. These heart-taxing efforts need a sustaining service to prevent burnout. The church service performances serve that purpose, not just for its members but for activists and progressives of many stripes.

We have come to the portion of the service where a member of the activist community is beatified as a Saint of the Church of Life After Shopping. It is usually an under-sung and consistent, long-time activist who has shown dedication and devotion for many years in their cause. Today, Bobbie Lasko is called up onto the stage. A city clerk and long-time in-the-streets activist, Bobbie is beaming and a bit overwhelmed by the applause of the hundreds of faithful. As the Reverend lovingly extols Lasko's record of service to the community and many progressive causes, and as the choir sings in his honor, he receives something more immediate, more warm and communal, than Warhol's cynical "fifteen minutes of fame." He is seen. He is recognized. He is celebrated and thanked. And he is joyful.[8]

Years later, in May 2011 at Theatre 80 in the East Village, the Billionaires for Bush were beatified collectively as Saints in the Church – and the event had a different feel. It was sillier but still heartfelt. Billionaires, including myself, showed up in their oligarchical drag and were given opportunities to speak in ironic character through the service. Billy himself acknowledged the differences between his project and B4B in his sainting sermon:

> The Church of Stop Shopping and the Billionaires, we were always parallel to each other, but as Larry Bogad, Ben Shepard, and Steve Duncombe . . . would tell you, we've always been at cross purposes. The frontier for *us* is to become more and more sincere . . . to discover a real faith, like raving agnostics or something, while the frontier for the Billionaires is to become more and more absurdly true to the billionaire culture. We've always been going in opposite directions, but we love each other as we disappear on opposite horizons, and tonight you are our saints! Amen! Hallelujah![9]

At this point the choir removed their robes to reveal that they were wearing billionaire-style costumes on underneath, a strong gesture of love for the ironic from the sincere. All went on stage and began to sing and celebrate together.

What do these sainting ceremonies do? "Preaching to the choir" is a phrase used to criticize actions that speak solely to the "converted" rather than reaching out to new converts or striking blows directly against an opponent. But the choir – whether literally a choir or the larger activist community, or, in this case, both – needs attention and love, too, in order to keep on singing and struggling in the long run through all the discouragement and despair. In this, the Reverend proves, literally and metaphorically, that preaching to the choir has its place and purpose.

If "choir members" are meant to volunteer countless hours and energy in service of an electoral campaign so draining that the candidate's heart staggers and stammers to a rock-and-roll beat, a Zinnian campaign not meant to win but as a performance for a future audience, with a sort of Brownian motion-notion of social change, whereby detemporalized progress will evolve from the imperceptible conversational osmosis of many "everyday people" rubbing together in the parks, the subways, and on street corners . . . well, then, an occasional sainting, some applause and some tribal warmth and singing, are going to be necessary. "Permaculture" and "sustainability" apply not only to the Earth and the biosphere as a whole: they are values for our own bodies and beings to embrace, so we can last past the first few years of fervent action.

The Church continues now, with an ecological focus, increasingly sincere in the tone of its sermons, zeroing in on corporate actions that are causing climate disaster such as mountaintop removal. Golden Frogs, performers in full head masks, move through the

**4.2 "Golden Toads" swarm a Chase bank to protest the species-threatening investments policies of that bank, while Reverend Billy is confronted by the NYPD. The Reverend felt more comfortable doing this kind of creative direct action than on the conventional election trail**

Photo by Erik McGregor

audience, haunting the space while the real amphibians are dying out. The Reverend describes more and more militant action, about the need to "put the 'urgency' back in 'emergency,'" before the disaster is complete, fantasizing about standing naked on the desk of the CEO of Citibank, not angry, but resolute, confrontational, wholly and Holily Odd.[10]

This wild act might not have flown during the election campaign, but it flies on this liberated stage, flies deliberately and gleefully in the face of "reason" – the reason that logically spawned Fordism, containerization, the supermall. It takes flight into that face of reason, and through it into the mind behind, to inspire, and sustain, action outside of the Church and out on the street.

We are left with a few takeaway lessons in activist praxis from the case study of Reverend Billy's campaign for Mayor:

- Thinking like De Certau, be open to the arrival of an *occasion* – a tactical opportunity for intervention. Learn to recognize them and act on them. For example, the unpopular, term-limit violating re-election campaign of billionaire Bloomberg – seen as a "cheat" but also inevitable by many, in the throes of a massive economic crisis – was an opportunity for the Church to make an intervention and find many sympathetic ears.
- At the same time, recognize when you are not on your own comfortable terrain – or when you are "taken out of your game," as the Reverend and Savitri D put it, and find ways to maintain your own creative momentum in a more stifling context such as electoral politics.
- Create play-spaces for protesters' expression, like the throwing of the shoes at the Bloomberg effigy – something that encourages people to step outside of the "protest cage" and give personal voice to their own concerns and hopes.
- Recognize your own limitations – sustainability and permaculture apply to your body and mind, not just to the earth as a whole. Your heart attack, your ulcer, your nervous breakdown or your burnout, do not help the cause.

### Ecosexual weddings, commitment ceremonies to the biosphere

A similar use of agnostic/pagan/playfully earnest spirituality that nurtures and celebrates commitment to activism are the "ecosexual" mass weddings created by Annie Sprinkle and Beth Stephens. Over a several year period, these performance artists staged mass weddings, during which they, and all the attendants and audience, would marry the Earth, or the moon, the sea, the sky, a specific mountain slated for obliteration by a mining company in West Virginia, the coal in the mountains, or the sun.

They referred to themselves as "ecosexual" – "Queer is old, honey, we're ecosexuals!" exclaimed Stephens mischievously – finding erotic joy and attachment to the natural world. They argue that the Mother Earth paradigm has clearly not worked – people seem to see this "Mother" as a being you can endlessly take from and never give back. But "Lover Earth," their paradigm, calls for mutuality, communication, reciprocation and actual caretaking and sustenance. It is a clever, and profound, paradigm shift. The weddings are playful and participatory and even absurdist at times, with many friends and colleagues called on stage in succession to perform original works around the central wedding theme.[11] But like with the Church of Life After Shopping, there is deep sincerity in the middle of all the playful sexuality and antics. It is, in effect, a mass ceremony of commitment, not to one other individual in a wedding life contract, but to the ecological cause, and to the local, specific activist concerns that are taken up during the performance.

- Choose from tactics and aesthetics thoughtfully to fit your goals. Allow yourself to evolve. Reverend Billy's first action at the Disney Store many years ago involved carrying a large cross with Mickey Mouse crucified on it into the store. This is a far cry from his later aesthetics of reverence – for the grassroots activists he saints into the Church, for the Golden Frogs, or for the mountains and river valleys slated for total destruction by mining companies.
- Use each campaign as a way to build infrastructure and coalitions for future actions, so that the exercise is not just a reactive, predictable, and costly incursion into heavily fortified enemy territory.

# Conclusion

## A tricky new play

Electoral guerrilla theatre is an innovation in the repertoire of contention of social movements in universal-suffrage democracies, reflecting a disillusionment with conventional participation in the electoral process among some marginalized counterpublics. Some electoral guerrillas seek to mock the entire electoral system through participation; others, like Pauline Pantsdown, use the highly mediated ritual in an unconventional way to lampoon a specific political target. Because this is such a modular tactic, it can be used by a wide variety of agents with many different goals. Like all performances, it is altered by and must be adapted to the demands and limits of each contingent context.

On a strategic level, this context is defined by each nation's greater electoral system and media structure. As Che Guevara might have put it, these are the "objective conditions" of the electoral guerrilla's art. One of the primary "subjective factors" is the individual guerrilla's campaign goals. These goals may in turn be influenced by the needs and desires of the guerrilla's backing organization, if any. The three major case studies in this book reflect a variety of these objective and subjective factors, in order to see how electoral guerrillas have adapted to and acted upon those conditions.

While all three electoral guerrillas were deeply critical of the commercial mass media, they all felt that media coverage, however shallow or biased, was important for the visibility of their campaigns. The more open and democratic electoral systems of Australia and the Netherlands enabled Pauline Pantsdown and the Kabouters, respectively, to gain ballot access. This in turn helped them to get more media exposure, as the legitimizing sanction of the ballot combined with the outrageousness of their performances made a worthy novelty item for the networks and print media. Australia's preference system enabled Pantsdown both to endorse friendly "real" candidates and to ask voters to put her nemesis, One Nation, last on their ballots. Automatic voter registration and mandatory voting meant that these requests were relevant to most people she spoke to on the street. The Dutch system, with its proportional representation, was so open that it resulted in the Kabouters winning numerous seats. The resultant problematic escalation of their performance into the city council was a primary factor in the dispersal of the movement. JettBlakk did manage to receive press and media coverage as well, both in her counterpublic's press and to a lesser extent in the mainstream media, but ballot access was much more difficult in the United States. This meant that fewer citizens outside of the queer counterpublic knew about her campaign. JettBlakk's event-crashing tactic was a low-budget way to overcome this barrier, cheerfully confronting audiences outside of her own subculture.

Besides seeking media coverage, all three of these electoral guerrilla projects used live performance to galvanize and entertain their own counterpublics, to reach out to wider local audiences, and to humorously critique their targets. All three had few illusions about the capitalist media, but all were hoping to use them to promote their performances. While directly playing to their allied subcultures and counterpublics, they also wanted to reach larger, broader audiences with the cutting humor of their sharp satire. They did this while continuing to participate in the separate and oppositional discourses of their own counterpublics: the Dutch extraparliamentary Left; the US radical queer community; and the anti-One Nation multicultural activist coalition in Australia, respectively.

There was a significant variation in campaign goals. Joan JettBlakk's overarching goal was widely defined: to promote Queer visibility and mock the US electoral system by using the electoral ritual itself as a media draw. The Kabouters' goal was also rather wide and yet tied to specific organizational aims: they hoped to satirize and undermine Dutch capitalist society and enlist greater participation in their extraparliamentary, anarchist counter-institutions. Both of these campaigns also hoped to use their electoral status as protection from police brutality during their street actions. Pauline Pantsdown's goal was the narrowest: to politically sabotage Pauline Hanson's One Nation Party, and to expose the constructed nature of Hanson's "authenticity" by parodying her in the electoral public arena. This parody (exaggerating negative aspects of Hanson's public persona through live performance, media appearances, and two wildly popular dance songs) undermined Hanson's attempt to be taken seriously in mainstream Australian politics. In this sense, Pantsdown is the only guerrilla in this study who actually used the mainstream media to help defeat a specific target on the far Right. Based on these case studies, it seems that the more focused a guerrilla's goal, the less chance there will be for "mission creep" or confusion. Also, it is harder to determine and maintain a focused goal as the size of the organization, or the number of electoral guerrillas, increases (e.g. the conflicts between the many council-Kabouters).

Membership in affinity groups or larger movement organizations further complicates campaign goals. The JettBlakk and Kabouter campaigns were troubled by contradictory desires within their organizations. Many members of Queer Nation/Chicago wanted the campaign to operate as a consensus-run collective creative process, in the hopes that this would serve the internal purpose of making their activist organization more egalitarian and less of a "boys' club." This did not fit in with the desires of JettBlakk and her campaign committee, creating an energy-draining split. Within the Kabouter movement, the unexpected electoral victories brought out an ideological conflict which perhaps was already there. Some members found themselves wanting to escalate their foray into the electoral sphere, in effect turning the guerrilla effort into a bona fide parliamentary venture, albeit a countercultural, New Left one. Parallel to the JettBlakk case, the majority of the Kabouters were disturbed that the council-Kabouters were not being responsive to their desires and ideology. Like Queer Nation, they were a consensus-run collective that found themselves being indirectly represented rather than constantly consulted and obeyed by their electioneering members. They also opposed the Federal campaign as a betrayal of their anti-parliamentary agenda (the difference between "strategic anarchists" and "ludic strategists"). This conflict was only exacerbated by the battle among the council-Kabouters, which pitted dreamy orators against performers of spectacular disruption. Pauline Pantsdown, who operated as a solo performer in solidarity with the multicultural anti-racist and anti-homophobic movement, rather than as a member-representative, faced few problems of this nature.

The distinction between electoral guerrillas and emergent parties can become blurry, especially when there is a backing organization that can end up being treated like a constituency. This is caused by a gradual shift from consensual, creative processes and fantastic agendas to representative and/or power-based politics. Any performance may come apart when the artists' vision shifts gears in the middle of the production, though much can be learned from the ensuing trouble. An electoral guerrilla who begins to receive media attention, or even becomes elected, may become answerable to a backing organization as a public representative, just like any politician, even if the initial intention was to perform a public prank. To some extent, this is what happened to the Kabouters as they began to straddle the line between a sharp satirical electoral guerrilla operation and an emergent political party. It was also part of the problem for Queer Nation/Chicago, as the JettBlakk campaign committee became autonomous in its increasingly public creative activities while still using Queer Nation's name. Remember Hildegaard Wassenaar's denunciation of this process: "Kabouters cannot represent other Kabouters." This was an astute summary of the conflict between anarchists looking to lampoon representative parliamentarianism and electoral guerrillas who were becoming public figures (or even politicans).

The cost of internal argument was higher for the Kabouters, an ironic result of the larger size of their organization and their electoral success. Because they had won so many seats in the municipal campaign, their representatives were the focus of a great deal of media attention. Unfortunately, this media attention was equally intense when it focused on their squabbling. On the other hand, Joan JettBlakk's efforts remained below the radar of most major media, despite her impressive "party-crashing" tactics. The result of this was that the Queer Nation/campaign committee split remained mostly an internal problem.

These dangers are inherent to electoral guerrilla theatre, an oppositional tactic that involves jumping boldly into a political process that is heavily ritualized, symbolic, and well equipped to co-opt all newcomers to the game. While the idea is to alienate these seductive, legitimizing rituals and expose their normalized shortcomings and exclusions, ironic participation can lead to involvement and even implicit endorsement. Some guerrilla campaigns replicate "straight" campaigns while maintaining an ironic twist, with the hope that this will garner a stronger response from their various audiences. Of course, this proximity to the thing imitated brings new problems. Electoral guerrillas may find themselves encircled, or worse, wearing the stolen uniforms of the enemy with less irony than originally intended.

*Verfremdungseffekt*, spectactorship, and the carnivalesque are vital but unstable elements in the electoral guerrilla's repertoire. *V-effekt* is a constant, inherent part of the work. However, the latter two elements offer special risks and gains. Campaigns that successfully enlist outrageous, irreverent, mass-participatory creativity, as the Kabouters did in their first election campaign, actually perform proto-alternatives to indirect, representative democracy and its stale ritual contests. They demonstrate to the greater public nascent, ludic visions of what a direct, participatory society might look like. However, the very structure of elections, with their rigid schedules, demand for quick decisions, and events structured around individual, symbolic candidate-celebrities, can reproduce the hierarchical dynamics of representative politics despite the intentions of the movement. It takes a great deal of focus and conscious "checking in" to sustain carnivalesque openness, multivocality, and mass participation in the midst of the electoral process. The electoral guerrilla may just decide to cut those cords with any base and perform as an individual gadfly.

Despite these pitfalls, the Kabouters further democratized Amsterdam's local political system and laid the foundation for many worthy reforms in Dutch society. JettBlakk stretched the definition of "normality" for many Americans, confronted head-on the ideology of gay assimilationism and public heteronormativity, and gave many queers hope and a good show. Pantsdown had a powerful negative affect on the fortunes of One Nation, and provided new music and a new cartoon character for the multicultural movement of her country. All of these accomplishments came from groups and individuals with few resources save their creative, activist energy. They danced their way through the rituals of power, improvising around the established rhythms, and, on occasion, tripping over themselves. Their ironic acts had many unintended effects, not all of them desirable, across a wide variety of audiences. As with other innovators at the margin of the repertoire of contention, electoral guerrillas face the danger of their own tactic becoming stale, staid, or easily co-opted. Hopefully, future oppositional movements can learn from both their setbacks and their successes.

Since the first edition of this book was published ten years ago, many more electoral guerrilla campaigns have intervened in elections all over the world. It appears to be an ongoing innovation, a running joke about running for office in neoliberal contexts. As campaign finance is deregulated, and popular environmental, regulatory and labor laws are struck down by international agreements like NAFTA, GATT, and TPP the gap between citizens' aggregate policy desires and the actual policies pursued by the state widens, and skews towards the interests of major corporations and oligarchies.[1]

This problem has only gotten more dire, particularly in the United States where the *Citizens United* ruling has eliminated all limits on campaign donations, and even made them anonymous and unaccountable, and where the recent evisceration of the Civil Rights-era Voter Rights Act has enabled state governments to further disenfranchise the poor and people of color.[2]

Many other countries have been confronted with the crises of neoliberalism and its clash with democratic desire and well-being. Iceland is one of the key examples. Iceland's economic crash in the Fall of 2008 was the canary in the coalmine for the entire over-speculated and deregulated global finance system. The small economy was bloated with a wild international investment bubble; when the bubble burst, bank crises spread to the UK.[3] The Icelandic people responded, not with a grumbling acceptance of a publicly-funded bailout of the banks, but with an massive, sustained, nonviolent uprising that included occupying the government buildings and city square in Reykjavik. The movement forced the resignation (and ultimately the conviction and imprisonment) of the Prime Minister that had presided over the speculation and crash, and who had advocated for an acceptance of neoliberal practice (i.e. the voters bail out the banks, and no one responsible goes to jail). Icelanders further voted in a referendum to refuse to pay for foreign banks' lost investments in Iceland, a very controversial move that went against the hegemonic assumptions followed by the United States and most countries impacted by the crash. The population of this small country (320,000 people) was clearly radicalized, activated, and mobilized by the crisis. And yet, in the next round of elections, the two "progressive parties" were advocating the same neoliberal medicine as the two "conservative" parties that had just been thrown out. What were the voters to do?

Enter the Best Party.[4]

The Best Party, an "anarcho-surrealist" party,[5] led by comedian/author John Gnarr, sprung up in 2009 in response to this crisis and the disillusionment with all "legitimate" parties. Like Jello Biafra's campaign for Mayor of San Francisco described in this book's Introduction, this was a radically satirical candidacy born out of a crisis for which no party seemed to be offering a solution. Their campaign was absurd like Biafra's but with a bit less of an edge to its humor. It was more whimsical and warm, not as cutting as Biafra's campaign, coming from a less violent context than the assassination and riot-torn San Francisco of 1979. In its more gentle absurdism, it was almost as if it was letting the crisis and the people's mass nonviolent uprising speak for itself. Like Biafra, they promised to solve the problem of corruption by being openly corrupt (remember Biafra's proposed Board of Bribery). Their ten point platform had 13 points and like Biafra's combined whimsy (free towels at every swimming pool) with serious points (e.g. the cancellation of all debt). As Dominic Boyer points out, they refused to choose between satire and sincerity, embracing both at once, and they saw their ludic actions as practical incursions into the strange and disturbing world of politics. In this they resembled the Kabouters, with their "two-handed strategy" combining corrosive critique with earnest ideas for radical change, but without the Kabouters' ingredient of disruptive direct action.

On 30 May 2010, the Best Party won 34.7 percent of the vote in Reykjavik, winning the Mayorship for Gnarr and six of the 15 city council seats of the city. They were even more electorally successful than the Kabouters. And they chose to govern. Gnarr mixed absurd but pointed allusions to elves, trolls and Schrodinger's cat in his public addresses with an actual (if painful and uncomfortable) engagement with the political system, including making difficult choices such as budget cuts and layoffs. With a collective emphasis on humility and human warmth, vulnerability and laughter, the Best Party managed the city for a full four year term (better than most Reykjavik Mayors in recent history); Gnarr decided not to run for a second term, but many people involved in the Best Party have now decided to help create a less surreal and perhaps more lasting party, Bright Future, which currently holds six seats in the national parliament.

The Best Party refused categorization not only in terms of satire versus earnestness, but also in terms of working inside or outside of the system. Unlike the Kabouters, they did not collapse into fighting among themselves and they did govern and transition to a progressive party. They successfully navigated this difficult political borderland, crossing back and forth, in a context of debt refusal and actual resistance to the very neoliberalism that had subverted their (and global) democracy.

*Die Partei* (literally, "The Party"), has operated in Germany since its founding in 2004 with less of a desire to engage or govern, and a more general mission to satirize the entire electoral apparatus and Germany's political history. Led by comedian Martin Sonnenborn, and coming out of the satirical magazine *Titanic*, which serves as its official media organ, its name echoes the dark totalitarian pasts of Nazi and East Germany, where the one ruling party would often simply be referred to as "the Party."

There was a "neoDada" aspect to their nonsense, as revealed by their spurious acronym. In German the letters of *Partei* supposedly stand for the contradictory principles of "Party for Work, Rule-of-Law, Protection of Animals, Advancement of Elites, and Grassroot-Democratic Initiative." When, in 2009, they were refused access to the federal ballot as a "frivolous party," this provided them with an opportunity for lawsuits and further high jinks that advanced the visibility of their ongoing prank. As often is the case, the action was in the reaction – they benefitted from being banned. Overall, The Party, with its generalized satire, serves to advertise the comedic chops of Sonnenborn (who is now a member of the European Parliament) and *Titanic*.

Antanas Mockus, in his two terms as mayor of Bogota in Colombia (1995–7 and 2001–3), provides an example of the use of innovative theatrics in earnest engagement with electoral and political systems. He ran with the intention to win, and he governed with the intention to make his city safer and more sustainable ecologically. Mockus dressed in superhero and other exuberant costumes as part of his campaigns. As mayor he famously employed hundreds of mimes to mock traffic violators rather than fine or arrest them – which successfully reduced traffic violations. With similar examples of serious play and creative and festive community engagement, Mockus' administration achieved significant reforms – water waste was vastly reduced, while water service was expanded to all homes, traffic deaths were cut almost in half and most importantly the homicide rate fell by 70 percent. Mockus was not an electoral guerrilla but an innovator at the margins of municipal politics – categorically a cousin of Boal, who did not intend to win in

Rio de Janiero, but then created Legislative Theatre as a collective direct-democratic tool with which to insinuate the people's desires into the formal structures of power.

Superbarrio, the masked *lucha libre* hero of the working people of Mexico, and indeed, the entire world, ran for President of North America in 1996, and toured all over the continent making speeches in character and costume. He provided a compassionate and fierce perspective on issues such as NAFTA, racism, and U.S. hemispheric domination.[6] At a speech at Dartmouth College for a Politics and Performance conference, for example, Superbarrio said:

> . . . What have the other candidates who have campaigned here proposed? They offer fear . . . the politics of fear only work in a climate of ignorance. Friends!!! I come from far away, but that's much closer than any of you might imagine. I come from everyday life . . . family, city parks, neighborhood parks, the workplace, the library, the classroom. I come from the places where we tend to look at the world from the bottom up, from south to north . . . where hardship has caused millions of people to cross borders leaving home, family, and culture behind them in search of work . . . I bring a message from the South to the North. The United States must open its mind and not close in upon itself provincially . . . NAFTA does not work well because it is a trans-national pact between trans-national corporations . . .

In contrast to those corporate interests, Superbarrio unified the exploited of all the Americas:

> We ask to join with us: the miners of Bolivia and Appalachia, the peasants of Chile and Ohio, those who live in the shanty-towns of Brazil, Los Angeles, and the ghettoes of Washington D.C., the undernourished children of Peru and Virginia, the indigenous people of Chiapas and North Dakota . . .

And in an ironic gesture to the anonymous and mythic sincerity of his own costume mask, he warned: "Distrust all politicians who wear masks and do not show their true faces."

Superbarrio denounced in detail the faults of NAFTA, the US policy of domination of its southern neighbors, and the depredations of transnational corporations and xenophobic culture. He closed by calling upon the names of revolutionary heroes from all the Americas, names like Simon Bolivar and Emiliano Zapata, but also Rosa Parks, Emma Goldman and Sojourner Truth.

Superbarrio levelled a critique of *Yanqui* power and paranoia from a Mexican perspective. His mythos is that of a fearless hero of the barrio, who, in the ring, draws his fighting power from the support of the working people of Mexico, and the world. This masked warrior radicalized the popular form of *lucha libre*, and was performed at different times by as many as three different costumed performers. As a poetic political candidate, he provided a prefigurative vision of a Western Hemisphere free of hegemony and exploitation.

In 2007 and 2011, Stephen Colbert also ran for office, wearing a mask of sorts – his own face deadpanning ironically. His campaigns may have been less poetic and sincere than Superbarrio but they were fuelled by his high-octane celebrity.

In the fall of 2007, Colbert ran for President for about two and a half weeks. He wanted to run on both Republican and Democratic tickets in his home state of South Carolina. His official sponsor was Doritos, and in a speech at Cornell University to promote his new book and discuss his campaign, he gleefully announced "I will be as good for the country as Doritos are for your body."[7] When it turned out that he would have to give $35,000 to the Republican party to get on their ticket, and the Democrats announced they would not let him on their ticket because he was not a serious candidate, he ended his brief but glorious campaign.

Colbert's campaign in 2011–2012 was more sustained and pointed. It targeted the *Citizen's United* Supreme Court ruling and its impact on campaign finance. By forming his own Super PAC (called "Americans for A Better Tomorrow, Tomorrow") and covering that PAC on his own popular TV show, Colbert educated millions of viewers on the ramifications of the Supreme Court ruling – namely that it essentially eliminated any limits or accountability for campaign contributions. He had Trevor Potter, a former Chairman of the Federal Elections Commission, on his show to help him fill out the paperwork – and with plenty of jokes in between, thus taught the audience how little regulation there was against corruption and bribery with unlimited cash-flow in politics. Potter later helped Colbert to set up a shell corporation, "Colbert Super PAC S.H.H.," so that corporations could contribute anonymously to his campaign. As Colbert said,

> We raised [over a million dollars] on my show and used it to materially influence the elections – in full accordance with the law. It's the way our founding fathers would have wanted it, if they had founded corporations instead of just a country.[8]

In the end, Colbert raised $1.2 million, spent about a third of it on absurd TV ads, and donated the rest to causes ranging from campaign finance reform to veteran's welfare. This campaign received a Peabody Award for its successful exposure of the troubling practical implications of *Citizen's United* on U.S. democracy. Colbert's playful participation was a form of investigative journalism that was unequalled on this issue in terms of mass exposure. He leveraged his celebrity, with the technique of satirical participation, to push a substantial critique into the national conversation.

On the flip side of the celebrity–grassroots divide, Occupy activists in Oakland ran their dog, Einstein, for Mayor in 2014 against incumbent Mayor Jean Quan and 18 other candidates. With the slogan of "He's a good dog. He'll make a very good mayor," this campaign ran on the internet and radio, with live appearances at candidate debates and other campaign events. Einstein was not allowed into the official candidate debates, but at The Omni Commons, a venue that hosts the popular show "Oakland Nights Live," he was on the stage with his human companion, Ed Biow, and four human politicians, for a "meet the candidates" event. The event was festive, with the other candidates appreciating the inherent humor and referring to Einstein in their answers. A visionary Occupy-style platform was thus successfully represented to a large audience by Einstein and Ed.

Their platform evoked some classic techniques of the form and added its own unique twists, reminiscient of the "Pigasus for President" campaign mentioned in the Introduction.[9] The lovely dog, Einstein, had actually attended Occupy actions and had experienced the tear gassing and flash-bombing by the Oakland PD of the Occupy camp in Frank Ogawa Plaza in front of City Hall. In fact, Biow had trained Einstein to bark and run around whenever he said "Jean Quan," the name of the liberal Mayor who had presided over the destruction of the Occupy encampment.

Einstein and his human companions declared his canine candidacy on the steps of City Hall with a platform that combined silly and serious in a familiar mixture.[10] "I like to run. A lot! I mean A LOT! So make no mistake, I can make it all the way to the finish line," affirms Einstein on his website. The platform includes prefigurative ideas for Oakland – one in which the police live in the city they patrol (a plank shared by Biafra a generation earlier), single-payer healthcare, living wage and maximum wage laws, a dismantling

**C.1 Campaign poster image for Einstein for Mayor**
Courtesy of the Einstein for Mayor campaign

of the surveillance state, and some serious planks about animal rights. The platform also asked larger questions coming from the Occupy movement's horizontal position: is it really wise or even possible to place so much power in the hands of one politician? Einstein advocated devolving that executive power to local control in the form of a 500-member city council.[11] As Einstein's political advisor Michael Wilson said, "We wanted to give a vision of the city we'd like to see."[12] While Einstein did not win – and indeed as a nonhuman, he faced species-ist discrimination and would not have been allowed to take office – this low-budget, creative intervention raised alternative visions and possibilities to a large audience of Oakland voters.[13]

Even when movements have lost steam, dissipated, and the cycles of contention that were their heyday have run their course, they can still leave behind social connections, lingering oppositional loyalties and solidarities, and permanent expansions in the field of popular political participation, pop culture, and ideology. Jello Biafra said that, many years after his anarchistic, absurdist run for Mayor of San Francisco in 1979, he still occasionally ran into somebody who would say "Oh, hey, I voted for you" (Biafra 1992). Memories of a faded campaign can linger as part of the cultural identity of an oppositional group, a favorite old war story, part of the movement's folklore. This experience can also be preserved and stored in the repertoire of resistance, as a tactic to be re-employed at a later date, as oppositional, performative "restored behavior" which alludes to the past even as it creates and improvises in the present. Equally important, this type of creative action is *a good time*, or at least it should be. Even if it has little immediate impact on the outside power structure, it can be personally liberating. As a joyful action for the performers and the affinity groups of activists involved, it can make the long, arduous struggle more sustainable. That alone may make it worthwhile, regardless of the actual number of votes cast for gnomes, queens, punks, and other wise fools.

# Notes

## Introduction: electoral guerrilla theatre in recent democracies: speaking mirth to power

1 Actually, Moore's information was outdated; it turned out that Freylinghuysen did face a challenger in the Republican primary who was not a plant.

2 See Bogad 2005. This is not to play down the experience of those taking part in contemporary oppositional carnivalesque events. The experiential, unmediated, personal element of tactical carnival is a powerful force in current movement building – indeed in our more specialized and alienated society it is a deeply politicizing experience for protestors and helps to sustain and build the movement in an immediatist sense (Bey 1994).

3 For Habermas, the bourgeois public sphere was a sort of golden moment of rational civil discourse: never perfect, exclusive, and all-too-fleeting, but nevertheless a tenuous, partial model for a future, better, and more participatory democracy. It was only the development of early capitalism that created a civil society separate from the monarchical/feudal state. A public sphere arose in which bourgeois individuals and artisans could meet *as if equals* to discuss policy and engage in rational, critical debate on the basis of quality of argument, not status. The bourgeois public sphere became an independent base for opposition to the state. According to Habermas, this public sphere was diluted by the increased participation of the working class, since the quality of debate was lowered as the quantity of participants increased. The public sphere was also corrupted as social democracy interfered with free discourse. As the state became the welfare patron of the working class, the public sphere became a mere haggling market of conflicting interests, in which negotiation overcame rational debate. Habermas's ideal context for rational discussion, where the best-argued definition of the society's "collective interest" would triumph regardless of the social status of the arguer, had been degraded by the increase of private corporations' power over the public on the one hand and the modest successes of the reformist/nationalist social-democratic parties of the Second International on the other. He referred to this process as the "refeudalization of society" (Habermas 1989; Calhoun 1992: Chapter 1; Fraser 1997: Chapter 3).

4 Nancy Herbst's concept of the "parallel public sphere" builds on and diverges from Fraser's subaltern counterpublic. As is suggested by the difference between the words "parallel" and "counter," Herbst's vision is slightly less oppositional, emphasizing dialogue over dialectic. Herbst recognizes the marginalization of certain groups in liberal democracies: "Social groups are marginal . . . when conventional institutions . . . attempt to *silence* them" (1994: 10, Herbst's emphasis). For Herbst, marginalized groups need to construct public spheres parallel to the center as a separate base of operations for three purposes: (a) building community; (b) articulating dissent and influencing mainstream discourse; and (c) negotiating with the political center through back channels of communication (1994: 4, 166). The similarities between Fraser's and Herbst's visions are strong. Both insist that marginalized populations must build an alternative public sphere with which to develop their own community and discourse.

This alternative, subversive discourse resembles J.C. Scott's "hidden transcript." For Fraser, the oppressed need

> venues in which to undertake communicative processes that were not, as it were, under the supervision of dominant groups [or else they would be] less able than otherwise to articulate and defend their interests in the comprehensive public sphere. They would be less able than otherwise to expose modes of deliberation that mask domination by absorbing the less powerful into a false "we" that reflects the more powerful.
>
> (Fraser 1997: 81)

Scott agrees, laceratingly questioning "Habermas' tendency to treat civil and political society as if it ought to be the perfect graduate student seminar" (Scott 1990: 115). For Scott, all social interaction between oppressor and oppressed is laden with power-necessitated deception. "Hidden transcripts" are the highly articulated and stealthily nurtured world-view and grievance list of the oppressed. In his study of feudal, slave, and authoritarian societies, he notes that:

> The elaboration of hidden transcripts depends not only on the creation of relatively unmonitored physical locations and free time but also on active human agents who create and disseminate them. The carriers are likely to be as socially marginal as the places where they gather.
>
> (123)

This necessary private space is an extremely hedged in and underground version of the subaltern counterpublic's alternative discursive space.

While Scott focuses on the agency of desperately oppressed people (slaves, proletarians, servants), some of his ideas are still relevant to marginalized people in liberal, industrial/post-industrial societies. Subaltern counterpublics do have their own hidden transcripts. They may not always be as carefully hidden as they have to be in more authoritarian/totalitarian power structures, but nevertheless they are unique, complex, and well-preserved lists of grievances and utopian visions/inversions. Hidden transcripts are a way of preserving this oppositional discourse until it can be brought out on a special "tactical" "occasion" or opportunity (de Certeau 1984). A radical performer can appeal to the hidden transcript by giving it an unexpected, outrageous, and carnivalesque voice in the official, hallowed/hollow, and symbol/ritual-laden electoral public sphere.

5 It is worth noting the distinction between those excluded for reason of identity, such as race, and those who are marginalized for reasons of ideology (for example, anarchists in the modern United States).

## 1 A prank too far? The Kabouters' electoral guerilla theatre, Amsterdam 1970–71

1 Please note that Van Duijn spelled his name "Van Duyn" during the Provo period. Since the Kabouter period, he has spelled it "Van Duijn." However, the press did not always spell his name correctly. This explains any spelling inconsistencies in this chapter.

2 Note that, in Dutch, there are two words for white – one designating race (*blanc*) and one for color (*wit*). Therefore the Provo use of *wit* (the term for color) was not as racially loaded as it might be in the United States (Tasman 2000b)

3 An even more mocking pamphlet suggests:

> ASK THE WHITE CHICKEN FOR CHICKEN
> [. . .] Outside the Magic Centre's canal area the so-called police cars can be used as 'tinned chicken'. The white chicken is unarmed and instead will carry a bag containing medicine, aspirin, matches, little orange slices with chicken meat.
>
> The French King Henri IV formulated the materialistic ideal as: 'A chicken in the pot every day'. White chicken is the cheapest kind of meat with the necessary animal protein. It will be issued by the municipality and distributed by Amsterdam's social workers among the suffering population.
>
> WHY NOT HAVE FUN
> CHICKEN IS IN
> CHICKEN IS FUN
> CHICKEN IS GOOD FOR YOU
>
> (Mairowitz and Stansill 1971: 33)

4 Richard Kempton, in his dissertation, goes so far as to suggest that the "Claus"–Claus coincidence is the single factor that guaranteed the Provos a place in world history (Kempton: 231).

5 The Orange Free State gained money for such materials by a windfall from the capitalist state: a computer error led The Hague to bestow 35,000 guilders upon the alternative radio station Radio 2000, which immediately passed on most of the money to the Orange Free State. "The rest of the money was used as legal funds for arrested squatters and for printing a 2,000 guilder bank note (there is no such currency, although the note looks like authentic Dutch

money).” Inspired by the Yippies’ act of dumping dollar bills on the floor of the New York Stock Exchange, some Kabouters tried to dump the convincing 2,000 guilder notes onto the Dutch Stock Exchange. They were denied entrance, so they dumped the fake money from the top of the Exchange’s tower onto the street below, puzzling many a passerby. The Kabouters also used some of the Radio 2000 swag to set up their own newspaper, *Kabouterkrant*, as well as several services: a housing bureau, cheap clothing shop, bio-dynamic food shop, etc. (Tasman 2000a).

6 Even this nursery rhyme was used in a playful/confrontational way later – as activist and long-time commune inhabitant Ans Alkemade told me, the “Cuckoo!” refrain in the song was often directed mockingly at the police during Kabouter-cop confrontations (Alkemade 2000).

7 This theme of “turning on” the forces of reaction, and the rest of the nation, through ludic joy and good deeds is further illustrated in a Kabouter cartoon in *ALOHA*, a national countercultural magazine that, for a time, was an organ of the Orange Free State. In the cartoon, a group of Kabouters, in need of a home, break into an abandoned house (with a nocturnal “KRAAAK!” playing on the word for breaking-in/squatting, “krak”). They make friends with their elderly, conservative neighbors, helping them by painting their house and other good deeds. The neighbors then stand up for the Kabouters in a confrontation with the police. The cheerful Kabouter-narrator then turns to the reader and says, “So remember folks, it’s important to turn on the neighbors!” (Ridder 1970).

8 The “Abbey Rood” occupation is typical of Action ’70’s high-stakes satire. Abbey Bank had a huge building downtown that they were no longer using, having moved their headquarters to the outskirts of town. The Kabouters occupied it, and then released a press release thanking Abbey for being so wise as to acknowledge the horrible housing shortage and agreeing to use their now-deserted building for free housing and other progressive uses. The Kabouters hung a banner from the building saying “Abbey Rood,” a pun on the Beatles’ song and a political irony – “Rood” is Dutch for “Red.” The police threw them out of the building fairly quickly. However, they pulled a similar stunt with an old Heineken brewery, and sent the spoof press release to the PR department of that company. Heineken negotiated with them concerning alternative uses of their space (Hakkenberg 2000b).

9 *Krakking* and squatting refer to the same action, but *krakking* has a stronger connotation, since it emphasizes the act of breaking-in, not just occupying. The VPRO video *Is it a Sin to be Subjective?* made this clear: “They advocate *krakking*, not for burglary, but for places to live” (Coehlo and Doebloet 1970).

10 *Het Vrij Volk* called the victory of the Kabouters almost a fairy tale, chiding the voters for playing such a negative role. “The only positive thing counteracting it is the victory of the Communist Party and the VVD, but, to be honest, we couldn’t call that positive.”

*De Nieuwe Rotterdamse Courant* tried to analyze the Kabouters’ politics in practical terms: “If . . . [the Kabouters have] formed an anarchist movement with a friendly mask, then they are more dangerous than had-je-me-maar [a vagrant who, in the Thirties, had run for city council. He was elected, but did not take his seat] . . . the fact remains that we can't progress very quickly with a group who want to make Arcadia out of a very densely populated, industrialized country that must work very hard to live decently" ("Fairytale" 1970).

11 *De Telegraf* had supported the Nazi occupation, had been trashed by striking construction workers after falsely blaming the death of one of their striking comrades on them in 1966, and had called for the Provos and Kabouters to be put in labor camps.

12 Hakkenberg, a radical architect, stayed in the city council for the rest of the term, instead of rotating out after a year. He did this because the Kabouter movement had dispersed and he therefore felt that there was no organization left to answer to. Hakkenberg, during his tenure in the city council, tried to work with the Communists, despite their hostility to the Kabouters as an organization, and especially to Roel van Duijn. Hakkenberg explained that, since he didn't desire to make a career out of politics, he wasn't too worried about getting credit for all of his ideas. So if he had to feed ideas to CPN members and let them gain the credit, that was fine as long as his radical proposals on housing design and other issues could be moved forward. Hakkenberg alluded to yet another aspect of the kabouter as folkloric symbol to explain this: "a kabouter comes in through the keyhole, does good deeds, and disappears. Nobody knows who did it but it gets done. This is how to do things in the city council as a Kabouter" (Hakkenberg 2000b). It is interesting to note that, since Hakkenberg was not invested in the Kabouters as a political entity, he felt no need to play party politics against the Kabouters' most strident foe on the left, the CPN. This was yet another source of disagreement between council-Kabouters.

13 The detailed history of the many Kabouters who served in the city council can be found in Tasman 1996. Van Duijn came back again over the protests of many Kabouters, but then switched to the PPR. Simen de Jong served twice, including one time when, after being nastily upbraided by the Mayor himself, he protested with demonstrative silence for six months.

14 In Polish, "*krasnale*," which can be translated variously as gnomes, dwarves, elves, etc.

## 2 *Sturm und Drag*: the fabulous camp-pains of Miss Joan JettBlakk

1 JettBlakk preferred to spell her last name with no space in the middle; however, journalists and even other Queer Nation activists usually spelled it "Jett Blakk." This explains any spelling inconsistencies.

2 The meaning of the term "queer" is partly defined by the constant contestation of that meaning. In this context I wish to contrast "queer" resistance of social, economic, and cultural regimes of the normal on one hand and assimilationist gay strategy/ideology on the other (Crimp 1993).

3 Whether intentionally or not, this title evokes the "Mayor of Bronzeville" campaigns held by the African-American readers of the *Chicago Defender* decades earlier (Herbst 1994). However, unlike the "Bronzeville" campaigners, JettBlakk did not limit herself to a parallel "shadow" campaign, but participated mockingly in the "real" campaign.

4 The Chicago River is dyed green every St Patrick's Day.

5 The two exceptions are Maine and Nebraska, who split their electoral college votes proportionately.

6 This broad approach is also exemplified by Church Ladies for Choice's satirical abortion clinic defenses (Cohen-Cruz 1998).

7 For a longer discussion about this, see Butler 1990. To read about Sylvia Rivera, another working-class queer of color who was attacked in the queer community for her transgender clothing and persona, see Shepard 2004.

### 3 Electoral guerrilla theatre in Australia: Pauline Hanson vs. Pauline Pantsdown

1 Or, as Jan Cohen-Cruz puts it, "Brechtian drag" (Cohen-Cruz 1998).

2 For more information about Sleaze Balls, see Bollen 1994.

3 This is the same "I find this very hard" from the *60 Minutes* interview (Wilkinson 1996). Hunt extracted Hanson phrases for his songs from many different interviews and speeches on TV and radio.

4 In fact, this was a faulty crediting. Hunt produced the song, while Vanessa Wagner produced the live performance.

5 It is still not clear how Hanson, who is widely understood to be a female of the species, could be understood to fit under this definition of "potato," even if such a definition existed, which seemingly it does not.

6 Ironically, the rulings of Simon Hunt's father, once a pre-eminent conservative Australian justice known for his judgments in defamation hearings, were cited in this case. After Hunt's identity was uncovered by a tricky reporter, Hunt's father, who was sitting on the International War Crimes Tribunal in The Hague, expressed unqualified support for his son's activities.

7 Right-wing Prime Minister John Howard, that is. A constant aim of Pantsdown's performances, both recorded and live, was to tie Hanson's blatant racism to Howard's more low-key anti-Asian immigrant/Aboriginal Reconciliation policies – to argue that Howard quietly benefitted from the attention which Hanson received on these issues while he actually implemented policies that had some elements in common with One Nation's (Hunt 1999c).

8 This is a reference to conservative politician Alexander Downer, at the time (and still) Foreign Minister and, according to Hunt, considered a bit of an also-ran in his career (Hunt 1999c).

9 Pantsdown actually received about 2,500 first-preference votes, four times as many as any other "below-the-line" candidate. His One Nation opponent, David Oldfield, failed to win a Senate seat.

10 Interview with the author, 29 April 2015.

## 4 EARTHALUJAH! The importance of being earnest with the Church of Life After Shopping

1 Talen, Bill. *What Should I Do If Reverend Billy Is In My Store?* New York: New Press, 2003, and the film *What Would Jesus Buy?* Rob VanAlkemade, dir. 2007. The Church changes its name to fit the issues of the times; it has also been known as the Church of Stop Bombing, and the Church of the First Amendment, for example.

2 When I first met Bill Talen, on the street during a Reclaim the Streets action in early 2001, he remarked that he was considering staging the Reverend's assassination, and moving on from the character. He clearly made another choice – not to kill, but to enter fully into the life of, the Reverend.

3 Interview with author, Summer 2009.

4 See: VanAlkemade, Siegel, Scheier, Weidner, White.

5 "Destemporalizarse," Tattoo on the torso of, and verbal explanation to the author by, performance artist Natalie Brewster Nguyen.

6 Interview with author, 2010.

7 Emails with author, 13 May 2015.

8 For more on Bobbie Lesko: www.nytimes.com/2009/02/28/nyregion/28protester.html

9 Author's fieldnotes.

10 As seen by the author at a performance in San Francisco, Spring 2013.

11 I delivered the Orbital Exhortation at the Marriage to the Moon in the character of a Cosmonaut who, forgotten by the Kremlin during the chaos of the Soviet Union's collapse, had spent 20 years circling the moon and earth until finally and coincidentally crash landing just in time to arrive at the wedding. It was ridiculous, and had a Planet-of-the-Apes style twist at the end, but it seemed to fit in with the playful and open rhythm of the night's offerings.

## Conclusion: a tricky new play

1 Martin Gilens and Benjamin I. Page (2014). "Testing Theories of American Politics: Elites, Interest Groups, and Average Citizens." *Perspectives on Politics*, 12, pp 564–581. Also, my own boardgame and video game-in-development, *Buypartisan*, attempts to show through strategic gaming how policy skews away from the democratic mean towards the big donors' desires.

2 Liebelson, Dana. "The Supreme Court Gutted the Voting Rights Act. What Happened Next in These 8 States Will Not Shock You." Mother Jones, 8 April 2014. www.motherjones.com/politics/2014/04/republican-voting-rights-supreme-court-id. Accessed 20 May 2015.

3 Rebecca Solnit and I were in Iceland just before the crash working on different projects, and we both experienced Icelanders looking around at all the new luxury cars, $20 hamburgers, etc., leaning into us and confiding, "this can't last."

4 Boyer, D. (2013) "Simply the Best: Parody and Political Sincerity in Iceland," in *American Ethnologist*, 40(2): 276–287.

5 Perhaps echoing the "socialist surrealism" of the Orange Alternative?

6 Also known as his unmasked alter ego, Marco Rascón Córdova.

7 Rice, Melissa. "Stephen Colbert gives CU a double dose of 'truthiness.'" Cornell Chronicle. 29 October 2007. www.news.cornell.edu/stories/2007/10/stephen-colbert-gives-cu-double-dose-truthiness. Accessed May 22, 2015.

8 Nir, Sarah Maslin. "Colbert's Super PAC Raises More Than $1 Million" *New York Times*, 31 January 2012. http://thecaucus.blogs.nytimes.com/2012/01/31/colberts-super-pac-raises-more-than-1-million-dollars/?_r=0

9 In which uber-Yippies Abbie Hoffman and Jerry Rubin actually argued about which pig to buy from a farmer – should the pig look ugly and mean? Or happy and friendly?

10 http://sanfrancisco.cbslocal.com/2014/10/01/dog-candidate-to-officially-announce-run-at-oakland-mayors-office-thursday/

11 www.huffingtonpost.com/2014/10/03/einstein-dog-oakland-mayo_n_5921798.html, accessed 21 May 2015.

12 Interview with Author, 18 May 2015.

13 The "Twit Wit" radio show on KPFA got a kick out of Einstein's campaign and wrote an entire musical drama for their show about it, in which Mayor Quan was the antagonist. At one point "Quan" says, "I never thought I would be sitting on a panel with a socialist dog!" At which point someone helpfully points out "He's not a socialist, he's a responsible anarchist." Later, someone muses "He might hump your leg, but he won't lie. Dogs don't do corruption." (www.kpfa.org/archive/id/108086)

# References

"A Queen in the White House" (1991) *National Examiner*, 31 December: n.p.

Alkemade, A. (2000) Interview with the author. Amsterdam, The Netherlands: 18 June.

Allen, M. (2003) "The Bird was Perfect but not for Dinner: In Iraq Picture, Bush is Holding the Centerpiece," *Washington Post*, 3 December. At: www.washingtonpost.com/ac2/wp-dyn/A33090-2003Dec3?language=printer, accessed 4 August 2004.

Australian Electoral Commission Website (2000) At: www.aec.gov.au, accessed 23 December 2000.

Bagdikian, B. (1990) *The Media Monopoly*, Boston, MA: Beacon Press.

Bakhtin, M.M. (1968) *Rabelais and His World*, trans. H. Iswolsky, Cambridge, MA: MIT Press.

Berlant, L. (1997) *The Queen of America Goes to Washington City: Essays on Sex and Citizenship*, Durham, NC: Duke University Press.

—— and Freeman, E. (1993) "Queer Nationality," in M. Warner (ed.) *Fear of a Queer Planet*, Minneapolis, MN: University of Minnesota Press. Reprinted in J. Cohen-Cruz (ed.) *Radical Street Performance* (1998), New York: Routledge.

Bey, H. (1994) *Immediatism*, Oakland, CA: AK Press.

Biafra, J. (1992) *I Blow Minds for a Living*, Spoken Word Album, San Francisco, CA: Alternative Tentacles.

Boal, A. (1985) *Theatre of the Oppressed*, New York: Theatre Communications Group.

—— (1998) *Legislative Theatre: Using Performance to Make Politics*, New York: Routledge.

Bogad, L.M. (2005) "Tactical Carnival: Social Movements, Demonstrations, and Dialogical Performance," in J. Cohen-Cruz and M. Schutzman (eds) *A Boal Companion*, London: Routledge.

Bollen, J. (1994) "Sexing the Dance at Sleaze Ball 1994," in *TDR*, 40.3: 166–91.

Boyer, D. (2013) "Simply the Best: Parody and Political Sincerity in Iceland," *American Ethnologist*, 40(2): 276–87.

Brecht, B. (1964) *Brecht on Theatre: The Development of an Aesthetic*, trans. J. Willett, New York: Hill & Wang.

Brestoff, R. (1995) *The Great Acting Teachers and Their Methods*, Lyme, NH: Smith & Kraus.

Burbank, C.E. (1998) "Ladies Against Women: Theatre Activism, Parody, and the Public Construction of Citizenship in U.S. Feminism's Second Wave," Dissertation, Northwestern University, IL.

Burgler, R. (2000) Phone interview with the author. Amsterdam, The Netherlands: 17 June.

Butler, J. (1990) *Gender Trouble: Feminism and the Subversion of Identity*, London: Routledge.

Calhoun, C. (1992) *Habermas and the Public Sphere*, Cambridge, MA: MIT Press.

Chomsky, N. (1989) *Necessary Illusions: Thought Control in Democratic Societies*, Boston, MA: South End Press.

Coehlo, R. and Doebloet, D. (dirs) (1970) *Is it a Sin to be Subjective?* Video, trans. S. Frieling, Amsterdam, The Netherlands: VPRO.

Cogswell, K. (2001) "Labor's Queer Irish Troubles," in *The Gully.com*: 20 March. At: www.thegully.com/essays/america/nyc/010320labor_gays_irish.html, accessed 4 August 2004.

Cohen-Cruz, J. (1998) "At Cross-Purposes: The Church Ladies for Choice," in J. Cohen-Cruz (ed.) *Radical Street Performance: An International Anthology*, New York: Routledge.

Convery, G. (ed.) (1998) *Pauline Pantsdown Fanclub Webpage*. At: http://members.tripod.com/reconciliation/pantsdown6.htm, accessed 17 July 2004.

Crimp, D. (1993) "Right on Girlfriend," in M. Warner (ed.) *Fear of a Queer Planet*, Minneapolis, MN: University of Minnesota Press.

Davis, T. (2002) "Theatricality and Civil Society," in T. Davis and T. Postlewait, *Theories of Theatricality*, Cambridge: Cambridge University Press, Chapter 5.

de Certeau, M. (1984) *The Practice of Everyday Life*, Berkeley, CA: University of California Press.

DeGrane, S. (1992) "Drag Race," *New City*, 23 January: n.p.

De Jong, S. (2000) Interview with the author. Amsterdam, The Netherlands: 21 June.

*Delta* (1967) *Untitled insert*. Autumn: 110–11.

Dubin, S.C. (1999) "Who Censors the Censors?" Lecture Handout, Northwestern University, IL, Center for the Humanities: 8 November.

Duijn, R. Van (1967) *Het Witte Gevaar* [*The White Danger*], Amsterdam, The Netherlands: Meulenhoff.

—— (1970a) "Alderman for Welfare," *Kabouterkrant*, 6: 7.

—— (1970b) *Schuldbekente nis van een Ambassadeur* [*Confessions of an Ambassador*], trans. S. Frieling, Amsterdam, The Netherlands: Meulenhof.

—— (1971) "Letter from the Future," speech, translated text from the archive at the International Institute for Social History, Amsterdam, The Netherlands.

—— (1972) *Message of a Wise Kabouter*, trans. H. Hoskins, London: Duckworth.

—— (2000) Interview with the author. Amsterdam, The Netherlands: 19 July.

Duncombe, S. (2006) *Dream: Reimagining Progressive Politics in an Age of Fantasy*, New York: New Press.

Durkee, S. Interview with the author. 28 July 2009.
Duynstee, F. "Uitgangspunt Kabouters – Irrationeel en Negativistisch [The Point of Departure of the Kabouters – Irrational and Negative]," trans. A. Nassuth, *De Telegraf*, n.d.: n.p.
Ernsting, M. (2000) Interview with the author. Amsterdam, The Netherlands: 27 July.
"Fairytale Writing on the Wall" (1970), trans. A. Nassuth, *Trouw*, 5 June: 2.
Felshman, J. (1992) "Lick Bush in '92!" *The Chicago Reader*, 24 January: n.p.
Fitzgerald, T. (1998) "Telling the Truth, Laughing," *Communications Update* 150: 11–14.
Ford, R. (1991) "Making for Strange Bedfellows," *The Advocate*, 19 November: n.p.
Fox, G. (1973) "The Kabouters Demystified," in *ROOTS*: 29–42.
"Frans, je moet om negen uur naar de raad . . .!" ["Frans, you have to get up to go to the council . . .!"] cartoon. *Volkskrant*, 5 June: n.p.
Fraser, N. (1997) *Justice Interruptus: Critical Reflections on the "Postsocialist" Condition*, London: Routledge.
Freire, P. (1989) *Pedagogy of the Oppressed*, New York: Continuum Publishing Co.
Futrelle, D. (1992) "Drag Queen Vows Campy Campaign Against Bush," *The Guardian*, 29 January: n.p.
"Gemeenteraads Filosofieën [City Council Philosophies]" (1970), trans. Coen Tasman, *Kabouterkrant* 6: 6–7.
Gilens, M. and B.I. Page (2014). "Testing Theories of American Politics: Elites, Interest Groups, and Average Citizens," *Perspectives on Politics*, 12: 564–81.
Gilliam, T. and Jones, T. (dirs) (1974) *Monty Python and the Holy Grail*, Python (Monty) Pictures.
Gomez, G. and kydd, E. (dirs) (1991) *Drag In' For Votes*. Video. Heart of the Empire Productions.
—— (1992) Unedited video footage (35 hours) from the *Lick Bush in '92* project. Personal archive of Elspeth kydd, University of Toledo, OH. Accessed October 1999.
—— (1994) *Lick Bush in '92*. Video. Heart of the Empire Productions.
Gregory, D. (1968) *Write Me In!* J.R. McGraw (ed.), New York: Bantam Books.
Guevara, E. (1961) *Guerrilla Warfare*, New York: Monthly Review Press.
Habermas, J. (1989) *The Structural Transformation of the Public Sphere: An Inquiry into a Category of Bourgeois Society*, trans. T. Burger with F. Lawrence, Cambridge, MA: MIT Press.
Hakkenberg, P. (2000a) Interview with the author. Amsterdam, The Netherlands: 16 June.
—— (2000b) Interview with the author. Amsterdam, The Netherlands: 26 June.
Hamsen, H.L. (1967) "Provocation and Poetry: A Letter from Amsterdam," *Delta*, Summer: 1991–3.
Hamsher, J. and Murray, E. (1979) "Jello Biafra," *San Francisco Bay Guardian*, 26 September–5 October: A11–A13.

Hanson, P. (1998) *Pauline Lee Hanson v. Australian Broadcasting Corporation, Writ No. 7681 or 1997*. Statement of Claim, filed in the Supreme Court of Queensland, Australia: 23 September.
Heart of the Empire Productions (1994) "Lick Bush in '92!" pamphlet.
Herbst, S. (1994) *Politics at the Margin: Historical Studies of Public Expression Outside the Mainstream*, New York: Cambridge University Press.
Hill, L. (2001) "Suffragettes Invented Performance Art," in *The Routledge Performance Reader*, London and New York: Routledge.
Hoge, W. (1999) "Screaming Lord Sutch, 58; Eccentric Even for England," *New York Times*, 18 June: A33.
Hunt, S. (1997) "Backdoor Man." Bootleg copy of CD.
—— (1998) "I Don't Like It," TWA Records.
—— (1999a) Interview from tape recorded 23 March 1999, "at Bob Humphries' House." Hunt's video archive. Sydney, Australia.
—— (1999b) Lecture at the College of Fine Arts. Video, Sydney, Australia: 15 August.
—— (1999c) Interview with the author. Sydney, Australia: 29 August.
—— and Regan, S. (dirs) (1998) *Send in the Clown: The Pauline Pantsdown Story*. Unfinished documentary video, Regan, S. (prod.), accessed August 2015.
Hutcheon, L. (1994) *Irony's Edge: The Theory and Politics of Irony*, New York: Routledge.
—— (1985) *A Theory of Parody: The Teachings of Twentieth-Century Art Forms*. London: Methuen.
"Ik, Ik, Ik . . ." (1970) Altered cover. *Kabouterkrant* 10.
Jackson, H. (2000) "Election Officials Reject Tree as Candidate," *The Record*, 14 April: n.p.
JettBlakk, J. (1992) "I Want You, Honey!" pamphlet.
"Kabouterraadslid Guy Kilian" (1970) Photograph, in *Rottterdamse Courant*, 17 September: n.p.
Kalk, E. (1970) "Dwarf Revolution," *Agenor: European Review*, No. 18 (June): 9.
Kempton, R. (n.d.) "The Provos: Amsterdam's Anarchist Revolt." Dissertation, from the archive at the International Institute of Social History in Amsterdam, The Netherlands.
Kenney, P. (2002) *A Carnival of Revolution: Central Europe* 1989, Princeton, NJ: Princeton University Press.
Kertzer, D.I. (1988) *Ritual, Politics and Power*, New Haven, CT: Yale University Press.
Kilian, G. (2000) Interview with the author. Amsterdam, The Netherlands: 21 July.
kydd, E. (2001) Telephone interview with the author. 31 January.
Lammers, H. (1970) "I see in the Kabouters . . .," trans. S. Frieling, *Parool*, n.p.: 5 June.
Lantigua, J. (2001) "How the GOP Gamed the System in Florida," *The Nation*. At: www.thenation.com/doc.mhtml%3Fi=20010430&s=lantigua, accessed 25 July 2004.

"Lawholder is too Authoritarian" (1970) pamphlet, trans. S. Frieling, Amsterdam: n.p.
Ledbetter, L. (1979) "San Francisco Tense as Violence Follows Murder Trial," *New York Times*, 31 May: A1.
Lelyveld, J. (1966) "Dadaists in Politics," *New York Times Magazine*, 2 October: 32–5.
Letton, B. (2003) "Hanson Faces the Music." At: www.abc.net.au/dig/stories/s771229.htm, accessed 17 June 2004.
"Lick Bush in '92." Pamphlet. n.a. n.p.: n.d.
Liebelson, D. "The Supreme Court Gutted the Voting Rights Act. What Happened Next in These 8 States Will Not Shock You." Mother Jones, 8 April 2014. At: www.motherjones.com/politics/2014/04/republican-voting-rights-supreme-court-id, accessed 20 May 2015.
Liebert, L. (1979a) "An Eclectic Bunch of Mayoral Also-Rans," *San Francisco Chronicle*, 25 October: 5.
—— (1979b) "Lots of Apathy and Cynicism over S.F.'s Election," *San Francisco Chronicle*, 2 November: 26.
"Maar Lieve Smurfen! [Dear Smurfs!]" (1970) cartoon, trans. S. Frieling, *Kabouterkrant* 3: 7.
Mairowitz, D.Z. (1970) "Amsterdam: Pop Terror in the Magic Circle," *Friends*, 12 June: 14–15.
—— and Stansill, P. (eds) (1971) *BAMN: Outlaw Manifestos and Ephemera 1965–7*, Baltimore, MD: Penguin Books.
Meyer, D. (2004) "Defending Dean's Scream," on CBSnews.com. At: www.cbsnews.com/stories/2004/01/23/opinion/meyer/main595508.shtml: 23 Jan, accessed 5 August 2004.
Meyer, M. (1994) *The Poetics and Politics of Camp*, New York: Routledge.
"Misschien helpt het voor 1971 [Maybe this will help for 1971]" (1970) cartoon, from the personal archive of Coen Tasman.
Monty Python (1994) *Monty Python Live at Drury Lane. 1974*. New York: Caroline Records.
Morris, J.A. Jr. (1970) "The Kabouters: Dwarf Power – Zany Politics Dazzles Dutch," *Los Angeles Times*, 9 July: 1.
Murphy, J. (2009) *Other Davids Ready their Slings in Run for Mayor*, At: www.citylimits.org, accessed 29 June 2009.
"Nachtwachtzaal Weer Bezet" (1970) *Der Tijd*, 12 June.
Newton, E. (1979) *Mother Camp: Female Impersonators in America*, Chicago, IL: University of Chicago Press.
*Nightlines* (1991) "Gossip," photograph by Scout, 10 April: 10.
Nir, S.M. "Colbert's Super PAC Raises More Than $1 Million" *New York Times*, 31 January 2012. At: http://thecaucus.blogs.nytimes.com/2012/01/ 31/colberts-super-pac-raises-more-than-1-million-dollars/?_r=0, accessed May 22, 2015.
Notes From Nowhere (eds) (2003) *We are Everywhere: The Irrestible Rise of Global Anticapitalism*, New York: Verso.

O'Connor, D. (1992) "Joan JettBlakk Throws her Wig in the Ring," *Windy City Times*, 23 January: 15.

Opland (1970) "Haya en de Lilliputters" ["Haya and the Liliputians"]. Cartoon, in *Volkskrant*, 6 June: n.p.

*Outlines* (1991) "Hero of the Month." Photo by Scout. May: 44.

Palmer, R. (prod.) (1997) *TODAY Show*, Host T. Grimshaw, Channel 9 Australia: 29 August.

"Pixie Power in Amsterdam" (1971) *Time*, 15 June: 33.

"The Pixie Prophet" (1971) *The Observer*, 16 May: 9.

Plant, S. (1992) *The Most Radical Gesture: The Situationist International in a Postmodern Age*, New York: Routledge.

"Politiek Amsterdam Geschokt door Grote Winst Kabouters" ["Political Amsterdam Shocked by the Great Victory of the Kabouters"] (1971) trans. S Frieling, *De Tijd*, 4 June: n.p.

*Provo* (1965–7) Pamphlets, from the archive of the International Institute of Social History.

Queer Nation (1991a) "Welcome to History in the Making!" Press release. Chicago, IL.

—— (1991b) "Dear Queer Nation." Memo. Chicago, IL: 27 July.

—— (1991c) "For Immediate Release." Press Releases. Chicago, IL: 4 and 16 July.

—— (1992) "After Prolonged and Serious Discussion." Press Release. Chicago, IL: 11 August.

Read, M. Interview with the author. 7 July 2010.

Rice, M. "Stephen Colbert gives CU a double dose of 'truthiness." Cornell Chronicle. 29 October 2007. At: www.news.cornell.edu/stories/2007/10/stephen-colbert-gives-cu-double-dose-truthiness, accessed May 22, 2015.

Ridder, W. de (1970) "Oranje Vrijstaat Strip." Cartoon in *Aloha* 37, 18 September: 15.

Rodrich, S. (1991) "King & Queen: Queer and Loafing in the Victory 'Camps' of Queen Joan Jett Blackk and King Richard the Second," *New City*, 11 April: 7–8.

Rogier, J. (1970) "De Grootste Handicap van de Kabouters is Dat Za niet Negatief Genoeg Zijn" ["The Greatest Handicap of the Kabouters is That They Are Not Negative Enough"], trans. A. Nassuth, *Vrij Nederland*, 13 June: n.p.

Schechner, R. (1985) *Between Theatre and Anthropology*, Philadelphia, PA: University of Pennsylvania Press.

Schechter, J. (1994) *Satiric Impersonations: From Aristophanes to the Guerrilla Girls*, Carbondale, IL: Southern Illinois University Press.

Scheier, J. (2009) "The Church of Stop Bloomberg: Reverend Billy Launches Longshot Mayoral Bid," *The Indypendent*, 20 March 2009.

Schimmelpennink, L. (2000) Interview with the author. Amsterdam, The Netherlands: 7 July.

Scott, J.C. (1990) *Domination and the Arts of Resistance*, New Haven, CT: Yale University Press.

Sedgwick, E.K. (1990) *Epistemology of the Closet*, Berkeley, CA: University of California Press.
Shapiro, E. (1994) "Shapiro for Sheriff: Vote Nihilist '94." At: http://members.aol.com/nihilist01/sheriff.html, accessed 17 July 2004.
Shepard, B. (1997) *White Nights and Ascending Shadows: An Oral History of the San Francisco AIDS Epidemic*, Washington, DC: Cassel.
—— (2001) "The Queer/Gay Assimilationist Split: The Suits vs. the Sluts," *Monthly Review*, Vol. 53, No. 1 (May). At: www.monthlyreview.org/0501.shepard.htm, accessed 23 July 2004.
—— (2004) "Sylvia and Sylvia's Children," in M. Bernstein Sycamore (ed.) *That's Revolting! Queer Strategy for Resisting Assimilation*, Brooklyn, NY: Soft Skull Press.
Siegel, J. (2009) "Mayor-alujah! Reverend Billy is running as a Green," *The Villager*, 78(39), 4–10 March.
Stallybrass, P. and White, A. (1986) *The Politics & Poetics of Transgression*, Ithaca, NY: Cornell University Press.
Stein, A. (1998) "The Decentering of Lesbian Feminism," in P.M. Nardis and B.E. Schneider (eds) *Social Perspectives in Lesbian and Gay Studies: A Reader*, London: Routledge.
Straat, van de (1970) Cartoon, in *Parool*, 3 June: n.p.
Stratton, J. (1999) "'I Don't Like It': Pauline Pantsdown and the Politics of Inauthenticity," *Perfect Beat: The Pacific Journal of Research into Contemporary Music and Popular Culture*, 4.4: 3–29.
—— (1998) *Race Daze: Australia in Identity Crisis*. Annandale, NSW: Pluto Press.
Talen, B. (2003) *What Should I Do If Reverend Billy Is In My Store?* New York: New Press.
Talen, B. (2009) "Why would I Run for Mayor?" *Metro International*, 20 July.
—— Interview with the author. 28 July 2009.
—— Interview with the author. 17 February 2010.
Tarrow, S. (1998) *Power in Movement: Social Movements and Contentious Politics*, New York: Cambridge University Press.
Tasman, C. (1996) *Louter Kabouter: Kroniek van een Beweging [Only Kabouter: Chronicle of a Movement]*, trans. S. Frieling and A. Nassuth, Amsterdam, The Netherlands: Babylon-De-Geus.
—— (2000a) Interview with the author. Amsterdam, The Netherlands: 2 June.
—— (2000b) Interview with the author. Amsterdam, The Netherlands: 19 July.
Tendor, K. (2003) "America-Made Mystery: Speech Backdrop Snafu had White House Thinking out of the Box," ABCNews.com. At: http://abcnews.go.com/sections/us/DailyNews/madeinusa_030122.html, accessed 4 August 2004.
Tilly, C. (1995) *Popular Contention in Great Britain*, Cambridge, MA: Harvard University Press.
Tyler, C. (1991) "Boys Will Be Girls: The Politics of Gay Drag," in D. Fuss (ed.) *Inside/Out: Lesbian Theories, Gay Theories*, New York: Routledge.
Untitled (1970) cartoon, in *Vrij Nederland*, 13 June: n.p.

VanAlkemade, R. (dir.) (2007) *What Would Jesus Buy?* Documentary Film. Palisades Pictures, Warrior Poets, Werner Film.

*Weekly House Hansard* (1996) Pauline Hanson Speech in Parliament: 2 December. At: www.aph.gov.au/hansard/.

"Wegens Roken Hasjiesj, Kabouters in Raad Gearresteerd" ["Because of Smoking Hashish, Kabouters in Council Arrested"] (1970), trans. A. Nassuth, *Volkskrant* 17 September: n.p.

Weidner, D. (2009) "Reverend Billy's Bailout: One Street Preacher Makes the Case for Propping Up Community Banks," *Wall Street Journal*, 16 April 2009.

Weinraub, B. "Youths in Amsterdam 'Liberate' Empty Buildings," *New York Times* n.d: n.p.

White, R. (2009) "Backed by Green Party, Comic Pastor Runs for Mayor," *New York Times*, 2 March.

"Why One Must Vote Kabouter," trans. A. Nassuth. Pamphlet. n.p.: n.d.

"Why Vote Kabouter" (1970), trans. C. Tasman, in *Kabouterkrant* 5: n.p.

Wilkinson, P. (prod.) (1996) "The Hanson Phenomenon," on *60 Minutes*, Channel 9, Australia: 20 October.

Willem (n.d.). Cartoon. From the personal archive of Coen Tasman.

Williams, A. (1991) "Outspeak," *Windy City Times*, 18 July: n.p.

# Index